# THE FORM OF FAUST

HAROLD JANTZ

# THE FORM OF $\mathcal{F}$AUST

## The Work of Art and Its Intrinsic Structures

The Johns Hopkins University Press

BALTIMORE AND LONDON

Manufactured in the United States of America

The Johns Hopkins University Press, Baltimore, Maryland 21218
The Johns Hopkins Press Ltd., London

Library of Congress Catalog Card Number 78–1447
ISBN 0-8018-2080-4

Library of Congress Cataloging in Publication data will be found on the last printed page of this book.

# Contents

# Preface

Any new approach to an old classic is bound to encounter a three-fold difficulty. In the first place, one wants to be as clear as possible and thus can never come to an end with revising and rearranging to prevent any possibility of misunderstanding—while knowing full well that the unconventional is bound to be misunderstood, at least by some, at least in part, do what one may. This inquiry into the intrinsic form of *Faust* was essentially completed several years ago and needed (so I thought) only the usual last reading by a friend and colleague before being sent to the publisher. But added readings, during occasional interludes away from other duties, showed me that further revisions were necessary, mostly of smaller matters, but here and there of larger ones.

In the second place, any truly new approach brings with it a wealth of new insights to which more and more continue to be added, and one must take care to exclude from the text all but a careful selection of the most important and characteristic and interesting ones. In this way the reader will not be overwhelmed but will rather be given the opportunity of continuing creatively and coming to new insights of his own.

In the third place, any new approach cannot help but go counter to the traditional and conventional approaches. Would that it were only the old approaches that had to be countered, but alas, there are people behind them who have labored hard to attain them, who fervently believe in them, who do not want to be disturbed in them. If it were only a matter of small differences within a larger consensus, these could be pleasantly debated, but when basic premises and fundamental assumptions are put to question, this comes to be altogether too distressful and can lead to highly emotional reactions.

I wish it were not so, and I have done all I can to stay strictly with the issues and to avoid all personal references. It may seem like an extreme in this direction that there is not a single footnote in the whole volume and only one specific negative reference to an earlier *Faust* study, this reference unavoidable because here originated a factual error that has led to false conclusions of grave consequence. Actually, footnotes and specific references were hardly necessary, for the points at issue are not singular ones but such as were shared by several or many, as the reader can readily ascertain if he turns to the various modern *Faust* commentaries or to the recent collections of *Faust* essays, even to those that contain one or the other contribution from me.

And yet it is just in the recent and most recent literature that I find much to reassure me; though still in the minority, there is an increasing number of scholars and critics, often of quite different temperament and from quite different approaches, who are coming to the same or similar conclusions. There is even the happy instance of a prominent Goethe scholar, quite independently, coming to a radical conclusion on one of the great cruces in Faust criticism to which I came in a *Euphorion* article more than twenty years ago. Thus it may be that a new consensus is in the process of formation; if so, I may soon be in the same pleasant position with my Goethe studies as I am with my Baroque, comparative, and early American studies, which initially were even more upsetting in their contravention of established views and judgments.

I do hope that my lack of solemnity and my tendency to play with matters that others take seriously will not be cause for offense. What I am doing is simply following a good precedent, for Goethe himself perpetrated various jests in *Faust*, some obvious, others very subtly hidden, as a number of recent writers have discovered to their great delight. If Chapter Eleven especially arouses shock and indignation, I can only state that I was a bit shocked myself when it dawned on me by degrees what Goethe was contriving to do. Five or six years ago, in the process of major revisions, I noticed that I had unintentionally come close to devising a similar jest, and I could not resist undertaking the small amount of rearrangement required to perfect it. The gentle reader need not be distressed if he cannot find it, because the discovery of it is quite unessential. Eleven is the sensational chapter but not the important one.

As for the translations of the Goethean texts, one is faced with a dilemma. A truly spirited translation that flows along with the flair of the original is likely to be inaccurate. An accurate translation is likely to be more awkward. A further danger is encountered with regard to the language level: it is of utmost importance to translate a passage at its same level of seriousness or levity, dignity or vulgarity, for it is the language level that frequently determines the intent of a particular passage or scene—this a factor that several recent translators have quite disregarded. Furthermore, in a work so tightly woven contextually the verbal relations to other scenes (sometimes distant scenes) must not be overlooked, because word and phrase echoes are often signals to alert the reader to important interrelations that a free translation would effectively obscure. For present purposes it was accuracy for which I had to strive, but a part of accuracy is making the verse as decently literate as possible, thus using freer equivalents where meaning and intent would not be impaired.

After making my own translations I did examine the rich store of others from the past for hints toward improving my own. I made several discoveries. Some of the nineteenth-century translations, even or precisely the little known ones, are surprisingly good through long stretches, and if the occasional lapses and blunders in them could be eliminated, they would be better than many a modern one. Some of the modern translators have apparently been aware of these poetically superior passages and have borrowed quietly and generously from them. To be sure, there are a few passages that almost inevitably translate themselves into one elegant way with only slight variants, and most translators will naturally hit upon this one way. By contrast, there are other vexatious passages that resist the efforts of even the most ingenious translators and that after prodigious effort turn out in fifty different ways to be equally unsatisfactory. The Easter Choruses are one instance, and since the message they convey to Faust at this critical juncture is of central importance for the dramatic continuity, the freer, smoother translations all do violence to Goethe's intent and the more accurate ones seem doomed to suffer poetically.

My heartfelt thanks, however, to the able and ingenious translators of the past. Although for present purposes I could not take over a single passage or even a single line from them intact (except the few that nearly all translations have as a common treasure), and though I have had to find many a new solution of my own, I am grateful to be a follower in a long and worthy tradition.

My thanks go to the colleagues and friends with whom I have had the privilege of discussing these new approaches through the years and who have been very patient while final completion was postponed year after year. The students also who reacted with a feeling of relief at being liberated from the old dogmatic approaches and who felt free to embark on exploratory voyages of their own through the drama rewarded me richly with a series of keen observations in their discussions and in the papers they wrote. They made it clear to me that what I offer here is only a beginning, one that, in Goethe's words, "Ist fortzusetzen."

# Introduction

# Why It Was Necessary to
# Write Yet Another Book on Faust

My difficulty with the standard *Faust* interpretations began years ago when I decided to take seriously Goethe's very clear statement that *Faust* was not a philosophic poem and his several appeals in letters and conversations to take the drama as a work of art, to regard the artistic factors as the guiding and controlling elements. To be sure, most critics sincerely believed that this was what they were doing; in minor matters and some larger features this is what they actually were doing. But when it came to the analysis of the structure and the comprehension of the whole, the approach remained largely intellectualized: the psychology of the characters, the rationale of the plot, the idea of the parts, and (the ultimate abstraction) the idea of the whole were regarded as the decisive features. Even when the approach was claimed to be symbolical, the genuinely artistic symbols hardly emerged; all was abstracted into intellectual schemata deprived of the living pulse that suffuses the work and makes it an artistic entity. There even was, and there remains, a tacit or explicit denial that it is an artistic entity. Sometimes Part One is still dismissed as an adventitious conglomerate in which it is hopeless to look for a coherent structure. Part Two in the last decades has fared better and there have been valiant attempts to study it separately for its larger structures and imbuing symbolism. Just how insufficient such a fragmentary approach must remain will be apparent when we come to about the middle of this study and learn that the guiding themes for the whole work are quietly announced in the introductory sections of Part One. Part Two cannot be truly understood without an awareness of them; yet nowhere in any critical work I have seen are these guiding themes (with their associated symbolism) recognized, or even mentioned in passing.

This capital disregard of overall interrelations is not the result of any dullness or indolence, but rather the opposite: the critics have been too acutely analytical; they have cut right through and destroyed the artistic fabric of the work in their futile attempt to get at the idea, which Goethe warned them several times they would never find, simply because it is not there. Under the firm conviction that a work must have a leading or underlying idea, Goethe's admonition has been ignored and pushed aside, and the intellectual approach installed as the guiding one in literary criticism. Granted, there is much in *Faust* that is accessible to the intellect, much even that demands an intellectual approach. With such a great mind as Goethe's it could not be otherwise. But the intellectual is not the controlling and composing principle. The controlling principle, it will appear, is the symbolic-pictorial; the composing principle is the measural-harmonic in theme and development, in pattern and proportion. The ideological content is simply put to use poetically without essentially affecting the shape and sequence of the drama.

A claim of entirely different structural principles will strike the conventional *Faust* exegete as not worth entertaining even as a hypothesis. And yet, anyone who has read the work a number of times from beginning to end, who has variously studied and discussed its text, will readily or gradually have observed in it a variety of larger or smaller continuities. He will see themes announced and developed, patterns established and repeated and varied, larger contexts contributing to the interpretation of a particular passage. In brief, he will have first intimations of a larger form and structure in what still seems to be a complex and chaotic work. And he may come to wonder whether the drama might not on still closer study reveal overall patterns and structures that continue to lie concealed under its complexities.

When he turns to the interpreters and commentators for guidance, he soon finds that the consensus of opinion tends strongly toward the negative. Even the advocates of the larger or more general unity of *Faust* tend to be defensive in their claims, make crucial concessions to the fragmentists, and retreat to the allegation of a higher, less visible unity. Their efforts and partial successes have been largely confined to the second part; the first part still seems to disintegrate into the three preliminary sections, the three study scenes, the popular and diabolistic scenes, and the Gretchen tragedy, variously present and intermingled in the *Urfaust*, the *Fragment*, and the completed Part One.

This traditional critical consensus will stand firm against all assaults, so long as one concedes that the traditionally accepted basic premises are entirely valid and without reasonably acceptable alternatives. One questions and removes the basic premises, and all suddenly looks different. But here is where the real trouble begins: basic premises are usually hidden premises, unstated and unconsciously accepted by all engaged in the particular critical concern or problem. Whenever they are brought into the open by the skeptic and questioned by him, he is viewed with alarm, reacted to with fear as a threat to the essential critical "dialogue," and usually rejected with a highly surcharged emotionalism.

Nevertheless, there is always the small minority that has quiet misgivings, possibly about the accepted basic premises, certainly about some of the results that flow from these premises. For clearer perspectives let us have the spokesmen for the consensus formulate these premises, and do so quite plainly and openly:

1. The very genesis of *Faust* over a course of sixty years, its changed plans and intents, they say, would preclude any overall unity and consistent structure.

2. The only possible form the work could have, they imply, would be the usual dramatic form constructed of action and character development encompassed within a leading or underlying idea. Since it clearly has no such form, it is formless.

3. Goethe as an artist, they assert, belonged to the unconsciously creative, impulsive, inspirational type rather than to the consciously planning, shaping, revising type. He was often not even aware of inconsistencies in a work, and when he was, he shrugged them off as unimportant, if only the general mood and effect were right.

4. *Faust* is a philosophical poem, Goethe intended it as such, but he had never learned to think philosophically and consequentially. As a result, they assume, some of the worst inconsistencies in the work, from specific details to the general plan for the outcome, arise from failures in Goethe's thinking.

Such alien premises and false conclusions were already current during Goethe's lifetime and elicited an occasional drastic response from him, as in his late poem:

Aber ihr wollt besser wissen,
Was ich weiß, der ich bedachte,
Was Natur, für mich beflissen,
Schon zu meinem eigen machte.

Fühlt ihr auch dergleichen Stärke,
Nun, so fördert eure Sachen!
Seht ihr aber meine Werke,
Lernet erst: so wollt' er's machen.

*But you claim to know much better*
*What I know when I reflected*
*What from nature as her debtor*
*I have as my own selected.*

*If you feel a like vocation,*
*Then do your thing as you view it,*
*But when you see my creation,*
*Learn first: this is how he'd do it.*

This refusal of the critic to accept the creation the poet has given him, to learn how the poet made it and intended it, lies at the root of the trouble. And yet, there are mitigating circumstances. Even the most offensive *Besserwisser* will concede the poetic supremacy of many passages, scenes, and sequences in the work that add immeasurable riches to the anthology of world poetry. And the defensive admirers of the whole work never cease in their efforts to find excuses for the admitted shortcomings and inconsistencies. They even show, with true loving devotion, that the work transcends its flaws, that it is like a great work of nature rather than of art, and deservedly ranks among the supreme works of literature. There are even those who have shown that certain features of the work, long considered faulty, are actually quite all right and have only been misunderstood. This last insight, bearing witness to a new critical modesty in the service of the poetic work, represents a solid advance in these recent and present decades that are one hundred and thirty, forty, and fifty years after the first publication of the complete work. If continued, this new critical modesty will inevitably lead to a reexamination of the basic premises, which have developed from anything but modest critical attitudes.

It will help if we pause a moment and extend our perspectives farther into the past. All this has happened before. What was the state of Shakespeare criticism some one hundred and thirty, forty, and fifty years after the first folio appeared in 1623? Astonishingly like that of Goethe criticism until recently, with essentially the same basic premises as those listed above, except for the one point that Shakespeare was too hasty instead of too dilatory, but with similar results in that neither poet bothered much about revising or eliminating even glaring inconsistencies. Voltaire and the other smart critics thought of Shakespeare as something of an idiot genius, quite incapable of rational thought, with most of his works an intellectual mess, beclouded by fumbling ambiguities and deprived of the benefit of their own modern critical principles. The refined English poets and editors, from Dryden onward and downward, out of loyalty to their benighted countryman and true admiration for his poetic powers, undertook to "revise" Shakespeare's dramas, to tighten their form and illuminate their murkiness (a nearly hopeless task, bravely and devotedly undertaken), so that they would be fit to present to a less barbarous, more sophisticated audience. These "revised and improved" Shakespeare texts of the eighteenth century make us shudder now when they do not make us laugh. Just so the present performances of *Faust*, when preserved on film, together with the parallel "modern" interpretations, will be the gruesome delight and hilarious sport of future generations.

Even when the critical climate after mid-eighteenth century turned more favorable until it culminated in an enthusiastic Shakespearomania, most of the fervent new defenders of the poet could not free themselves from the established critical premises. They merely put positive signs where there had been negative ones: Shakespeare was a natural genius destined to "warble his native wood-notes wild," as Milton, even Milton, had already put it. His works were more works of nature than works of art and in their very ruggedness and imperfection revealed a higher truth than was possible in a sleek and contrived and calculated work that followed all the rules and lost its soul in the process. Thus the way was opened for the new revolutionary and then romantic glorification of the natural, instinctive, inspirational, and the admiration for the inchoate, fragmentary, irregular, disorderly. Such attitudes and modifications of them still survive in popular opinion, but, needless to say, they are quite remote from the insights and conclusions of present-day Shakespeare critics, insights and conclusions that have developed from very different basic premises.

Normal caution might therefore suggest to us that the presently accepted basic premises concerning *Faust* could be just as provisional and transitory as were the similar eighteenth-century premises concerning Shakespeare's major works, and that they might well be replaced by newer and more appropriate ones, not necessarily similar to those now prevailing in Shakespeare criticism, but parallel to them in their commensurately higher level of insight and lower level of arrogance.

What presently stands in the way of our reaching such a higher level of insight into the intrinsic nature of the Goethean work is a vast thicket of convictions and conclusions as to the nature of *Faust*, both in general and in a multitude of particulars—convictions and conclusions either derived from false basic assumptions or inserted into the work by alien and discrepant critical or philosophical systems. Such approaches refuse to accept the *Faust* on its own or on Goethe's terms, and their surrogate Fausts all too often appear in grotesque distortion and disproportion over against the real one. Some of the traditionally accepted convictions about the work are actually contrary to text, as we shall see; still more go clearly contrary to the context and are indeed the cause of the observed discrepancies rather than the result of any discrepancies that reside within the work.

Thus it will be necessary first to clear away this accumulated critical underbrush that is hiding the true form of *Faust*, and this task will take up the first and smaller part of the present study. To the left, the thorny undergrowth is populated by the diabolists who have always been unhappy at the way Goethe unhelled his *Faust* and have insisted on restoring the proper amount of brimstone and evil to bring it back into proper balance. There were these even during Goethe's lifetime; he directed the shafts of his humor against them, all to no avail, for they continue strong to this day. To the right in the thicket of fern and creeper lurk the sentimentalists who drool over several characters and scenes in the work with the warm mucilage of their outpouring feelings. Goethe saw them as such a serious impediment to the true understanding of his work that he early directed a poem against them and took other measures, again to no avail, for they continue influential. In the forefront is the bracken and brittle brushwood of the fragmentists, or, as one may fondly call them, the fragmentalists, since the disjunctions and discrepancies they perceive exist not in the work but in their own mentalities. Their complacent strictures and suggestions for "improvement" have been a continuing nuisance from Goethe's day to our own. Bringing up the rear is a mixed thicket of reductionists and schematists, among whom we shall find many a choice and singular botanical specimen, generally quick-growing and short-lived, yet adding nicely to the critical confusion.

In the end, the weedy obscurantists on all four sides are reductionists and schematists. All of them are, or rather would be, profoundly dissatisfied with the *Faust* as Goethe left it, except that they have never seen it the way he left it, because they have reshaped it according to their own minds or feelings, reshaped it so far as they have been able, and since they are not very able and most of *Faust* remains unaffected by their efforts, they have only managed to distort it superficially so that it seems malformed to them and to those who believe in them. This falsified *Faust* is passed off as the real *Faust* and then Goethe is roundly condemned as though he himself had perpetrated this botchery. If Faust were addressing not Wagner but them, he would have to vary his verdict only slightly from lines 577–85:

> *What you call "spirit of the play,"*
> *Is in effect the critics' self-display*
> *Wherein their spirits are reflected.*
> *Then often it is right pathetic,*
> *And at first sight one wants to run away.*
> *It's like a dustbin or a lumber attic,*
> *At best a stilted high-heroic play,*
> *Pragmatic maxims pompously emitting,*
> *Such as in puppets' mouths are most befitting.*

Is there any way out of this impasse? Must we forever persist in making a series of pseudomorphs out of *Faust* instead of allowing it to unfold before us in its proper shape and form, as the orthomorph it is? There is another way. Just as there is in Greek story a counterfigure to Procrustes, just so there is a critical method that will allow a work to appear in its own form instead of having an alien shape imposed upon it. This critical method, to be sure, has little chance of becoming popular, for reasons that will appear as we explain and apply it.

Procrustes, you will remember, was that hospitable gentleman who lived in a house by the side of the road and was a friend to man. His one slight aberration was that he was fonder of his guest bed than of his guests. Instead of making man the measure of all things, he made his bed the measure of all the men whom he could stretch or abridge into it. Ancestral Procrustes has pointed the way for abstract critical principles to promote dehumanization.

In place of the Procrustean method I should like to put another method, named after another distinguished Greek, Odysseus, for one of his most quiet and loving achievements, the creation of a bed of a different nature, as we hear in the twenty-third book of the epic. The measure was the marriage, and the whole was built onto the living post of the olive tree. It came from old life, it was fitted to life, and it led to new life. It did not dictate to its occupants, it served them, it enhanced them.

Of course, the Procrustean method is the more popular because it is far the easier and more universal. One merely has to learn a critical faith, with its full panoply of impressive vocabulary, and then one can proceed to accommodate any and every work of literature and really make it fit, more or less. The "sound" assumption is that if there is going to be any critical system at all, the work of art had better accommodate itself to it or be condemned for deviationism.

How much more awkward and impractical is the Odyssean method that requires a new and different critical approach be fitted to each new work of art. A wasteful procedure, not at all accommodated to our age of interchangeable parts and the adjustment of the flesh to the machine. And yet, all is not so hopeless and the outlook quite so bleak. There are still critics who prefer Odysseus to Procrustes, and some of the best designed modern furniture is very comfortable indeed because the true realists tend to make the adjustment toward the living flesh. So it may be that a criticism made to measure may find some approval over a measure made into a criticism, and it may not be so hopelessly old-fashioned when it does point a way out of the present cubicular discomfort.

With this modest hope and consolation I have ventured in the second and larger part of this study to explore the inner principles of form in the work, the primary themes and points of view, the pervasive principle of the interlude, together with the symmetrical and progressive sequences built around it; then the recurrent patterns and larger contexts and, separately, the remarkable phenomenon of echo structures; next the coordinating features of monodrama and polydrama; then the contextual configurations, the symbolic extensions and metamorphoses; thereupon the structure of time; and finally the all-encompassing framework of scenes with its revelation of balances and proportions—all these factors coming together in a careful coordination of form and function to constitute a masterful work of complexity controlled by harmony.

This may seem like an ambitious undertaking. To the fragmentalists it will seem a hopeless, even an absurd one—but only from their point of view, which may turn out to be impertinent. If the equivalent of the presently prevailing methods of *Faust* criticism were applied by the art critic to some great and complex work of art, a comparable confusion would result, a confusion that then consequentially would be blamed on the artist himself. Let us suppose that the normal approach to Raphael's *School of Athens* had been the intellectual, with the chief emphasis on its ideological significance, including an outline of the philosophical system of each of the persons represented in it, as though the ideological were the only possible approach to the picture. The next, higher school of critics would then come along and upon careful scrutiny find that Raphael had badly misplaced the personages in his picture, that their historical succession required a quite different arrangement. Then the next higher school of critics would come along and upon careful scrutiny find that Raphael had badly misplaced the personages in his picture, that their ideological positions required a quite different arrangement. Then the ultimate critic would come along and demonstrate that the whole picture was an absurd anachronism, that these people never came together in this way at all, that in fact they lived scattered over several centuries. Against him the other schools of criticism would rise in indignant or dignified refutation, and a long dispute would develop in which Raphael's right to bring these figures together would be defended and only the way he did it would be deplored.

All of the time the conflicting groups would be arguing on the basis of the same critical premises, would not realize that any other set of premises could exist, and would be utterly bewildered if an outsider were to suggest that they should instead take a symbolic pictorial approach to the work, forget the ideological factors as not centrally relevant, look instead at the abstract geometry of form and composition, the distribution of colors, the balance of bodies, the dynamics of grouping, the interplay of expression and gesture, not just fragmentarily or incidentally to prove a point, as heretofore, but comprehensively, from larger perspective, within the framework of the whole. Out of all this in the end some symbolic-ideological factors might well emerge as a valued secondary result. But they would be different from the old ones imposed from without; they would cautiously start from Raphael's own artistic statements and accord with the artist's own intent.

The final point is: the art critics have not been that foolish, at least not in our century. Do we in literary criticism, specifically in *Faust* criticism, need to be so far behind the art critics? Must we continue to remain subjected to the philosophical and sociological tyrannies that they have long since shaken off, while merely smiling at every new attempt to impose them? The philosophical stultification of *Faust* criti-

cism must some day come to an end, as must the arrogance of the
sapients, the *Besserwisser*, over against the poet.

No one, of course, would concede that a critical obtuseness similar
to the one imagined over against the *School of Athens* could ever occur
in *Faust* criticism. Allow me, therefore, to offer a small specific example
at this point (anticipating many another to come) of an early passage in
*Faust* that, firstly, continues to be misinterpreted; secondly, the misinterpretation then makes the imagery of the passage seem confused;
thirdly, this confusion is then attributed to a defect in the poetic imagination of Goethe; and even in the latest commentaries and critiques
there is no statement or suggestion that, fourthly and instead, a new and
different interpretation may be called for.

The passage, in the first monologue, is the one in which Faust views
the sign of the macrocosm (447–53):

> Wie alles sich zum Ganzen webt,
> Eins in dem andern wirkt und lebt!
> Wie Himmelskräfte auf und nieder steigen
> Und sich die goldnen Eimer reichen!
> Mit segenduftenden Schwingen
> Vom Himmel durch die Erde dringen,
> Harmonisch all das All durchklingen!

Most of the English versions are mistranslations, a confused mixture of
the Goethean text and the commentators' aberrant intrusions. A faithful,
uncontaminated rendering would run something like this:

> *How all into one whole here weaves,*
> *Each in the other works and lives.*
> *How heaven's powers rising and descending*
> *Each unto each the golden vessels lending,*
> *On bliss-filled fragrant pinions swinging*
> *From heaven through the earth awinging,*
> *Through all the All harmonious ringing.*

For the interpreters the only possible explanation is that Goethe was
here thinking of a kind of Jacob's ladder, a heavenly staircase, with
angels ascending and descending upon it. Confirmatory quotations for
such a celestial escalade are cited from mystical works such as the
Rosicrucian *Fama* of 1614 or Franciscus Mercurius van Helmont's *Para-
doxal Discourses* of 1685 (German 1692), and therewith most commentators rest content. Some of the older ones add that the angels pass
the golden urns or buckets on to one another after the manner of a
celestial fire brigade, but the more recent ones are generally silent on this
activity.

A few of the more thoughtful, however, have tried to visualize the whole configuration and find that it is a confused botchery—as the present reader will also if he tries to behold these heavenly procedures in motion before his mind's eye. How do the angels pass on the urns—forward, backward, or across from descending row to ascending row, or vice versa? If he were a film director, how would he arrange the action? He would find that it is impossible to do so without lapsing into slapstick comedy. Either the angels would have to stand still and pass on the urns, or they would have to stride up and down, with each keeping his urn on his shoulder. And how on earth or in heaven can they, while engaged in these activities, "with their benignantly fragrant wings penetrate from heaven through the earth"? The one or two students whose analysis has gone this far sadly concede that young Goethe, whose poetic imagery was usually so vivid and so just, here fumbled badly and this passage could only be considered a poetic failure.

If we take a fresh look at this description and have some understanding of the traditional connotations of its imagery, we shall come to quite different conclusions. First, one small observation: young Goethe did not write "heavenly powers," as the traditional explanations would demand, he wrote "heaven's powers," "powers of heaven." In the second place, to interpret the "golden urns" as some kind of celestial fire buckets is not only absurd and anachronistic, it also violates the poetic tradition of meanings associated with the term. From Aristophanes' *Clouds* onward through Milton's *Paradise Lost* the imagery of the golden urns was poetically associated with the planets. In the traditional cosmological setting the constellations, particularly the signs of the zodiac, are the "powers of heaven" that "rise and descend." Furthermore, it is the planets that are, in the course of the months and the years, passed on from one sign, one power of heaven, to the next. In the traditional poetic imagination (quite explicitly in Aristophanes and Milton) these "golden urns" fetch their light from the sun and radiate it forth again on their nocturnal course. In the last lines too all difficulties disappear in the established astrological context, for in the calculation of a horoscope the position of the zodiacal signs and of the planets below the horizon is also established since their radiant powers penetrate *through* the earth in the total celestial harmony.

And after all, what was and is a macrocosm other than the universe of sun, planets, and stars? Therefore also, the sign that Faust so eloquently and beautifully describes in the passage quoted and in the preceding eighteen lines cannot possibly be derived from any one of the dry simplistic designs such as the hexagram or any one of the mystic or alchemical diagrams that the commentators have brought forward. Indeed, in the whole consideration of the motifs of macrocosm and microcosm the lapses of the authorities are more frequent than their right understanding, with two further painful blunders being passed on un-questioningly from commentary to commentary right to the present day. The critics were searching only for the idea, one that is not even there, and totally failed to unfold their poetic pictorial imagination to see what actually is there. Such a failure to understand the planetary golden urns passed on from one constellation, one power of heaven, to the next in the macrocosm can stand as one specific example of what happens all too frequently and all too generally in *Faust* exegesis.

There is another related kind of fallacy that has occurred and re-curred in the study of *Faust*. The critic will find a discrepancy that really is there, and will then go on to the only explication that seems possible to him: Goethe with his usual carelessness did not notice the inconsis-tency or did not bother to correct it. The other possible explication seems hardly ever to occur to him: the poet was well aware of the discrepancy, he deliberately introduced it, he wanted the reader or listener to notice it, and then derive from it the conclusions proper to the total intent of the drama. Shockingly enough, two of the most persistent discrepancies, one of them running through the Gretchen tragedy, the other even fur-ther, seem not even to have been noticed in the German lands, although they have been by a few of the more sharply observant students in America. I refer to Goethe's fluctuating use of "Margarete" and "Gretchen" and to the form of address, fluctuating between "du" and "ihr," in the dialogues between Faust and Mephistopheles. Thus the poet's (very cogent) reasons for introducing these discrepancies have not even been put to question. However, one briefer, more specific in-stance will suffice for present purposes.

Near the beginning of Faust's first monologue, in summation of the total failure of his preceding academic career, he asserts (374–76):

> Auch hab' ich weder Gut noch Geld,
> Noch Ehr' und Herrlichkeit der Welt;
> Es möchte kein Hund so länger leben!

> *Nor have I goods or money's worth*
> *Or honor and glory of the earth.*
> *No dog would live thus any more.*

However, in the course of the Easter Walk we find him held in such honor and reverence by the people that Wagner in his description of Faust's progress through the crowd of merrymakers declares in conclu-sion (1018–21):

> Du gehst, in Reihen stehen sie,
> Die Mützen fliegen in die Höh':
> Und wenig fehlt, so beugten sich die Knie
> Als käm' das Venerabile.

*You go, they stand in rows to see,*
*The caps are lifted up on high;*
*A little more and they would bend the knee*
*As if the blessed Host came by.*

The few who have noticed the discrepancy content themselves with another "error" scored against Goethe and so miss the point. Once we have observed that one of the basic poetic principles of the drama is that of multiple points of view, serving as mutual critical correctives over against accepting any one point of view, we shall have the proper basis for the understanding of this and other inconsistencies in the text. What Goethe is doing here, and doing so very plainly, is allowing us to observe one of the crucial character traits of Faust. It is so crucial that if we fail to understand it, our whole understanding of the drama will be impaired. The point is that Faust is an exaggerator, he thinks and speaks in hyperboles, all the more so when he is under emotional stress. This hyperbolism of his together with his impatience, his precipitateness in action, we can observe throughout his career from the first monologue to the last. The poet wanted us to observe it and to be early aware of it. Wagner's description of the honor and respect in which Faust is held is an urgently necessary corrective at this point because it is immediately followed by Faust's description of his and his father's activities during the plague, a description that piles up bitter self-accusations in ever mounting exaggeration until it culminates in the wild absurdity of "die frechen Mörder," "the shameless murderers" (1055). Wagner, well aware of this tendency in the great man, gently, soothingly brings the whole matter back into the perspective of the gradual progress of knowledge in the arts and sciences (again revealing his own very different limitations); Faust simmers down to an elegiac lament on the lack of that which one needs most, and in a quiet mood goes over to the contemplation of the sunset.

    With such varied obstructions to our understanding removed, we should be able to proceed somewhat in the manner of a music critic when he is confronted by an extensive and complex composition, say a spacious tone poem or a great symphony, with its very different movements, its very different themes and ways of thematic development and interrelation, with all of its complexity and diversity going far beyond that of the normal classical symphony or suite. Does he dismiss it as intellectually and artistically unsound and despair of making any coherent sense out of such a bewildering diversity? If he is worth his salt, he will proceed to a careful search for structures, intrinsic musical structures of and in the work itself (without any preconceptions as to the kind that ought to be there), taking care in feeling his way into the work so that he will not obscure but will allow to emerge the symmetries and continuities that do after all masterfully control and shape the bewildering complexity.

That something analogous can be done for *Faust*, I hope to show in this study. The basic assumptions I make are fairly modest ones to which any sensible person can consent, at least provisionally, until it is clear how they will work out. In briefest form, they ask only that we have a decent respect for Goethe as a literary artist and an intelligent man who knew what he wanted to do and who was able to do it. Careful literary studies of other works of his have demonstrated, time and again, that he was a master of his art. Let us at least give him the chance to demonstrate that in *Faust* also he was the master. Let us not be romantic-atavistic in preferring the earlier, more imperfect versions of the work and judging the completed work from their vantage point. Let us instead, in proper courtesy and respect, agree that the final version he left us is the ultimate expression of his artistic will; let us assume that when he abandoned an old plan or an old sequence and adopted a new one, he did so for very good reasons, that his change of mind was in the service of a better realization of his larger intent. After all, this is no more than what Rembrandt did in several of his etchings when he quite changed smaller or larger details on the plate, all in the service of a higher realization of his artistic intent than he was able to achieve in the first draft. Above all, let us not confuse collector's rarity, in the first state, with artistic quality, in the final realization.

The results of a reformed critical attitude in this direction can be most fruitful. We shall see, again and again, that the larger and smaller revisions Goethe made were principally for sound aesthetic reasons. In the contextual approach we shall see his principle of *wiederholte Spiegelung* becoming operative in the mutual illumination that related scenes shed upon one another. In this Goethean light many an established interpretation will have to be abandoned, to be sure, but this loss will be more than compensated for by the new insights and more pertinent interpretations that will emerge naturally out of the new coherences, by new interrelations that will become manifest, and by erstwhile ambiguities that will be clarified. We shall even see aspects of his careful and exact artistic mastery that we could not possibly have anticipated.

# I

## The *Faust* of the Critics versus the *Faust* of Goethe

# 1

# The Diabolists

N THEATRICAL PERFORMANCES of Goethe's *Faust* the high point of involuntary humor is reached when Gretchen, in the course of questioning Faust about his religion, confides to him (3471 ff.) her intuitive aversion to Mephistopheles, and when Faust, after evasive answers, is impelled to exclaim (3494):

Du ahnungsvoller Engel du!

*You intuitive angel, you.*

After one has for quite some time in the previous scenes observed the typical stage Mephistopheles in at least semidiabolic make-up and costume, slinking, hissing, and leering, one cannot possibly credit Gretchen with any higher intuitive powers in having sensed his sinister nature. Indeed it would take a rather feeble-minded girl not to get the point of the actor's blatant hellishness. And, of course, Goethe never intended to present Gretchen as feeble-minded or Faust as overcome with astonishment to find even this small ray of intelligence in her.

Now the most alarming aspect of this patent absurdity is not simply that one never hears a single member of a German audience laugh or even snicker at this point, one never even hears of a single drama critic writing in protest against this perversion of the drama's intent. The intent is easy enough to ascertain: one need only turn to the text itself to learn that Mephisto in the first confrontation with Faust appears as a wandering scholar and in the next as an elegant cavalier on the grand tour. On top of this there is all the external evidence pointing in the same direction: that Goethe intended a subtle, sophisticated realization of the role. More than once in the past all this has been pointed out, perhaps too quietly, certainly without effect. Quite likely the chief reason is that the readers and the critics have not been willing to accept the

Mephistopheles that Goethe gave them but have insisted on putting another Mephistopheles in his place.

This unwillingness to agree to the character that Goethe had intended goes back to the time of the published *Fragment* of 1790 and the completed *Part One* of 1808. The young romantics especially wanted a greater dose of diabolism, and Goethe remarked with good humored indulgence that Madame de Staël demanded a "much fiercer" Mephistopheles. He does so in an amusing context to which we shall return.

1

Goethe, of course, never yielded to these demands and the Mephisto of his intent was generally the one that appeared on the stage during the first performances of the drama, in 1829. For the very first, at Braunschweig, January 19, the director, August Klingemann, prescribed (Gräf II, 2, 476) that the actor is to perform the role of Mephistopheles "with the avoidance of everything gruesome and frightening, instead to carry it through dashingly, adroitly, with sparkling humor and in the diction of an elegantly profligate man of the world." For the Weimar performance, August 29, 1829, the great Carl La Roche played the role. He was then in the early years of a long career that was to carry him from triumph to triumph at the Burgtheater in Vienna. Fortunately, there is a detailed eyewitness account of the performance by a distinguished writer, Carl von Holtei. He had himself prepared a stage version of the *Faust* and had talked about it with Goethe on several occasions. Furthermore, he was a personal friend of La Roche, and the two men no doubt also discussed the Goethean interpretation of the role. Thus it is not merely a momentary impressionistic report that we have from Holtei but a solidly considered and informed one.

After this good start there follows a sad course of events, beginning with the subsequent career of La Roche at the Burgtheater, when the hostility toward his Goethean interpretation can first be observed, and going on to the final triumph of the opposition in imposing an unGoethean realization of the role upon all German audiences to this day, with the actors, directors, and critics in the opposition quite complacently certain that they were right and that La Roche, and Goethe, were wrong.

The sinister significance of all this goes far beyond the theatre deep into literary criticism and the concept the educated world has of one of its literary masterpieces. A Mephisto such as the actors project is indeed conceivable in another *Faust* written by another poet with another set of basic attitudes and intentions. If the romantics had produced a poet of stature to write a *Faust* that could have rivaled Goethe's, the diabolist urge of nineteenth- and twentieth-century Europe could have been satisfied. But sad to say, the best they could do was Nicolaus Lenau's *Faust*, followed by a descending order of even less adequate Fausts. Thus all that was left for them was to twist the Goethean Faust and Mephistopheles into an approximation of the Faust and Mephistopheles they longed for.

Just how dreadful the results have been, one can perhaps best illustrate by an analogy. Let us suppose that the critics in Leonardo's time and since were deeply dissatisfied with the representation of Judas in the *Last Supper* and that finally Cerano or Tanzio was commissioned to repaint the figure with a more viciously striking expression of villainy. Approximately this is what has happened to Goethe's *Faust* under the tender ministrations of actors and critics. There is an artistic discrepancy, a poetic disharmony in the drama as most people know it. And the crowning irony is that this disharmony is blamed on Goethe's poetic incompetence rather than on the critics' and actors' interpretative incompetence. The case of Mephistopheles is the most glaring and crucial instance of the critical misinterpretation that has stood between us and the *Faust* that Goethe actually wrote. Only after the overpainting of the ignorant or contrary-minded "restorers" has been removed can we go over to the study of the character that the poet himself had in mind. In extenuation two further observations should be added. Most of the critics and scholars who write about *Faust* have since childhood seen nothing but the diabolistic realization of the role and other, accompanying perversions of the drama; thus presumably they have become inured, perhaps desensitized to the discrepancies. And yet, the best of them quite apparently have not. In their writings, and also in conversations with artistically sensitive persons, I have noticed a feeling of unease, however subliminal, at the usual representation of the character, a feeling of disharmony, "hier stimmt etwas nicht," something is out of tune here.

Critics and observers of this kind may welcome what now follows, the removal of the alien overpainting and the showing of the whole figure (and eventually the whole work) in Goethe's original coloring and composition. Just as faithful early copies often tell us what a painting, later maltreated, originally looked like, just so the early report of Carl von Holtei, together with other related evidence, will tell us how Goethe himself wished his drama, specifically the role of Mephistopheles, to be realized. What lends it all further power of conviction is that in its illumination of the basic intent the previously disturbing disharmonies and discrepancies are shown to be later obtrusions, easily removed, leaving a consistent composition and harmonious coloration to delight the observer.

Nevertheless, our course will not be a clear and easy one, for the

advocates of the diabolistic interpretation have seized on one discrepancy and attempted through it to dissociate the La Roche evocation
from the Goethean intention. Later in life, when the actor came under
attack for his performance of the role, he defended himself by maintaining that what he did was in accordance with Goethe's specific direction,
that the poet had first, before the rehearsals began, assembled the actors
and read the play to them by way of interpretation, and that he later
coached La Roche down to the finest nuances of the performance of the
role. This claim has always been a stumbling block to the few among the
diabolistic critics who realized that the claim had even been made, and
naturally there was a valiant attempt to discredit this claim, with some
slight success to be sure, but with essential failure, as will appear.

The points that were scored against La Roche were these: (1)
Goethe's diaries at this time were especially rich and detailed, yet they
contain not a word about a preliminary meeting to gain his consent to
the Weimar performance, or about the poet's reading of the drama to
the assembled actors, or about his coaching of La Roche. (2) Goethe,
nearly eighty years old, would hardly have had the voice for such an
extended and animated reading as La Roche describes. (3) The Weimar
actor, Franz Eduard Genast, later asserted expressly that Friedrich Wilhelm Riemer was in charge as Goethe's representative and that the poet
himself unconcernedly let him do as he pleased.

Jacob Minor made these points in his *Aus dem alten und neuen
Burgtheater* (1920, 243–47), and the few who have looked into the
matter subsequently have unquestioningly and uncritically accepted his
verdict. And yet, a critical scrutiny of the total available evidence will
show them to be more than dubious. On the third point it is clear that
Genast was poorly informed or had a lapse of memory or misrepre-
sented. From Johann Peter Eckermann's letters to Auguste Kladzig at
this very time, we receive the firsthand and quite contradictory information that Goethe was personally interested and did directly participate;
more important, the still extant prompter's book contains directive notes
in Goethe's own handwriting; and most important, the poet exactly defined the extent of his participation in his letter to Johann Friedrich
Rochlitz, September 2, 1829, telling him that the *Faust* had also been
performed at Weimar "without any initiative of mine, but not against
my will and not without my consent as to the way and manner in which
the whole is to be conducted." No question, Goethe's guiding hand was
clearly present, thus also in the realization of the Mephistopheles role.

As for the second point, we have abundant witness from a series of
visitors to Weimar just at this time that Goethe was in unusually fine
health and vigor, with a remarkably strong, clear, flexible, melodic voice.
It is only necessary to read their accounts for 1828–29, as Heinz
Amelung has assembled them in his *Goethe als Persönlichkeit* (1925, III,

162–97), for instance, those of Immanuel Ilmoni, Christian Schuchardt (especially in Robert Springer's report), and Willibald Alexis, to realize that he was quite capable of such a feat. And naturally he would not have read the whole of Part One but only the stringently abridged version intended for the performance.

As for the first point, the completeness of Goethe's diaries at this time, more especially the assertion that a larger assembly of people could not have escaped being noted in it, let us merely look at the record for one vital date, August 29. It ends: "Alone that evening. Performance of *Faust* at the theater." True, Goethe did not attend the performance and was probably alone until after nine o'clock that evening. But immediately thereafter, as we know from several witnesses, there was a soirée at Goethe's house in which he participated in an active and animated way. Elsewhere also in the diary of this year there is frequently no record of what happened in the evening, sometimes even no record of what happened afternoon and evening.

We are thus forced to the conclusion that this supposed refutation of Carl La Roche's claims was merely a weak though seemingly plausible attempt to bolster the diabolist cause by discrediting this actor's all-too-clear exposition of Goethe's true intent. The most that can be said for that side is that La Roche later in life may have overstated his direct dependence on Goethe as a defensive exaggeration at the time the diabolist interpretation of the role was triumphing and his own interpretation was being denied its validity and primordiality. In sum, on the side of the diabolist interpretation there is no incontrovertible evidence; on the side of the more worldly and complex interpretation there is both the internal evidence of the text itself and the external evidence of Goethe's various sarcastic remarks about Madame de Staël and the other advocates of a diabolistic interpretation, all going to show that Carl La Roche was indeed carrying through the role according to Goethe's clear intent.

With the objections to Carl La Roche's validity disposed of, we can now safely turn to Carl von Holtei for an account of the way the actor played his role. In the course of a critique in which he censures various shortcomings of the performance, among them Durand's interpretation of the role of Faust, he singles out for special praise the masterly staging by Kobler and the excellent acting of Caroline Lortzing as Gretchen and of La Roche as Mephistopheles. The latter he describes thus (*Der Salon*, III [1868], 679–80; see also Schroer, I, CXIV, and Gräf, II, 2, 507):

> To my way of thinking, La Roche presented the devil as no one else has before him or after him. Whoever has, as I have . . . given public readings of Goethe's *Faust*, cannot possibly be unaware of the difficulty of actually embodying this "spirit who denies," and that "as a rascal," this "breath of evil" who involuntarily creates the good, this sublimest poetic creation of all time. I had never quite been able to imagine how to

manage that justice should be done to the outer appearance and how at the same time the higher intellectual magic power should be preserved so that it would not be dragged down into the dust of materialism. Very famous actors have attempted the experiment and have, rewarded by the applause of the multitude, gone so far as to act contrary to Mephisto's own declaration as to the "long since vanished Northern phantom" and to present precisely this. They have purred, spit, growled, they have limped as though on horse's hoof (a wonder that they did not put horns on), have grimaced, making faces to scare children out of their wits, so that Faust truly had no reason for calling Gretchen an "intuitive angel" because of her inexplicable aversion toward his friend.

La Roche by contrast abstained from all such revolting, evil-smelling household remedies and concoctions. He strictly followed the directions implicit in the poem and remained throughout the humorously negating, wittily mocking, merrily skeptical, craftily spying spirit. In harmony with this were his gestures, his elegantly free deportment, his masterfully simple speech, which was neither strongly emphatic, nor pompously elevated, nor straining for effect, but always fluent, impressive, intelligible, and according to Hamlet's precept pronounced "trippingly on the tongue." His Mephistopheles was no devil of flesh and blood who roams about like a roaring lion seeking whom he may devour. It was a symbolic phenomenon standing at the pinnacle of the poem. Indeed, if I may speak frankly, a phenomenon that perhaps did not belong on the real stage any more than did the poem itself. In this case highest praise for the actor who esteemed the literary work above the striking effect.

Just one further neat little indication of the actor's direct relationship to the poet at this time: the Goethe entry in the autograph album of La Roche is dated the day before the performance, that is, on Goethe's eightieth birthday, August 28, 1829. It is printed in Eduard Mautner's *Carl La Roche. Gedenkblätter* (Vienna, 1873, page 23), and repeatedly in the later Goethe literature.

All this information on the side of the more worldly, more complicated interpretation of the role of Mephistopheles (that turns out to be Goethe's own interpretation) has long since been available, though just a bit scattered. That no one has till now gone to the slight labor of putting it together, that no one has been interested in doing so, may be an indication of the hold that a tradition, however false, can have on the mind of man. The rest of the story is, in part, more difficult to come by, although much of it can be reconstructed from the reports and critiques gathered by Monty Jacobs in his *Deutsche Schauspielkunst*. It is the sad story of an otherwise celebrated and successful actor who, because he remained faithful to the precepts of Goethe and the clear indications of the text, had to endure the continuing invidious objections of critics and fellow actors who thought they knew better how Mephistopheles should be portrayed, less smoothly and elegantly, more demonically and diabolically. The histories of *Faust* on the German stage perpetrate the bias, at least passively, by slighting or even omitting the early defenses of the Goethe-La Roche interpretation, or actively, by endorsing the critical fallacies of the diabolists. La Roche had no equally able successor to carry on the Goethean interpretation, and so in the tragically inevitable course of time the opposition triumphed, to such an extent that apparently no present actor of the role, no present director of the play is even aware that an alternate and more authentic realization of the role ever existed.

Quite early, in 1832, Carl Ludwig Costenoble through his misunderstanding succinctly revealed the attitude of the opposition and its false basic premises. He does not realize that his demand for a diabolic mask runs contrary to Goethe's intent:

> La Roche as Mephistopheles was not lively and malicious enough. Also his intonation was too candid, sometimes even too woeful. . . . His delivery corresponded to his costume and make-up, which were definitely not diabolic. He played the part gently and much more slowly than was necessary, but effectively even so.

Ludwig Speidel, after citing La Roche's statement that his Mephistopheles was entirely Goethean, advances to the point of doubting the poet's own judgment about his work. This smug self-conceit became a critical tradition:

> That presumably is credible, for La Roche's Mephisto was a decidedly moderate comfortable devil, as might well correspond to the concept of Goethe in his old age. . . .
> If we make an effort to recall to memory the somewhat faded figure of La Roche's Mephisto, there is nothing to prevent us from tracing it back to Goethe and his authority. It had little of the poisonous sharpness, the superacuteness, and the cynicism with which other actors usually endow Mephisto. La Roche was a devil who would be presentable in good society. He was no sarcastic vulgarian but an ironist who even found it difficult to become menacing.

The opposition found its focus and rallying point in the next notable portrayor of the role on the German stage, Carl Seydelmann. This actor wrote a defense of his interpretation, one that developed from his simplistic concept of Mephistopheles as *the* devil:

> If we follow this devil through the whole poem, however, we shall find him not only not tame, but even bold and nasty and dirty. Just as bold and nasty and dirty as witty, burning, and corrosive, just like the devil. Only a few centuries later, modernized for the fun of it, but quite the old familiar devil. And Goethe who, even for his enlightened public, used the folk legend in almost all its details, did not want him otherwise.
> I don't give a damn about what he may later have said about it to

the contrary, when it's my task to play the devil the way he wrote him.

I adhere strictly to the costume and make-up prescribed by the poet himself and, in accordance with the spirit and its development, I play the devil.

As we shall see a bit later, August Lewald admiringly described this stage presence that Seydelmann considered to be so authentic. When we compare it with the presence so clearly prescribed and inferred in the Goethean text, we can only conclude that the poor man had a reading problem.

The great Eduard Devrient clearly recognized that Seydelmann's realization was contrary to the Goethean text:

> Seydelmann defended his role in a letter. He insisted on playing the devil of the folk legend and reducing Goethe's wonderful poem to the crude realism of a superstitious collier. . . . These utterances show above all that Seydelmann was totally deluded about the effect of his Mephistopheles. No one was really frightened at him; the impression he conveyed was merely that of the repulsive, the grotesque, even the ridiculous. . . . It was Goethe's intent to present the devil as a distinguished nobleman with an irony just as devastating as it was graceful.

Karl Immermann showed an equally clear discernment and was not taken in by the admittedly powerful talent of Seydelmann:

> Out of Mephistopheles he made an earthy, creaking spirit, with rigid consistency to be sure. But where was the Marinelli of Hell whom Goethe had in mind? Seydelmann was not at all refined or diplomatic, but heavy, with a diabolic-feral tone. . . . He stands in a demolished world of art. . . . He makes himself the focal point in order at least to be something himself where the work is reduced to a nothing. . . . When style is ruined, whim takes over.

This concluding reflection brings to mind a modern parallel, to judge from some accounts (laudatory ones, alas): Gustaf Gründgens in his representation also achieved the demolition of *Faust* as a work of art in order to make himself the focal point.

Unlike Immermann, Karl Gutzkow yielded to the power of Seydelmann's interpretation and had reservations only in particulars:

> You know in what high esteem I have always held Seydelmann's Mephistopheles. In the past six years I have seen several devils on the stage, but in my opinion Seydelmann's ranks first. . . . I know that this excellent artist and his Mephisto encountered strong opposition in Berlin. . . . I suppose that here they want the devil as civilized as possible, more "Squire Voland" with the cock's feather, the "Baron" rather than the terrible elemental spirit who is not only the devil but also Hell.

August Lewald succumbed completely and uncritically to the diabolistic interpretation, and his vivid description of Seydelmann's realization of the role indicates ominously the romantic smoke screen that had settled between the Goethean work and its beholder:

> He is Mephisto through and through, so great, so alien, so wild, so mocking, as only the most fervid imagination is able to depict him. . . . His costume is of a bright red shimmering fabric with yellow decorations, the cape "of stiff silk" grass green, his unusually long waist girded with a narrow black sword belt. This body is of a wasplike thinness, the fingers are bent like claws, in walking the horse's hoof is dragged along with elegant *grandezza*. His skull is covered with stubbly black hair, his eyes are squinting and crossed, his mouth bares his teeth and is turned up at the corners, the most terrible scorn speaks out from it, his nose sinks in crass shapelessness to his chin. Only the nose and the hair are artificial, all the rest is artistry, that is, Seydelmann produces the illusion without external aid, only through distortion of his facial muscles, and maintains it with incredible consistency during the long course of the play.
>
> . . . He places the jewels in the cupboard, but before he leaves [Gretchen's] room, he concentrates on suffusing the air with his breath. This blowing and puffing has something frightening about it, and we react sympathetically to poor Gretchen's words, "How close and sultry is the air."

However, Seydelmann was not the only Mephistopheles who aroused critical attention around mid-century. A critic of lesser stature than the preceding ones, Carl Wexel, does give us a comparative view of five different actors in the role, but, characteristically, he too concedes the crown to Seydelmann:

> Döring's conception of Mephisto tended throughout toward the humorous, and he gave him only so much diabolic coloration as seemed consistent with his intentions. . . . I have seen various great actors in the role of Mephisto: Weidner, Grunert, Marr, Dawison and—I salute the learned gentleman—Carl Seydelmann, a prince of Hell, as he stands in the book. Weidner made him pedantic with a kind of gruesome school-master's dignity; Grunert doctrinaire, more a professor of Hell; Marr more the cavalier, but with the demonic streak of Squire Voland; Dawison "the misbegotten freak of dirt and fire," but too subaltern, too insipid; and Seydelmann; his hellish majesty with the whole apparatus of the abyss, trailing lightning, thunder, and sulphur, with shudder and fright to the right of him, the howling and the gnashing teeth of the damned to the left of him; and yet of the five it was he who gave freest play to humor and satire.

Further descriptions of the role as played by such actors as Theodor Döring, Heinrich Marr, Bogumil Dawison indicate that when the diabolistic was not emphasised, the grotesque-comic was. For Döring and his comic talents Théophile Gautier had words of praise on his visit to Munich in 1854. However, it is the account of Eugen Guglia of

Friedrich Mitterwurzer's performance a quarter of a century later that reveals, by contrast, to what depths other Mephisto performances had sunk by this time:

> In the later scenes likewise Mitterwurzer did not employ the traditional Mephisto mask, not the red cap drawn over the forehead so that all the hair is covered, not the angled eyebrows running together over the nose; he simply used very pale make-up on his face and perhaps a few wrinkles at the corners of his mouth, but his forehead remained free, his unkempt hair visible; he did not distort his countenance in any manner.

Just after the turn of the century Josef Kainz aroused especial interest, but the contrasting accounts of Alfred Kerr and Arthur Eloesser indicate how uncertain, fluctuating, dubious the interpretation of the role (or the critical view of the interpretation of the role) had become:

> *Kerr:* That was . . . a figure not from Goethe, but perhaps from Byron. A Lucifer [from Byron]. An angel. One of the damned even while smiling. In mockery and agility with melancholy flashing and fluttering about him.

> *Eloesser:* . . . he abjured the elegant man of the world, the grandiose cynic. In which direction then did he draw the figure? Did he draw it toward the elemental, the grotesque, did he erupt with dirt and fire as lord of the rats and lice, as Reinhardt had once attempted? That too was not for him. Kainz maintained the middle way, a way otherwise alien to one of his vigor; he did not reach deep enough downward as the strange son of chaos nor high enough upward as the supreme critic of the course of the world. . . . This squire with his thick smirking lips was actually amusing only when he is associating with people of lower rank.

There is no need to go on. When Gründgens made headlines with the cheap atomic claptrap of the study scenes, the most ominous result was that even the critics who objected to this demented perversion of our artistic heritage were not able to reassert the original will that imbues the drama, the original poetic intent in the figures of the protagonist and the antagonist. Actors, directors, audience, critics have generally preferred a counterfeit Mephistopheles to the genuine Goethean one. And if the accounts of recent *Faust* performances in the *Goethe* yearbook for 1970 are symptomatic, we have little to look forward to in the immediate future. What a pity. We are being cheated out of most of the subtlety, most of the wit, most of the complexity of extension and limitation with which the poet endowed this fascinating character.

After reviewing this sad course of events over the past century and a half, one cannot help wonder what it would be like (and wish that it were possible) to see again a truly polished performance, in the genuine succession of La Roche and in the genuine intent of Goethe. This should not be too much to expect when one thinks of another eighteenth-century work with an equal sophistication and elegance in its presentation of evil (and gallant courage in a losing cause), I mean da Ponte's and Mozart's *Don Giovanni*. There are, of course, on to the present day, the vulgarizers and brutalizers of the Don Giovanni role, but there are also the interpreters of power and elegance, and to have seen one of these in a consummate performance can be among the great theatrical experiences of a lifetime. That Goethe himself saw analogies, comes out clearly in his conversation with Eckermann, February 12, 1829, on musical aspects of his drama: "The music would have to be in the character of *Don Giovanni*, Mozart would have been the one to set the *Faust* to music." Here another piece of evidence of how different the poet's own vision of his work was from that of subsequent times. Further evidence lies about in abundance inside and outside the work.

It may seem strange that among the people connected with the stage it was apparently an Italian actor who first in our time again had the right concept of the role, and that, ironically, not in the Goethean *Faust* but in the musical adaptation of Gounod. To be sure, Cesare Siepi was helped toward his bold reinterpretation both by his stellar performances in the *Don Giovanni* and by his early reading of Goethe's masterpiece. Here again is an example of where a thoughtful and sensitive artist can come to critical insights that have eluded all but a few of the earnest students of the work. In an interview with the artist, Mary Campbell reported for Associated Press on the last "opening night" of the old Metropolitan Opera House (the *Baltimore Sun*, June 17, 1965). She inquired about his "witty, agile interpretation" of the role and the critical controversy as to whether his "debonair" Mephistopheles was "a triumph over cliché" or was "sadly lacking in venom and demonic fire." He answered that he was unshaken by the adverse criticism; he had years before read Goethe's *Faust* and had come to the conclusion that the diabolist interpretation, costume, and make-up are an absurdity. He went on to describe how out of place all this is and how crudely inadequate; indeed, "You see we are dealing with a literary masterpiece." In conclusion he maintains, "People's taste is definitely becoming more refined." We can only hope that he is right and that in Germany too we may soon see the drama in something like its original form and intent.

2

Now that the crude overlay of demonics has been laboriously removed from the figure of Mephistopheles, the view is open for the understanding of the more subtle evil to be found in him, an evil passed over unseeingly as long as the diabolist overpainting intervened. It appears in two ways. The first is clearly visible and has indeed been correctly seen before, but only in its separate manifestations rather than with the larger perspective that brings all these together and leads to insight into a basic trait of character and trend of action. A clear understanding of this trait of character and trend of action is necessary if we are to discern the dynamics of the relationship to the protagonist, especially the chief device Mephistopheles uses to try to demean Faust, to make him "eat dust," "and with pleasure," as he vowed to do in the "Prologue in Heaven" (334).

The individual instances are quite obvious and well known. According to the terms of his wager with Faust, Mephisto must serve Faust on earth and carry out his every wish until such a time as the latter becomes complacent and content (the sign being Faust's saying to the present moment, "Stay, thou art so fair"), at which time Faust would lose his wager. Mephisto does carry through every wish, but almost always he does so in a way that will involve Faust in guilt, will lower his human dignity, will bring indignity upon him, will gradually, he hopes, dull his human sensibilities, blunt his conscience, inure him to wrong, and thus little by little remove him from the human toward the brutal where he would indeed easily become addicted to sensual pleasure and yearn for its continuance.

The first instance is a seemingly minor one and involves only the telling of a "white lie," as a kind of social expedient, easily condoned as doing no one any harm. Faust wants to meet Gretchen, Mephistopheles makes the arrangements, not the simple and direct ones that could easily have been made, but, more in character, elaborate and roundabout arrangements, the kind that will leave room for introducing some evil or perversion into the whole. So the arrangements are made through Martha, and Faust must as part of the scheme confirm Mephisto's story about the death of Martha's husband in Padua. He does not lightly consent to do so, for to him this is plainly bearing false witness. Mephisto's sophistical arguments he rejects (as he always does), but in his desire for Gretchen and in his impatience to see her he yields, with a frank admission of his weakness, free of sham and gloss (3071 f.):

> Und komm, ich hab' des Schwätzens Überdruß,
> Denn du hast recht, vorzüglich weil ich muß.

> *So come, this chatter fills me with disgust,*
> *For you are right, especially since I must.*

For Mephisto's designs Gretchen is clearly the wrong girl; he therefore has to devise ways of separating her from Faust and of involving both of them in guilt. Thus the supposedly harmless sleeping potion that he provides for Faust, and Faust passes on to Gretchen, results in the death of her mother, this only the first in a series of involvements clearly designed to lead a girl of her sensitive and dependent nature to the verge of madness and over it. In the scene, "Night. Street before Gretchen's Door" (3620 ff.), if we are to understand its true import, we need to observe clearly two factors that have been regularly overlooked. The first factor, plainly evident in the speeches of the protagonist, is Faust's abstraction, his dreamy reverie, his total remoteness from the time and place of action. It would be rewarding for the critic to reread these first speeches of Faust in context. Mephisto takes sinister advantage of this abstraction; with the sudden intrusion of Valentin he shocks Faust out of his reverie and, like Iago with Cassio, manipulates an innocent man into committing a homicide. The result is also well calculated: with Faust's involvement the blood ban is upon him, and since this is a sacred juridical act, Mephisto is powerless to protect him against it (3715); Faust must flee, he must desert Gretchen, he is helpless to do anything for her. Later when he learns of her fate and commands a return, Mephisto reconfirms his powerlessness over against the blood ban in even more emphatic words (prose scene, "Dreary Day") and can only limitedly and through minor magic carry out his orders.

By the time near the end of his life, when Faust gives his fateful order for the removal of Philemon and Baucis to the new estate he had prepared for them, he would certainly know Mephisto well enough to realize that his orders would be carried through not straightforwardly but with a sinister twist to bring upon him yet another degradation of human right and dignity. With such knowledge comes responsibility, and it will not do to excuse Faust because he gave clear, explicit directions for the safe removal of the old couple (11275 ff.) and because Mephisto perverted these orders. What dulled Faust's awareness this time was another kind of absent-mindedness, a deep involvement in a soul crisis, an inner sense of lack, which he in fatal error mistook for an external lack, projecting it upon the old estate on the dunes, as we shall see in the next chapter. When we observe that his besetting fault of impatience is added to his fatefully subjective self-involvement here, we only observe, we do not condone. We also observe how Mephisto for the last time uses a technique that he has used repeatedly against Faust, several times (far from always) with the limited success of involving him in guilt, never with the larger intended result of thereby brutalizing, dehumanizing him, bringing him to grovel and revel in the dust.

Mephisto's second kind of evil trickery is far less sinister and far more amusing, though it has, in fact, done incalculable damage to the interpretation of the work. It has naturally been least observed by those whom it has most affected, the critics and interpreters. All the way through the drama the old rascal indulges in a great variety of comments and "asides," usually at the end of scenes; from the "Prologue in Heaven" onward he frequently has the "last word" and tells the listener how he should understand and interpret what has just transpired. Now these are some of the most witty and entertaining bits in the whole drama, and

such are their charm and power of persuasion that many critics have
been inclined to accept at least some if not most of these as true and
sound, have interpreted large portions of the drama in accordance with
them, and have in innocent confidence cited his statements as "proofs"
for their various interpretations and conclusions. Indeed, it has been my
observation that many if not most of the wrong interpretations of *Faust*
are based on an all-too-gullible acceptance of Mephisto's twistings and
perversions as true interpretations.

In striking contrast to such critics stands Faust who maintains the
utmost degree of skepticism over against the distortions and sophistries
of Mephisto. If we review the drama, we shall see that Faust does so
time and again throughout both parts. Even on those few occasions
where Mephisto is under obligation, by the laws of the spirit world, to
tell the truth, Faust doubts him until he has reason to think otherwise.
Such truthful and reliable statements of the old rascal, the important
ones at any rate, can be discerned if we examine them in the context of
the whole, for the poet took care to have them confirmed elsewhere in
the drama by trustworthy witnesses, above all by the Lord in the "Prologue."

To cite an extreme instance of critical innocence, it seems almost
incredible that any alert and observant person could believe in Mephisto's "interpretation" of the song of the spirits (1607–26) that follows
immediately upon Faust's great curse. What the spirits actually sang
stands in such obvious contradiction to what Mephisto claims they sang
that one is left marveling at the earnest students who have weighed his
words and weightily decided for or against their credibility, much to the
obscuring of the intent of the scene, particularly of the nature and function of the aerial spirits.

Actually, this is perhaps Mephisto's most inept and unconvincing bit
of twisting; he knows it is and hastily changes both subject and tone. It
is inept because he was taken by surprise at the unexpected and inop-
portune intrusion of the aerial spirits at this point and had to improvise
quickly in order to cover up. What do they sing? After they express their
woe at Faust's destructive nihilistic curse, they call upon him to reconstruct the world, to lead a life of renewed creativity. Nothing could be
more contrary to Mephisto's nature and intent than creativity, as we
know from the immediately preceding scene and from the Prologue. His
claim that these are his minions and that they are summoning Faust into
the world of pleasure and activity is about as feeble an effort in interpretative twisting as this rogue ever perpetrated. If such a crude trap
can be effective, what then are we to expect from his better prepared
and far more clever efforts?

Our worst fears are confirmed when we look at the critical comments on Mephisto's "asides" and "last words" all the way from the

"Prologue in Heaven" to his final comments on Faust's last earthly activities (11530, 11544–50, 11595–603). Strange how a whole school of modern interpreters has cited these final comments (with the careful omission of the last, to be sure) as the "proof" that Faust's final creative achievements are futile and chimerical. If the critic trusts Mephisto more than the Lord of the "Prologue," he will reap his reward in a commensurate misunderstanding of the drama. It is time for us to replace this naive gullibility with some of the sound skepticism of Faust and a sharper analysis of the sophistries involved. Doing so will free us from most of the particular misunderstandings of separate scenes as well as from many a larger misunderstanding. It will also increase our enjoyment of some of the most delightful features of the play. We shall observe the clever old rascal repeatedly laying traps for the unwary, his more cunning ones arousing our grudging admiration. And it is, of course, more fun to detect them than to fall into them.

Nevertheless, it is a well grounded and generally accepted critical observation that Mephistopheles does occasionally tell the truth, that his statements can at times be relied on. To be sure, we have seen that these occasions are rarer than is generally assumed and that impressively numerous critical blunders continue to result from an all too trusting reliance upon the comments and interpretations he makes at various points throughout the drama. Then also there is the complication that he may occasionally tell the truth not from motives of pure candor but in order to obfuscate a confused situation still more, that he may occasionally utter a cynical truth simply to prick the bubble of Faust's or another's self-conceit or overexaltation, or that he may make a quip just for the fun of it, not failing occasionally even to laugh at himself. How then can we distinguish the times when he is being reliable from the times when he is leading us by the nose? There are two ways, fortunately, and they can often be used in combination for greater certitude.

There is, first of all, the larger context, and this is the critical criterion we have been using up to this point. When Mephisto describes himself to Faust as "the spirit that ever denies" (1338) and so forth, this turns out to be in close agreement with what the Lord had said about him in the "Prologue" and disagrees in no particular except in the appropriately negative, anti-creative bias. When he describes the realm of the Mothers, his report is found to be in general agreement with Faust's upon return, and beyond that, in the larger context, with the whole continuum of the feminine creative throughout the drama. It would seem then that when Mephistopheles is speaking about the laws of his function and place in the spirit world, its conditions and relations, he is under higher obligation to speak the truth. Likewise, when Mephisto's capabilities are not equal to Faust's demands and when he needs the assistance of spirit worlds and forces beyond his own, he must be straightforward and truthful, albeit with the added ingredient of his usual slant or slur.

There is a second way to distinguish between the reliable and the unreliable statements of Mephistopheles. It is based upon a careful, sensitive listening to the language level, to the tone and diction of Mephistopheles' statements. Even by itself alone this approach can lead to generally reliable results, as Kurt May has demonstrated in his *Faust II.Teil in der Sprachform gedeutet*. His observation of the elevated and serious tone that prevails in Mephisto's speeches in the Mothers scene ("A Dark Gallery") and his description of quite different tones in the speeches elsewhere are for the most part right, and we can on their basis make reasonably good judgments as to the intent and the degree of reliability of this character at a particular point.

This is equally the case in Part One. If we look at the diction of Mephisto's self-description in the study scene of his first encounter with Faust, we find a careful, dignified choice of words with none of the scurrilities of phrase or implication he indulges in so frequently elsewhere. On the other hand, at the end of the next study scene, when his statement about seeing the small and then the great world occurs in combination with the inelegant "munching through this course" (2054), then let the critic beware: the old rascal is setting yet another trap for the simply trusting. All the more so when he later refers to the great world and the small world in the "Walpurgis Night" (4045), while he is reflecting on the sex life of the upper classes, and immediately appends remarks on the dress and undress of witches; then an elevated intellectual vision is hardly the critical instrument to deal with the situation.


3


With the removal of the crude overlay of diabolistics we come not only to new insights into the subtler evil of Mephistopheles or into his hilarious devices for hoodwinking reader and critic, we come also to new insights into his weaknesses and inadequacies. If we fail to take note of his personal and mental limitations and of the blunders that result from them, the possibilities for misinterpretation are even further extended.

Significantly, and with the poet's design no doubt, Mephistopheles enters the Faust action with a blunder. Disguised as a poodle, he fails to notice that he is accidentally walking into the study through the open peak of a pentagram and so (by the laws of the spirit world) is entrapped there. Once in the study, he realizes that his timing also is bad: he has not foreseen Faust's change of mood from despair to serenity and a yearning for the divine. Thus all his ingenuity has to be expended in securing his own release and evading issues with Faust till a more fa-

vorable occasion. As we shall see, it is not only in this first scene that
Mephistopheles has to concentrate on saving himself, to the neglect of
his main intent, this also happens to him in his last scene. Quite clearly,
the poet has established an ironic framework around the Mephisto action. And it is important that we realize this, first of all for our understanding of the function and larger intent of this scene.

A more favorable occasion than that exalted night after the Easter
Walk comes the next morning when Faust, quite understandably, is
again plunged into the black despair that carries him on recklessly to his
great curse. Even after the monitory hortatory song of the aerial spirits
Faust remains ready to sign the usual kind of a quid-pro-quo compact.
However, at that point Mephistopheles is, first of all, disconcerted by
this song summoning Faust to a new life of reconstruction and creativity.
He is thrown off balance and in his moment of panic improvises an
"interpretation" so implausible that it should never have deceived any-
body, and then furthermore feels compelled quickly to cover up this
makeshift again in his "hearty," "man-to-man" exhortation to Faust to
surmount his grief.

Through the scene Mephisto never quite recovers from the nasty
surprise of the spirit chorus, and this early he commits the blunder that
he repeats several more times in the course of the scene, the second and
third time crucially, for the blunder results in his losing the chance of
attaining a firm quid-pro-quo compact with Faust and forces him to
accept Faust's counter-proposal of an open-ended wager (winner take
all, loser lose all). At this point critical confusion will readily give way to
clarity if one carefully observes what happens in the order in which it
happens, and also observes why there is a sudden shift from an expected
compact to an unexpected wager. The first time Mephisto makes the
blunder, he quickly covers over (1637–40):

> Die schlechteste Gesellschaft läßt dich fühlen,
> Daß du ein Mensch mit Menschen bist.
> Doch so ist's nicht gemeint,
> Dich unter das Pack zu stoßen.

> *No company so vile but lets you feel*
> *You are a man with other men.*
> *Yet that's not my intention*
> *To thrust you forth into the rabble.*

Then comes the discussion of the originally intended compact. With
Faust recklessly disregarding the future consequences, Mephisto sees
victory at hand and, to clinch the bargain, holds out delightful prospects
for Faust (1671–74):

> In diesem Sinne kannst du's wagen.
> Verbinde dich; du sollst, in diesen Tagen,

Mit Freuden meine Künste sehn,
Ich gebe dir, was noch kein Mensch gesehn.

*In this sense you can go these ways.*
*Commit yourself. You shall in these next days*
*Behold my arts, with pleasure too;*
*What no man yet has seen I'll give to you.*

Ironically, however, these words turn out not to be the final inducement
to persuade Faust to agree to a compact; they turn out to be Mephisto's
major blunder, a badly miscalculated case of "overselling." Faust's very
next words show his towering indignation at this insult to his intelligence. He had earlier taken the correct measure of Mephisto's powers
and limitations and is indignant that he should be thought so gullible.
Contemptuously he retorts (1675–77):

Was willst du armer Teufel geben?
Ward eines Menschen Geist, in seinem hohen Streben,
Von deinesgleichen je gefaßt?

*And what would you, poor devil, give me ever?*
*When would a human spirit in its high endeavor*
*Be understood by such a one as you?*

Mephisto's reply shows that this was not simply a momentary lapse on
his part but an intrinsic blunder that had deep-seated origins in character and insight. He truly does, as Faust (and earlier the Lord) observes,
lack understanding for man's higher aspirations and he reduces everything to the pleasure principle. So he goes on to aggravate his blunder to
the point of putting a compact quite out of reach and being forced by
Faust's next response to accept a wager in its stead.

Although Faust has by now twice tried to correct Mephisto's misapprehension, this is not the end of the latter's stupidity. Not once more,
but three times more in this scene he repeats his blunder, even though
Faust wearily tries again to set his thinking straight. Surely, the poet was
intent on making it abundantly clear where Mephisto's blind spot lay and
equally surely it was not his fault if reader and critic have continued to
miss the point. What has stood in the way has been the non-Goethean
diabolism and the folk-book atavism. These have allowed otherwise intelligent persons seriously to believe that a compact was actually concluded in this scene (and even more preposterously, that Mephisto had
actually concluded, not merely proposed, a wager with the Lord in the
"Prologue in Heaven").

Mephisto's limitations in scope, range, knowledge, and understanding are even more drastically exposed in Act Two of Part Two, in the
first Homunculus scene, so drastically indeed that even he is embar-
rassed and in the end resorts to a mendacity, a misrepresentation of the

events that is almost as weak and silly as his misrepresentation of what the spirits had sung after Faust's great curse.

The old rascal, having in his helplessness brought back the unconscious Faust to his old study, had already suffered a smaller humiliation during his interview with the Bachelor of Arts. At an earlier stage, when this glorious creature was a mere freshman, Mephisto had led him toward a perversion of his higher faculties in the temptation toward the sensual rewards of a medical career; thus at this later date it must have been disconcerting to him to find his finest temptation outtopped by a still more seductive temptation, that of the transcendental subjective philosophy. This may have made it all the harder for his vanity to bear the humiliation of Homunculus' witty, good-natured, but devastating exposure of his limitations, indeed total helplessness in the present dilemma of Faust's deadly dangerous faint. Only Homunculus has the intelligence, knowledge, and understanding to propose and enact a way out of the dilemma. This way, moreover, is one that will carry Mephisto completely beyond his borders, out of his depth, and he is battered about in a series of further humiliations, culminating in his encounter with the Lamias, until finally he finds a point of rest with the Phorkyads in the primordial shadows at the edge of chaos. With Homunculus in charge, all that Mephistopheles can do is trail along and conclude this last study scene with a sheepish twisted half-admission addressed to the audience (7003–4):

Am Ende hängen wir doch ab
Von Kreaturen, die wir machten.

*And finally we do depend*
*Upon the creatures we have made.*

How anyone could give credence to this spurious claim to creativity after a close reading of the scene as a whole, especially after Homunculus' words (confirmed by the continuing context), would surpass our understanding if we did not here have, as so often before, the intrusion of a crude diabolism that has concealed not only the subtler evils but also the limitations, stupidities, and blind spots. Far from being a monolith of infernal evil, Mephistopheles is endowed with a complexity of character that has a greater diversity of strengths and weaknesses than has ever been realized.

4

Beyond these insights, what we still lack toward a fuller and juster understanding is a compensatory consideration of certain more positive traits that are also present in his character, at least potentially. We shall best have access to these if we examine more closely the poet's original intentions with regard to Mephisto and then the somewhat revised destiny toward which he allowed him to go. Goethe does all this in the form of a jest, a jest that was an outrageously exuberant one in his young and middle years and came to be modified to the final, subtle, smiling jest that he introduced into his great work. This final extension of our symbolic understanding of Mephistopheles will reflect back on several earlier scenes and episodes; it will make clear and fitting certain remarks of his that till now have had to be considered out of character. It is not untypical of the poet to present us with these final insights in the form of a jest, though it was certainly not his intent that the jest should have been missed through a hundred and fifty long years. One reason why it has been missed can be observed in the sad specific example of a critique a few decades ago in which the comic-grotesque sequence in the poodle-transformation (and Bible-translation) scene is regarded as proof positive that the scene as a whole is trivial, an awkward transition, a mere expedient, and devoid of deeper purpose. Its compositional function in the framework for the whole Mephistopheles action has simply gone unobserved.

Neither Goethe nor his great master Shakespeare was inclined to use the comic scene in serious setting for any mere purpose of entertainment or "relief." This function is fulfilled, of course, but so is, usually, a far greater and deeper and subtler one, namely, the revelation of the irony of life itself and the wildly comic way in which some of its central crises transpire. In Shakespeare, almost immediately after Macbeth has murdered his king, Fate comes knocking at the door in the figure of the future avenger Macduff. And who comes to open the door? A drunken dallying porter, amusing himself by playing the role of gatekeeper of Hell. Schiller, alas, either missed the point in his elevated idealism or, more likely, feared that the audiences of his day would miss it; in his version of *Macbeth* he took out the drunken scalawagery of the porter and substituted a sober morning song, also deeply ironic but no longer grotesquely comic. That is the kind of concession to negative good taste that Goethe would not make, even at the risk of a century and more of misunderstanding.

In the text itself of the last great jest lies the crux of the matter. One idiom, one verb complex, can in its larger textual setting be correctly interpreted only as a medical metaphor. Only once or twice has there been any notice of this, and then merely in isolation, without any understanding of the implications in the larger context. Thus the point of the jest has been missed and therewith the point of the whole scene.

Here, as always, Goethe played fair with his audience, his readers. The words of the Lord in the "Prologue in Heaven" prepare us, though somewhat indirectly, for the great comic scene where Mephisto contends with the angels and the fire of heavenly love. What is more, Goethe, early in life, plainly stated his intent in this scene—with a confirmation of this intent coming about forty years later. That this statement has been overlooked is one of the ironic accidents of *Faust* scholarship.

The accident happened in this way: Hans Gerhard Gräf overlooked the important statement of young Goethe, and the *Faust* volume of his great compilation, *Goethe über seine Dichtungen*, issued in 1904, does not contain it. Everyone since then has naturally relied on Gräf; everyone since then has also missed it. A further irony is that, although the statement is to be found in that other great Goethe compilation, Biedermann's edition of the conversations (1909–11), it is tucked away in a supplement and does not appear in the index at the proper place.

Let us then look at the pertinent texts and see what they have to tell us. The first is a report from Wieland about Goethe's early years at Weimar when he gave readings from his *Faust* but would not disclose his plan for the whole except on one occasion. The report comes through Bernhard Rudolf Abeken who relates a conversation with Wieland in 1809 (Biedermann I, 134): "Goethe never divulged his intentions about the *Faust*; only once in ebullient company he said, 'You think the devil is going to fetch Faust. Quite the contrary: Faust is going to fetch the devil.'"

This sounds like an authentic report; certainly it comes from reliable sources; the outburst is just the kind of drastic, paradoxical one that would be characteristic for Goethe around 1775/76. Certainly the notion behind it is one with which he was familiar since 1770; in one of his favorite books of that time, Gottfried Arnold's *Unparteyische Kirchen- und Ketzer-Historie*, he could read, for instance, in the section on the Greek church father Origen, that the fallen angels also could be saved by an act of God's grace. Then, of course, there is the childhood memory of Klopstock's remorseful fallen angel, Abbadona.

We have clear evidence as late as 1816 that Goethe continued to relish the thought of shocking the public by hauling the old reprobate up to heaven in the end. As Johannes Daniel Falk recorded it in his conversation of about June 21, 1816 (Biedermann IV, 473–74):

> When finally in the continuation of *Faust* [the Germans] happen upon the place where the devil himself finds grace and mercy before God, that, I do think, they will not soon forgive me. . . . Even the perceptive Madame de Staël took it amiss that after the song of the angels [in the "Prologue in Heaven"] I made the devil so good natured over against God the Father. She wanted him much fiercer. What is going to happen when she encounters him again on a still higher level and perhaps even in heaven?

But is there any indication in the *Faust* itself that Goethe carried out any such plan? Carried it out fully? No. Suggested and began to

carry it out? Yes. It is the cream of the jest that in the end Mephistopheles comes perilously close to being saved by the grace and love of
God, and it is only by a supreme effort of his brilliant perverted intellect
that he manages to evade this dreadful fate and save himself for further
deviltry. Goethe had quietly prepared the way for such a perilously close
and uncertain outcome in the "Prologue in Heaven" when the Lord says
to Mephistopheles (337–39):

> Ich habe deinesgleichen nie gehaßt.
> Von allen Geistern, die verneinen,
> Ist mir der Schalk am wenigsten zur Last.

> *I never have abhorred the like of thee.*
> *Of all the spirits who deny*
> *The scamp has been least onerous to me.*

He goes on to describe such a rascal's function in keeping mankind from
falling into sloth (343):

> Der reizt und wirkt und muß als Teufel schaffen.

> *Who stirs and prods and must create, as devil.*

We must admit that he has performed his rascally assignment well,
according to the Lord's intent, and certainly deserves some reward for
his pains ultimately, even though the reward here offered strikes him
rather as a dirty trick. He is a good sport, however; when he is the loser
through what he regards as a piece of heavenly chicanery, he comments
with a good-humored shrug and a quip (11837):

> Ein großer Aufwand, schmählich! ist vertan.

> *A lavish outlay, shamefully, is lost.*

And anyway, he had just previously managed to save his soul from the
fires of heavenly love. Let us see how he managed to do that. The
sequence is familiar enough up to the climax, but here the point is easily
missed, in part because the exact order of events has not been accurately
observed.

After Mephistopheles has deployed his short-fat and long-thin assistants about the body of the expired Faust to watch for his emerging soul,
the heavenly hosts descend strewing roses, amid his offbeat commentary
on the dissonant music and the simpering sanctimony, culminating in his
devastating, wrong-side-out characterization (11696):

> Es sind auch Teufel, doch verkappt.

> *They're devils also, only in disguise.*

When the assistants flinch under the sting of the descending roses, puff
them into flame, and then retreat in panic into their more comfortable

type of flame, Mephisto stands his ground courageously and defiantly (11739–40):

Gesegn' euch das verdiente heiße Bad!
Ich aber bleib' auf meiner Stelle.

*Blessed be your well-earned scalding bath.*
*But as for me, I'll keep my station.*

He is, however, sore beset with the penetrating flames of heavenly love descending upon him despite all his efforts to fend them off. The angels explicate, and we must carefully heed their words, especially in the third and fifth lines (11745–52):

Was euch nicht angehört,
Müsset ihr meiden,
Was euch das Innre stört,
Dürft ihr nicht leiden.
Dringt es gewaltig ein,
Müssen wir tüchtig sein.
Liebe nur Liebende
Führet herein!

*What you've no tenure to,*
*You must beware it.*
*What stirs the depths of you,*
*You may not bear it.*
*If it pervade with might,*
*We must effect aright.*
*Only the loving ones*
*Love leads to light.*

Here there is no talk of a surface effect, but of something that disturbs the inner self, that penetrates powerfully. In the next scene the Younger Angels make it abundantly clear that this is indeed the case (11949–52).

Mephistopheles' next words, with their wry twist, indicate that he is succumbing to the fire of love and now understands the woe of unhappy lovers. What to do now? His resourcefulness is not exhausted; he manages to stay in control of the situation by a final masterfully imaginative exertion of diabolical ingenuity. His own words about unhappy frustrated lovers give him the clue; he twists the love surging within him into a supremely hopeless pederastic passion for the boylike angels, and he churns this up through forty perverted lines—with ultimate success when the angels pronounce the verdict and summon back upward the descended flames of love, though their concluding words here indicate that this is not the last time Mephisto will have to sweat it out (11801–8):

Wendet zur Klarheit
Euch, liebende Flammen!
Die sich verdammen,
Heile die Wahrheit;
Daß sie vom Bösen
Froh sich erlösen,
Um in dem Allverein
Selig zu sein.

*Turn, clear revealing,*
*Flames loving, unhemmed.*
*And to the self-condemned*
*May truth bring healing,*
*That they from evil*
*Find glad retrieval,*
*That in All-Unity*
*Blessed they may be.*

As the flames of love leave their deep seat within him and emerge to the surface, something strange happens to the old rascal. We must listen carefully to his words and see them in their context and sequence (11809–16):

Wie wird mir! —Hiobsartig, Beul' an Beule
Der ganze Kerl, dem's vor sich selber graut,
Und triumphiert zugleich, wenn er sich ganz durchschaut,
Wenn er auf sich und seinen Stamm vertraut;
Gerettet sind die edlen Teufelsteile,
Der Liebespuk, er wirft sich auf die Haut;
Schon ausgebrannt sind die verruchten Flammen,
Und wie es sich gehört, fluch' ich euch allzusammen!

*What's happening to me!—Job-like, boil on boil*
*The entire fellow, that I shrink to view me,*
*Yet triumph still when I search through and through me*
*And place my trust in mine own self and kin.*
*My noble devil parts survive the broil,*
*The love spell it is thrown off on the skin;*
*Burnt out already are the atrocious flames,*
*And, one and all, I curse you as the instance claims.*

The crucial idiom is "sich werfen auf," and, for good measure, the confirmatory, sequential "ausgebrannt" is added in the next line. To my knowledge only two of the commentators explain this term correctly, but they do so only in passing while retaining the quite contradictory notion that the flames produce only a surface effect of singeing and blistering the skin. The translators follow the commentators, sometimes the worst of these, and so mistranslations result, like this relatively recent one: "The love spook went no deeper than my skin," or most recently and even worse: "It's only skin the love-spook knows to chafe." To my knowledge, only one recent translation reads more correctly: "The love infection breaks out through the skin." Actually, of course, the flames had descended earlier in the scene and had penetrated deeply into Mephisto, as the angels clearly indicate (11747 and 49) and he immediately confirms (11753):

Mir brennt der Kopf, das Herz, die Leber brennt.

*My head's aflame, my heart, my liver too.*

Only now, later in the scene, after the episode of perversion, upon the departure of the angels upward with the flames of love, do they *emerge* from him, do they raise up the boils. "Sich werfen auf," as a medical metaphor to describe this process, though there are instances of it from the seventeenth to the nineteenth century, has become rare. However, if one calls to mind the more common, nearly synonymous expression, "ausschlagen," "Ausschlag," "erupt," "eruption," the meaning and happening at once become clear. Mephistopheles is not alarmed when, Job-like, his skin bursts out in boils; it is gruesome, he admits, but in the very next phrase he expresses his sense of triumph at a nasty disease successfully "thrown off" through his abiding loyalty to his own nature and his own kind. Then comes his blasphemously witty anticipatory parody of the angels celebrating the salvation of Faust's soul. The angels sing later (11934–35):

Gerettet ist das edle Glied
Der Geisterwelt vom Bösen.

*The noble limb of the spirit world*
*Is rescued now from evil.*

Here Mephisto exults (11813):

Gerettet sind die edlen Teufelsteile.

*The noble devil parts are rescued now.*

The next line is couched in terms of still extant medical folklore, erstwhile medical science: the sign of a patient critically ill taking a turn for the better occurs when the inwardly consuming fever comes to the surface in the form of a skin eruption:

Der Liebespuk, er wirft sich auf die Haut;
Schon ausgebrannt sind die verruchten Flammen.

*The love spell it is thrown off on the skin;*
*Burnt out already are the atrocious flames.*

This is why Mephisto rejoices at what one might think of as highly alarming symptoms. He knows that now the worst is over. His supreme

imaginative effort at a perversion of heavenly love into a grotesque
parody of love has been successful. He has once more saved his soul
from a fate worse than hell. He can now continue in his delectable
career of raising the devil instead of warbling insipidly in the heavenly
choirs.

But it was a close call. His own "salvation" so completely summoned
to supreme effort all his resources of intelligence, imagination, concen-
tration that he had to neglect temporarily his plans for Faust's damna-
tion. Just as he is breathing a sigh of relief at having escaped, even
though not with a whole skin, the choir of angels rises upward with
Faust's soul. "Cunningly snatched away," "pfiffig weggepascht," is his
indignant comment. But the eternal "Schalk" and "jester" has to have his
fun right to the bitter end, even when it is at his own expense, though, as
so often previously, he twists the facts again, just as if this encounter
were analogous to his futile affair with the Lamias in the "Classical
Walpurgis Night." He comments (11834–43):

> Du bist getäuscht in deinen alten Tagen,
> Du hast's verdient, es geht dir grimmig schlecht.
> Ich habe schimpflich mißgehandelt,
> Ein großer Aufwand, schmählich! ist vertan;
> Gemein Gelüst, absurde Liebschaft wandelt
> Den ausgepichten Teufel an.
> Und hat mit diesem kindisch-tollen Ding
> Der Klugerfahrne sich beschäftigt,
> So ist fürwahr die Torheit nicht gering,
> Die seiner sich am Schluß bemächtigt.

> *In your old days you have been roundly cheated,*
> *But you deserve it, wretched is your plight.*
> *I have mismanaged in outrageous fashion,*
> *A lavish outlay, shamefully, is lost;*
> *A vulgar lust, an absurd lovesick passion*
> *The hardened devil to and fro has tossed.*
> *If from this childish foolish folderol*
> *His shrewd experience could not wrest him,*
> *Then verily the folly is not small*
> *That in conclusion has possessed him.*

When love hit the sophisticated old rascal, he behaved just as absurdly
as the youngest greenest lover in his first springtide—so this old confidence man claims, in his last attempt to hoodwink us. All that he has to
console himself is that, though he has lost Faust, he has saved himself.

Can it be that this is what Goethe meant when he wrote to Karl
Ernst Schubarth, November 3, 1820, no doubt with an inward chuckle:
"Mephistopheles may only half win his wager"? But this is not the place
to become involved in another crux of *Faust* interpretation, just as one is

about to close. Actually there is no need to do so; what we have before us is clear and sufficient. The wager that Faust had offered so scornfully, Mephistopheles had accepted confidently—overconfidently, as it turned out. For Faust himself, bearing half the guilt, as Goethe puts it in this letter to Schubarth, the Lord's mercy intervened. Divine grace also reached down to Mephisto, who, however, exercised his freedom of will and chose to reject it.

In the end the old poet was more kind to Mephistopheles than the young poet had intended to be. The engaging rascal was in mercy spared the ultimate humiliation of totally losing his wager with Faust: Faust did not fetch the devil after all.

# 2

# The Sentimentalists

N THE COURSE OF the *Faust* drama a young girl, a young boy, and an old couple, each in turn, comes to a tragic end that arouses the sorrowful sympathy of spectator and reader, all the more since Goethe's poetry achieves an imaginative realization of their fate that would make it difficult for anyone of normal human warmth to escape becoming emotionally involved. This is all very well, provided one takes this marvelous imaginative realization for the artistic achievement it is and does not mistake it for partisanship, for a summons to the reader to take sides. As a matter of sad fact, however, the reader has all too often taken sides, to the extent of twisting and perverting the poet's larger artistic intent.

The situation was, of course, far graver for the *Werther*, which the reading public took in exactly the opposite way from the one young Goethe had intended, in going over from sympathy with the protagonist to active approval and imitation of his pathological course toward self-destruction. For the second authorized edition, of 1775, Goethe added two quatrains as mottoes for the title pages of the two parts. The second ends with the admonition from Werther's shade: "Be a man and do not follow me." Goethe omitted these quatrains from later editions; as poetry they are a failure, in part because the author here broke his usual rule against a direct and open indication of how a work of his was to be interpreted. It is old artistic wisdom that an author shows but he does not tell.

1

Goethe did better in another early poem that indicated, this time by indirection and juxtaposition, just how the Gretchen episode in the Faust

30

was to be understood. He wrote it during his first years in Weimar, no doubt because he felt the need to oppose the sentimental reaction toward Gretchen that was already developing during the time of his early readings of the play before any part of it was published. If a circle of friends and acquaintances close around him could so mistake his intent, what could be expected from the larger, remoter public?

The strangest aspect of the whole matter is that in the extensive critical literature on the Gretchen tragedy there is, so far as I have been able to ascertain, not a single mention of this poem. We have thus been in the position of trying to assess the poet's intent in this episode while lacking one of the clearest and plainest indications of his intent. Perhaps it would be more accurate to say that we have never been sufficiently concerned with the poet's intent but have allowed ourselves to become so sympathetically, and sentimentally, involved in the movingly pathetic fate of this ineffably sweet and adorable creation of the poet that we have imperiously intruded our subjective involvement and participation into the interpretation of the character and the action and have thus overlooked not merely the outside poem in which Goethe indicates his attitude, but also the really obvious intimations within the Faustian text itself. In sum, much the same sentimental fallacy that caused successive generations of readers to misinterpret the Werther tragedy, greatly to Goethe's dismay, is to this day causing a widespread misinterpretation of the Gretchen tragedy. It would seem to be about time, or past time, to put aside our personal involvement and directive sympathies, long enough at least to ascertain the poet's own intent within these scenes themselves and for the drama as a whole.

As always, when we rise from our own dimensions to the poet's greater dimensions, we see that from the poet's standpoint the dramatic continuity here assumes greater and nobler proportions, opens up wider perspectives, and, most important of all, shows closer relation to the drama as a whole and seems far less episodic than heretofore. Furthermore, the grave misinterpretations that have arisen from the subjective sentimental approach are cleared away and we are able, almost for the first time, to view this wondrous poetic fabric in its relation to the total pattern.

One advance can be clearly and immediately made if we imagine how different the whole course of events would have been if Faust's Gretchen had been of approximately the same character and attitude as the heroine of another early Goethean drama, *Egmont*; here Klärchen defies convention and remains courageously active to the tragic end. With this contrastive instance in mind, we can see at once that the Gretchen tragedy is not a tragedy of circumstance, as has regularly been inferred, but rather that far deeper and subtler type of tragedy, the tragedy of character. The tragedy came about not because Faust seduced Gretchen, but because Gretchen was what she was, with her intrinsic being remote from and irreconcilable to Faust as he was. Fortunately, for our critical consideration, Goethe did delineate a girl who was brought into the same circumstances as was Gretchen but, with her very different character, responded quite differently to them. The moment we realize this, it becomes clear that we have grossly oversimplified matters by assuming that Faust's actions and Mephistopheles' intrigues alone and inevitably brought about the tragedy. We must face the fact that a main part of the tragic guilt resides in Gretchen herself, in a tragic flaw of character. Seen from this point of view, that of a truly innocent and virtuous character who nevertheless brings about a pitiable fate upon herself and those close to her, she rises to the status of a true tragic figure. We may even think of an ancient character, of comparable virtue and strict adherence to convention, who also brought a pitiable fate upon herself and those close to her, though no one of course would, beyond this analogy, think of equating Gretchen with Antigone.

It would seem that it was Goethe's intent to make clear, once and for all, that this was a tragedy of character when, in 1776 or 1777, he wrote his poem "Vor Gericht," "In Court." No doubt, the sentimental and subjective literary attitudes, prevalent in his time, were already developing the Gretchen image and interpretation that has remained standard to this day. With his reluctance about interpreting his own works, especially marked in his youth, and with the unfortunate instance of his *Werther* quatrains in mind, he may have thought it better to illustrate his intent with a vivid new and complementary creation rather than to explicate his own *Faust* text directly. At any rate, the intrinsic nature and clear intent of the poem make such an inference probable. The title gives the setting for what develops in the poem: a pregnant unwed girl has been brought to a court hearing, and pressure has been exerted by pastor and magistrate to make her reveal the name of the father. The poem consists of her defiant, courageously independent reply:

> Von wem ich es habe, das sag ich euch nicht,
> Das Kind in meinem Leib. —
> Pfuf! speit ihr aus: die Hure da! —
> Bin doch ein ehrlich Weib.

> Mit wem ich mich traute, das sag ich euch nicht.
> Mein Schatz ist lieb und gut,
> Trägt er eine goldene Kett am Hals,
> Trägt er einen strohernen Hut.

> Soll Spott und Hohn getragen sein,
> Trag ich allein den Hohn.
> Ich kenn ihn wohl, er kennt mich wohl,
> Und Gott weiß auch davon.

Herr Pfarrer und Herr Amtmann ihr,
Ich bitte, laßt mich in Ruh!
Es ist mein Kind, es bleibt mein Kind,
Ihr gebt mir ja nichts dazu.

*From whom I have it, the child in my womb,*
*That I will not confess.*
*"Fie," you spit out, "look at that whore!"*
*I'm honest never the less.*

*With whom I was wedded, I will not disclose.*
*My lover is bonnie and braw,*
*Whether he wears a golden chain,*
*Or else a hat of straw.*

*If mock and scorn are to be borne,*
*I'll bear them all alone.*
*I know him well, he knows me well,*
*God knows it too, I'll own.*

*Reverend Sir and Honorable Sir,*
*Leave me in peace, I pray,*
*It is my child, remains my child,*
*You'll help me in no way.*

Here is the plain indication of how different the outcome would be if a girl such as this, or such as Egmont's Klärchen, were Faust's beloved. The poem clearly conveys the young woman's independence, self-assurance, and self-sufficiency: she sincerely loves her man and is assured of his love, but she will not for a moment be weakly dependent on him or allow him to be drawn into a situation that could only hurt him without doing her or her coming child any good. Whereas to Gretchen the opinions of others are decisive, to this girl her own inner conviction of worth is all that counts. She is beholden to no one and is quite able to take care of herself.

Yet it was not a Klärchen, it was a Gretchen who was involved; and with a character such as Gretchen's the outcome, under the circumstances, could not be anything but tragic. She was weakly subject to her environment instead of strongly superior to it. A beautiful, adorable girl, perfectly adapted to the surroundings in which she grew up, with no capacity for transcending those surroundings or adjusting to circumstances or personalities beyond them, is required to do just that, and cannot. Even without the chain of misfortunes that came upon her (largely through the manipulations of Mephistopheles) she could never have adapted her way of life to Faust's, any more than he could have adapted his to hers. Even if Faust had succeeded in rescuing her and she had gone away with him, the ending would have been just as tragic, or more so. Existence for her is unthinkable outside her natural environment; she is as much confined to it as a plant is to its soil. The interpreta-

tion that Wilhelm Meister (not Goethe) gives to the character of
Hamlet offers something of an analogy: this was too delicate and finely
attuned a character to stand up under the demands that were put upon
it.

If we look for actual flaws of character in her, we have to search
hard before we find a few little ones. There is the incident of the second
casket of jewels, which she takes not to her mother, from whom she
would get the right advice, but to neighbor Martha, from whom she
would get the desired advice. Then there is her admission at the end of
the scene at the well that in earlier days, before her own fall, her attitude
toward those who had fallen had in it all the cruelty that was conventional to her time and place. Yet over against this there are such positive
virtues and graces in her that even Mephistopheles thrice lapses from his
usual cynical self into warm acknowledgment of them. Upon first entering her room he remarks (2686):

> Nicht jedes Mädchen hält so rein.
>
> *Not every girl keeps things so neat.*

And then at Martha's, after her innocent answer as to the state of her
heart, he is moved to an aside (3007):

> Du gut's, unschuldig's Kind!
>
> *You innocent good child!*

And in conclusion, countering her feeling of unworthiness, he exclaims
(3022):

> Vor keinem Könige der Erden.
>
> *Before no king upon this earth.*

The importance of these statements for the understanding of
Mephistopheles, in all his complexity and ultimate potentiality, became
apparent in the fourth section of the previous chapter. For Margarete
they serve as an extra highlight upon the grace nature had bestowed on
her, a grace appearing in so many different ways at every turn of the
action. If she had found her beloved within the environment in which
alone she could live and breathe, her life would have been a luminous
blessing to all. But instead, there was the fateful attraction to and from
Faust, and for this there was no happy solution possible upon this earth.
Both knew it, he more clearly and consciously, both acted against their
better insight and intuition, Faust tried ("Forest and Cavern") to remove himself and the danger to her, lacked the power to do so, bore
much the heavier share of the tragic guilt. She had already surrendered
to him in anticipation before his return; like him she foresaw the mortal
outcome; then, during her inquiry into his religion and about his sinister

companion, she showed more will to believe than caution at the warning signs against believing. And thus her character and circumstances led to her doom.

2

In the case of Faust's son, Euphorion, the issues are clearly and plainly stated. But all in vain. For readers and critics alike have refused to face the issues, have refused to accept the poet's solution of them. The several plain statements about Euphorion's nature and destiny within the last third of the third act are simply disregarded and the scene interpreted as though the intent were virtually the opposite of the stated one. The interpreters, the insistant ones at least, are biased in favor of transcendentalism and imperiously give positive values to that which the poet had endowed with negative values. The dramatic intent of the scene is made unmistakably clear even if we regard only two simple and unambiguous statements in it, first Faust's and Helen's warning to their dangerously hyperactive son that he is not a spirit of flight but a "son of earth" who has his strength from the earth, like Antaeus (9606–11). After he disregards their warnings, ventures to fly by a sheer act of will, he does not enter into the bright empyrian. Instead, "Euphorion's voice" comes up "from the depth" and his last words are (9905–06):

Laß mich im düstern Reich,
Mutter, mich nicht allein!

*Leave me not all alone,*
*Mother, in realm of gloom.*

Clearly, therefore, his will to transcendence ends in tragic failure, down in darksome Hades, in the realm of the dead, shut off from the light toward which he had tried to rise. Read the commentaries, and there is hardly a hint that this is the way it all ended, and that Euphorion in his inexperience had committed the error of transcendence that Faust from fuller life perspectives had avoided.

If we take the scene in even broader context, the intent of the author becomes all the clearer when we perceive that he fashioned a figure that stands in direct contrast to Euphorion. For over against Euphorion with his will to transcendence there is Homunculus with his will to immanence. The embodiment that Euphorion flung from himself in a headless, heedless moment of suicidal delusion, Homunculus sought to attain by entering into the organic life of the littoral sea and being willing to go through the long slow process of organic evolution. And as though to underscore even more fully and unmistakably the folly of transcendental attitudes, during the time when these attitudes were at the crest of esteem, the poet developed that delightfully hilarious parody on this intellectual fashion of the age in the figure of the Bachelor of Arts at his encounter with Mephistopheles, an encounter that bowls over even this casehardened old sophisticate, all the more because the worst temptation that he could put in the way of the naive beginning student of Part One is now proved to be sadly inferior to the seduction held out by the new philosophical mode.

This brief summary of the poet's intent with regard to Euphorion will, of course, not be believed after a century and a half of uncritical adulation of this figure to the point where a leading Germanistic periodical is named after him and where his (9821–22):

> Immer höher muß ich steigen,
> Immer weiter muß ich schaun.
>
> *Higher must I climb and higher,*
> *Ever farther must I gaze.*

has been adopted as a personal motto. Let us therefore examine the matter in closer detail so that there may be no mistake as to the author's intent and no escape from its implications.

Once it is pointed out, the significant relationship between Homunculus and Euphorion is at once apparent: each wanted what the other had, and each gave up his kind of existence in strong yearning for the other's kind. Homunculus, the spirit in the artificial embodiment of the vial, wanted to attain to the fullness of life through organic embodiment (7830–31):

> Ich . . . möchte gern im besten Sinn entstehn.
>
> *I'd . . . like, in the best sense, to come to be.*

Through repetition and variation this statement becomes a leitmotif of the concluding scenes of the "Classical Walpurgis Night." Homunculus sought out the best advice on how to enter into organic life; under the guidance of Thales and Proteus, under the inspiration of Eros he entered upon life's evolving cycle, the long course of evolution, at the foot of Galatea's throne. Euphorion, who as the son of Faust and Helen had attained to that organic embodiment, as his parents expressly declare, was restive under his earth-bound limitations, yearned to become a disembodied spirit, and in a fit of suicidal illusion hurled himself to his death and descended to the darksome realms of Hades.

Because these larger contexts have not been observed, it was inevitable that the fullness of Goethe's symbolic intention in creating these two contrasting figures has not been apprehended. As a further consequence, an important part of his intention in the drama as a whole and of his general attitude has been missed.

Since both Homunculus and Euphorion commit a kind of suicide, voluntarily leaving the form of existence they had (this with an essential difference), there is probably some relation to Faust's contemplated suicide on that critical night when we first meet him. Since Goethe quite clearly brings Homunculus into relation with the classical world and has him enter into the process of organic evolution, and since he equally clearly brings Euphorion into relation with Byron and makes him the epitome of romantic idealism, he is probably expressing here in symbolic terms his attitude toward classicism versus romanticism, hylozoism versus idealistic transcendentalism.

To avoid widely prevalent misinterpretations, especially as to Goethe's intention in Euphorion, we had best ascertain from the text itself the course and the end results of the superficially similar acts of the two characters. Proteus, the god of the constant cycle of life and organic change, told Homunculus how he could best enter into existence (8260–64):

> Im weiten Meere mußt du anbeginnen!
>
> . . . . . . . . . . . . . . . .
> Man wächst so nach und nach heran
> Und bildet sich zu höherem Vollbringen.
>
> *In the broad sea your being must commence.*
>
> . . . . . . . . . . . . . . . .
> *So gradually one grows and grows*
> *And forms oneself toward loftier achievement.*

and in summary (8319–20):

> Ich nehme dich auf meinem Rücken,
> Vermähle dich dem Ozean.
>
> *Upon my back I'll carry you,*
> *Join you in marriage to the sea.*

Thereupon Thales adds in approval (8321–26):

> Gib nach dem löblichen Verlangen,
> Von vorn die Schöpfung anzufangen!
> Zu raschem Wirken sei bereit!
> Da regst du dich nach ewigen Normen,
> Durch tausend, abertausend Formen,
> Und bis zum Menschen hast du Zeit.
>
> *Obey the noble aspiration*
> *And at its source begin creation.*
> *Be ready for the great emprise.*
> *By laws eternal still ascending,*
> *Through myriad forms of being wending,*
> *And take your time toward man to rise.*

As Homunculus in the ecstasy of his love for life is breaking his vial at the foot of Galatea's throne and is pouring forth his fiery spirit into the general organic life of the sea, Thales exclaims in apprehension (8469–73):

Homunculus ist es, von Proteus verführt . . .
Es sind die Symptome des herrischen Sehnens,
Mir ahnet das Ächzen beängsteten Dröhnens;
Er wird sich zerschellen am glänzenden Thron;
Jetzt flammt es, nun blitzt es, ergießet sich schon.

*Homunculus 'tis by Proteus seduced . . .*
*A yearning imperious these symptoms disclose,*
*I sense the lament of his agonized throes,*
*Against the bright throne he'll be shattered, no doubt;*
*Now the flame, now the flash, his own self is poured out.*

This must, of course, be interpreted in the context of the whole. The closing song and chorus, celebrating the elements of organic life, celebrating the author of its vital continuity (8478–79):

Und ringsum ist alles vom Feuer umronnen;
So herrsche denn Eros, der alles begonnen!

*And all things around are enclosed in the flame;*
*Let Eros prevail from whom everything came,*

reassure us that the act of Homunculus was not one of self-destruction, but one of an entrance into life, a "Stirb und werde," "die and become," as Goethe expressed it in his famous lyric, "Sagt es niemand," tell it to no one, or as he has the Earth Spirit state it near the beginning of the drama (504–507):

Geburt und Grab,
Ein ewiges Meer,
Ein wechselnd Weben,
Ein glühend Leben.

*Birth and the grave,*
*An endless sea,*
*A changeful weaving,*
*Effulgent living.*

As I have shown elsewhere, all this is ancient poetic image to express man's insight into the eternal cycle of life. It has found one of its renowned poetic formulations in the culminating synthesis of Ovid's *Metamorphoses*, the fifteenth book, most tersely in the words:

Omnia mutantur, nihil interit.

*All things change, nothing perishes.*

Shakespeare and many another poet has come back to this theme again and again as an expression of the continuity of life combined with constant cyclic change.

From another aspect, less abstract, more pictorial, the phenomenon described by Thales and in the concluding choruses of the act, namely, the phenomenon of monocellular luminescence, finds a remarkable parallel in a Venetian epigram of Goethe's, the ninety-sixth, perhaps the most beautiful of them. It dates from 1790 and again illustrates how many of the poetic visions in the *Faust* preexisted elsewhere in Goethe.

> Du erstaunst und zeigst mir das Meer; es scheinet zu brennen.
>   Wie bewegt sich die Flut flammend ums nächtliche Schiff!
> Mich verwundert es nicht, das Meer gebar Aphroditen,
>   Und entsprang nicht von ihr uns eine Flamme, der Sohn?

> *You are astonished and point to the sea, it seems to be burning.*
>   *How the flood moves aflame round the ship in the night.*
> *Me it does not astonish, the sea brought forth Aphrodite,*
>   *Did not from her for us spring forth a fire, her son?*

Nevertheless, it remains a fact that Thales expresses apprehension here ("von Proteus verführt," "by Proteus seduced"), and he has just reason for so doing: he himself has traversed completely the cyclic course upon which Homunculus has just entered, boldly and enthusiastically, and he knows well the agony of wandering its slow spiral up through its final and most painful turn in the cycle of human life. It is with this in mind that he says that Homunculus has been "seduced" by Proteus, the god of evolution, to enter upon the cycle of organic life, to which he is thenceforth irretrievably committed. Homunculus has impetuously yearned for embodied life, he has made his decision, and now can no longer withdraw from it.

Something of this is implied in Thales' words just previously addressed to Homunculus (8326):

> Und bis zum Menschen hast du Zeit.

> *And take your time toward man to rise.*

Proteus joins in approvingly and actually warns against striving toward the ultimate realization of organic life, in man (8330–32):

> Nur strebe nicht nach höheren Orden:
> Denn bist du erst ein Mensch geworden,
> Dann ist es völlig aus mit dir.

> *Yet do not strive toward higher order,*
> *For once you reach the human border,*
> *Then all is at an end with you.*

The implication seems to be that, once Homunculus reaches the end stage of organic evolution, there is no future left and life again enters into the spirit world.

Thales, however, though he does not contradict Proteus, does express his reservations: the kind of man one was on earth will determine the kind of afterlife he will have (8333–34):

> Nachdem es kommt; 's ist auch wohl fein,
> Ein wackrer Mann zu seiner Zeit zu sein.

> *That all depends; it's also good, I'd say,*
> *To be a worthy man in one's own day.*

Proteus heartily agrees to such exceptions from his general verdict (8335–38):

> So einer wohl von deinem Schlag!
> Das hält noch eine Weile nach;
> Denn unter bleichen Geisterscharen
> Seh' ich dich schon seit vielen hundert Jahren.

> *Well, one of your kind, to be sure.*
> *For quite a while such can endure;*
> *Whenever the pale ghostly throng appears,*
> *I've seen you now for many hundred years.*

Here we have the poetic expression of a belief in conditional immortality, in the preservation of an entelechy worthily and significantly developed on earth. It parallels Goethe's own extensive statement on the subject made to Johannes Daniel Falk on the day of Wieland's funeral, January 25, 1813, and also the poetic statement near the end of the next act of *Faust*, when Panthalis, the leader, calls upon the girls of the chorus to follow their mistress, Helen, to the shadowy realms of Hades. The girls prefer to lose their individual lives and merge with the general life upon the glad surface of the earth. Panthalis pronounces final judgment (9981–84):

> Wer keinen Namen sich erwarb noch Edles will,
> Gehört den Elementen an; so fahret hin!
> Mit meiner Königin zu sein, verlangt mich heiß;
> Nicht nur Verdienst, auch Treue wahrt uns die Person.

> *Whoever has not won a name or willed a noble deed,*
> *Belongs among the elements; therefore be gone.*
> *Ardent is my desire to go rejoin my queen.*
> *Not only merit, also troth preserves us personal.*

Therewith she goes to join Helen who has been drawn away from her renewed life on earth by the anguished cry of loneliness coming up from her son Euphorion in Hades.

Let us see now exactly what Goethe tells us about the brief life and tragic death of Euphorion. We know that he poetically conceived of Euphorion as having been in origin a spirit, and as having entered into organic life through having been born as the son of Faust and Helen. The spirit origin he indicated in his whimsical explanation to Eckermann, December 20, 1829, as to how Euphorion could have appeared as the Boy Charioteer in the carnival scene of the first act before he was born in the third act: "In this he is like the spirits, who can be present everywhere and appear at any hour." That Goethe poetically thought of him after his birth as subject to the laws of organic life can be seen in Faust's and Helen's apprehensive words of caution when Euphorion at once undertakes his daring leaps (9607–11):

Ängstlich ruft die Mutter: Springe wiederholt und nach Belieben,
Aber hüte dich, zu fliegen, freier Flug ist dir versagt.
Und so mahnt der treue Vater: In der Erde liegt die Schnellkraft,
Die dich aufwärts treibt; berühre mit der Zehe nur den Boden,
Wie der Erdensohn Antäus bist du alsobald gestärkt.

*Anxiously his mother tells him: Leap, and leap again at pleasure,*
*But beware, think not of flying, flight unhindered is denied you.*
*And his faithful father warns him: In the earth lies force elastic*
*That will send you upward bounding; touch the earth but with your*
    *toe-tips,*
*Like the son of earth, Antaeus, straightway is your strength renewed.*

Here then the epithet, "son of earth" (with the additional emphasis of the name Antaeus) is applied to Euphorion, as it had three times previously, with changing implications, been applied to his father Faust (617, 1618, 3266).

But the tension of the scene increases as Euphorion, only momentarily checked by the repeated warnings and pleadings of father and mother, mounts to ever greater heights of transcendent ecstasy (9713–16):

Zu allen Lüften
Hinaufzudringen,
Ist mir Begierde,
Sie faßt mich schon.

*To press on upward*
*Through all the ether*
*Is my desire,*
*It fills me now.*

Their admonitions that he belongs to them, that their life together depends on his safety, are of no avail, and Faust under the agony of apprehension exclaims (9752–54):

Wäre das doch vorbei!
Mich kann die Gaukelei
Gar nicht erfreun.

*Would this could ended be!*
*For this mad revelry*
*Brings me no joy.*

At the end of the wild chase when the untamable girl disappears in a
burst of flame, Euphorion can no longer be restrained in his heedless
course of self-destruction. The call of distance, the call of heights is
irresistible. His striving is an ironic parody of his father's (9821–22):

Immer höher muß ich steigen,
Immer weiter muß ich schaun.

*Higher must I climb and higher,*
*Ever farther must I gaze.*

For at once, most ominously, his ecstasy merges into a yearning for war
(9837, 9846, 9862):

Krieg! ist das Losungswort.
Verschwendrisch eignen Bluts.
Und ein jedes Kind ein Held.

*War is the rallying-cry.*
*Lavish of their own blood.*
*Every child a hero now.*

He grows into manhood, armed, bound toward self-destruction in a swift
blaze of glory, uttering the fateful nihilistic words (9888–90):

Und der Tod
Ist Gebot,
Das versteht sich nun einmal.

*Verily,*
*Death's the decree,*
*That of course is manifest.*

Therewith the yearning for flight, once so strong also in Faust, brings
him on his dizzy height to a final stage of self-delusion, as it never had
his father (9897–9900):

Doch!—und ein Flügelpaar
Faltet sich los!
Dorthin! Ich muß! ich muß!
Gönnt mir den Flug!

*Lo—see, a pair of wings*
*That now unfolds.*
*Onward! I must, I must,*
*Grant me the flight.*

But alas, the gods had not destined him for flight, and he crashed down to his death. Here Goethe symbolized the tragic personal outcome of the strange willful *Willensphilosophie* that he had observed arising all around him in the young literary generation. Euphorion did not then, released from his bodily encumbrance, rise freely into the air with a new song. The text tells us (after 9902) that the aureole (the poetic spirit) rises on high like a comet, the body falls at the feet of his parents but at once disappears, and a moment later we know that his soul has descended to the depths, from which his anguished cry arises (9905–06). His denial of his organic existence, his measures to overcome it, had turned out very badly.

This attempt of Euphorion to transcend his own potentialities, especially in the sheer act of will by which he attempts to give himself wings, sounds like a grim piteous parody of Faust's actions at the beginning of the drama when he tried to make the Earth Spirit give him answer by a sheer act of will and soon thereafter put the cup to his lips to gain release for his heaven-aspiring soul. In the first instance we also hear similar words (481):

Du mußt! du mußt! und kostet' es mein Leben!

*You must, you must, though life should be at stake.*

In the second instance Faust used the symbol of the beckoning sea, as did Euphorion (698–701 and 9815–18); and there was the same martial attitude of a heroic plunge into self-destruction (712–13, 718–19):

Hier ist es Zeit, durch Taten zu beweisen,
Daß Manneswürde nicht der Götterhöhe weicht

. . . . . . . . . . . . . . . . . . .
Zu diesem Schritt sich heiter zu entschließen,
Und wär' es mit Gefahr, ins Nichts dahinzufließen.

*Now is the time through deeds to demonstrate*
*That human dignity yields not to gods on high*

. . . . . . . . . . . . . . . . . . .
*And take this step with cheerful resolution,*
*Albeit with the risk of utter dissolution.*

But the point is that after his initial rejection by the Earth Spirit he learned the proper, gradual approach to him through a loving communion with created life in nature, as we see later in "Forest and Cavern." Furthermore, the crystal goblet out of which he intended to drink the poison summoned up in him happy memories of joyous festivals in his father's house, and when these perspectives were augmented by the reminder from the Eastern bells and choruses that this was the day on which Christ resumed his body of flesh, Faust, the son of earth, permanently dismissed all thought of suicide with the simple words (784):

die Erde hat mich wieder!

*The earth has hold of me again.*

He has turned away from the gates of death toward a new life on earth. And in the next scene, "Outside the City Gate," where his yearning for flight reaches its most impassioned utterance, he never for a moment deludes himself into believing that flight is attainable by a sheer act of will.

It is almost as though at every critical juncture his tutelary genius leads him away from the brink of destruction and gives him the courage and strength to go on living. His intuition always leads him back to life and to the fullness of vital experience. Euphorion lacks such a tutelary genius and his impulses, however splendidly phrased, are at bottom nihilistic ones.

And there we have it: the poet wanted to make very clear to us Faust's constructive impulses and his sure instinct for a life of long continued development by contrasting them with Euphorion's nihilistic impulses and his yearning for self-destruction in a flashing meteoric glory ("sein Haupt strahlt, ein Lichtschweif zieht nach," "his head is effulgent, a trail of light follows"). This characterization of Euphorion as bellicose and self-destructive is confirmed by Goethe himself in a conversation with Eckermann (July 5, 1827) in which he discusses his choice of Byron as the prototype for his Euphorion: "Furthermore, he was completely suitable because of his discontented nature and warlike tendency, from which he perished at Missolonghi."

By contrast, Faust's long, slow, painful course of development, starting with a desire to experience the fullness of life in joy and sorrow and ending with his strong statement of approval of life on earth, is given its parallel in Homunculus' impassioned entrance into life with the long prospect of organic evolution before him.

Perhaps we can best illustrate the contrast between Euphorion and Homunculus, between what Faust started to be and what he came to be, by means of an old poetic image, one that experienced a significant transformation in the works of the romantics. It is the image we have already encountered, the image of flight. For the romantics the necessary corollary of transcendence was disembodiment; for Goethe and a long line of poets before him the transcendent remained firmly integrated with the organic.

Since Goethe himself thought of Byron as a splendid example of the type he wished to portray in Euphorion, let us by way of illustration use a passage from *Childe Harold's Pilgrimage*, one that Goethe may possibly have even had in mind (III, 14):

> Could he have kept his spirit to that flight,
> He had been happy, but this clay will sink
> Its spark immortal, envying it the light
> To which it mounts, as if to break the link
> That keeps us from yon heaven which woos us to its brink.

This example of resentment against the body as impairing the free flight of the soul could be multiplied almost indefinitely from the works of the romantic and post-romantic poets. It is indeed so familiar to us that it seems to be the only poetic attitude possible in relation to transcendence and yearning for flight. Novalis in life as well as in poetic expression is an almost perfect example of the *Entgrenzungstrieb* that aims toward death.

Shelley began his ode "To a Skylark" with a flat denial of its organic nature:

> Hail to thee, blithe spirit!
> Bird thou never wert.

And it would seem philistine to remark that the skylark has to be a bird with powerful little lungs and a strong throat to produce the sounds it does. That would be beside the point for the romantic whose aim it is to deny or to transcend earthly limitations. In a later stanza the song of this "scorner of the ground" is inevitably connected with thoughts of death:

> Waking or asleep.
>     Thou of death must deem
> Things more true and deep
>     Than we mortals dream,
> Or how could thy notes flow in such a crystal stream?

Another poem of Shelley's, his "Adonais," offers us in a few familiar lines a neat epitome of what we have observed. It uses a different image (LII):

> The one remains, the many change and pass;
> Heaven's light forever shines, Earth's shadows fly;
> Life like a dome of many-coloured glass,
> Stains the white radiance of Eternity
> Until Death tramples it to fragments.—Die,
> If thou wouldst be with that which thou dost seek!
> Follow where all is fled!

How completely this contrasts with Faust's joyful acceptance of the variegated colors of the rainbow over the waterfall when he has turned blinded from the white radiance of supernal light which no mortal eye can bear (4715, 4721–22, 4725–27):

So bleibe denn die Sonne mir im Rücken!

. . . . . . . . . . . . . . . . . . . . .

Allein wie herrlich, diesem Sturm ersprießend,
Wölbt sich des bunten Bogens Wechseldauer,

. . . . . . . . . . . . . . . . . . . . . . . .

Der spiegelt ab das menschliche Bestreben.
Ihm sinne nach, und du begreifst genauer:
Am farbigen Abglanz haben wir das Leben.

*And therefore let the sun remain behind me*

. . . . . . . . . . . . . . . . . . . . . .

*Behold how glorious arching o'er this tumult*
*The many-colored rainbow's changeful being*

. . . . . . . . . . . . . . . . . . . . .

*Man's striving mirrored in it to perfection.*
*Take thought and you will understand more truly:*
*We have our life in many-hued reflection.*

In Shelley we can observe a return to the attitude of the ancient ascetics, pagan and Christian, for whom the world was an illusion, the report of the senses a lie, and the body the prison house of the soul. It should be added that this was not at all Jesus' own attitude and that it entered into Christianity through the epistles of St. Paul and the Apocalypse ascribed to St. John. Young Goethe had observed this discrepancy and gave expression to it in his letter to Johann Caspar Lavater of October 28, 1779:

> I am a very earthly man. For me the parable of the unjust steward, the prodigal son, the sower, the pearl of great price, the last piece of silver, etc. are more divine (if indeed something divine is to be there) than the seven bishops, candle sticks, horns, seals, stars, and woes. I feel that I too have share in the truth, but in the truth of the five senses, and may God have mercy with me as before.

Again from countless quotations in prose and verse this fundamental attitude of Goethe's could be illustrated, and on an earlier occasion I did present an adequate number of characteristic examples. His earth-centered, nonascetic attitude also has a long tradition behind it and can be traced back not only to the Renaissance, for instance in sonnets of Tansillo and Spenser, but also to antiquity, strikingly, for example, in a passage from the *Aetna* that anticipates old Faust's warm words of approval of an earth-centered life (11441–49). The *Aetna* poet writes:

> Yet this is man's more primary task—to know the earth and mark all the many wonders nature has yielded there. This is for us a task more akin than the stars of heaven. For what kind of hope is it for mortal man, what madness could be greater—that he should wish to wander and to explore in Jove's domain and yet pass by the mighty fabric before his feet and lose it by his negligence?

Earlier Pindar had phrased it this way: "O my soul, do not aspire to immortal life, but exhaust the limits of the possible." And later the *Dicta Catonis* expressed it just as tersely:

> Ask not if Gods exist or are Heaven's kings;
> As thou art mortal, think of mortal things.

This attitude likewise has become a tradition in German, and European, literature, to counterbalance the romantic variant of the transcendent attitude. The romantic type of transcendence is closely associated with nihilism and will inevitably lead to it, as we can see clearly in its twentieth-century outgrowths, and as Goethe had already illustrated prophetically in the figure of Euphorion. There is a beautiful German word for the Goethean attitude: *diesseitsfromm*, reverence for the here and now; and the thin strong thread of this tradition runs from Eduard Mörike and Gottfried Keller through Albert Schweitzer into our own time. That is why there have always been a few poets and critics at least (and probably many receptive readers) who have understood *Faust* in the following of Goethe, even though the consensus of the traditional romantic-nihilistic opinion was against them.

As we have already indicated, it would be unfair to make an abstract formulation and claim that the attitude of Euphorion is the romantic-Christian one and that the attitude of Homunculus is the classic-pagan one. Goethe, with his aversion to all abstract formulation, would never have allowed that. He knew (and we should know) that there were strong and valid nonascetic, nontranscendent strains in Christian tradition, and that these were sometimes expressed most sharply by the mystics in their call to practical piety. He also knew that there was a strong ascetic tradition in the Greco-Roman-Oriental pagan world, and that in it expressions of aversion and repugnance toward life on earth can be far stronger than those in the Christian tradition. And finally, he knew and practiced the other healthier kind of transcendence that looked upon the organic nature of man and upon the soul's return to earth after brief flight as something good and as a positive advantage. Herein he followed Christian Renaissance as well as ancient pagan tradition.

If, however, we speak of prevailing tone and dominant emphasis, and not in absolutes, we can claim with some reason that Euphorion expresses the ascendant Pauline Christian, romantic, antiorganic attitude, and that Homunculus expresses the main pagan, classic, organic attitude, in which the divine *Physis*, nature, is the chief goddess and the mother of man.

Quite in the spirit of this relativity, Faust the man is no pure parallel of either the symbol Euphorion or of the symbol Homunculus. Rather we can observe in him a mixture of both, though also, most decidedly, a

development from Euphorion-like attitudes in the beginning of the
drama to a complete and decisive approval of life on earth at the end of
the drama. This life, with all its inherent error and tragedy, can heartily
be affirmed as a good life. The concluding scene of the drama likewise is
in harmony with the ancient philosophies that believed that a man who
had developed his entelechy on earth to its fullest potentialities and
dimensions would enter upon a new life of more perfect activity in a
higher sphere. This final scene achieves that loving fusion of pagan and
Christian convictions in which Goethe as a new Hypsistarian found his
own final religious peace.

Faust enters upon his progress to higher spheres not after having
renounced the earth but after having reconfirmed its validity once more
(11441–48):

> Der Erdenkreis ist mir genug bekannt,
> Nach drüben ist die Aussicht uns verrannt;
> Tor, wer dorthin die Augen blinzelnd richtet,
> Sich über Wolken seinesgleichen dichtet!
> Er stehe fest und sehe hier sich um;
> Dem Tüchtigen ist diese Welt nicht stumm.
> Was braucht er in die Ewigkeit zu schweifen!
> Was er erkennt, läßt sich ergreifen.

> *I know enough the sphere of earth and men,*
> *The view beyond is barred from mortal ken.*
> *Fool, who would yonder turn his blinking eyes,*
> *Imagine his own kind within the skies.*
> *Let him stand firm, the prospect round him scan,*
> *The world's not mute unto a worthy man.*
> *Why need he soar through all eternity?*
> *Here he can grasp whate'er he knows to be.*

And old Goethe also reconfirmed the attitude that young Goethe had
expressed in his letter to Lavater, most memorably in his poem
"Vermächtnis," "Bequest," centering on its fourth stanza:

> Den Sinnen hast du dann zu trauen:
> Nichts Falsches lassen sie dich schauen,
> Wenn dein Verstand dich wach erhält.
> Mit frischem Blick bemerke freudig
> Und wandle, sicher wie geschmeidig,
> Durch Auen reichbegabter Welt.

> *Your senses then you well may trust:*
> *No falsehood will they on you thrust*
> *If wakeful reason keep its worth.*
> *With a fresh glance observe in pleasure*
> *And wander safely and at leisure*
> *Through meadows of this bounteous earth.*

## 3

Seemingly most firmly established and most unshakable of all is the prevailing sentimental interpretation of the Philemon and Baucis episode at the beginning of the last act. Indeed it will require a very close reading of the text and a very careful weighing of the psychological implications developed by the poet if we are to come to a fuller understanding of the larger intent. This deeper understanding will serve rather to enhance than to lower the dramatic importance of the old couple on the dunes, especially since it will open up, for the first time, the true symbolic implications of their persons and their fate.

Let us begin by looking more carefully at the details that are usually submerged in a milky haze of sentimentality, first the scene on the dune and then the crucial events at Faust's palace. The wanderer has arrived from the land side up the dunes to the dwelling of the old couple and expresses his gratitude to Baucis and then Philemon for what they had done many years earlier in saving him and his treasure, after storm and shipwreck, and restoring him to life. They allow him to go on to the crest of the dune where he expects to look out upon the boundless sea but, to his utter astonishment, beholds a large flourishing and cultivated realm. While Baucis is setting the table in the garden, Philemon explains to him what has happened, does so in entirely positive and approving terms.

However, most of the critics and commentators have silently passed over Philemon's account and have concentrated upon the account of Baucis, accepting it uncritically and unquestioningly. In their partisanship, they have not noticed the poet's irony in juxtaposing these two accounts, an irony with implications about the way in which history reports on great events. Here are two eyewitness accounts of the same events, observed and reported, moreover, by two people who have lived together for a long time in close mutual communication of thought and feeling. And yet these two accounts could not be more disparate; it is almost as though two entirely different events were being reported. As a parallel to this there is the well known episode in the life of Sir Walter Raleigh which Goethe brought up in the famous conversation with Heinrich Luden of August 10, 1806: while Raleigh was writing his history of the world, he witnessed an incident before his house, immediately interviewed the other eyewitnesses, received utterly discrepant accounts, and despaired of ever getting at the real truth in history.

Here, in this scene of the drama, Philemon reports the arrival of the imperial herald ceremonially announcing Faust's sovereignty over the strand; he tells of the first foothold of the new project near the old couple's dunes, with the erection of tents and huts. Where the sea had cast the wanderer on shore, there is now a paradisiacal garden. Philemon's only regret was that he was too old to participate when the bold servants of the wise master dug ditches, made dams and dikes, and pushed back the sea to the distant horizon. He points out the green meadows, fields, gardens, villages, and groves, in the far distance the sails of ships approaching the harbor, to right and left a populous realm.

Then at table Philemon with affectionate and gentle ridicule calls upon his talkative and superstitious wife to give her account of the events (11109–10):

> Möcht' er doch vom Wunder wissen;
> Sprichst so gerne, tu's ihm kund.
>
> *He would like to hear of wonders;*
> *You do like to talk, so tell him.*

The tale we hear from the old woman is prefaced by her dark suspicion that the whole affair was mighty strange (11113–14):

> Denn es ging das ganze Wesen
> Nicht mit rechten Dingen zu.
>
> *For the whole affair unfolded*
> *In a most uncanny way.*

To her mind the laborers working all day got nowhere, but at night the torches moved eerily about and in the morning there was a dam. Then she brings out a factor common to all great engineering projects: the toll of human lives through the inevitable mishaps; but she gives this report her own personal slant (11127–30):

> Menschenopfer mußten bluten,
> Nachts erscholl des Jammers Qual;
> Meerab flossen Feuergluten,
> Morgens war es ein Kanal.
>
> *Human victims doomed to bleeding,*
> *Wailing sounds were nightly borne;*
> *Seaward sped the flames, receding,*
> *A canal appeared at morn.*

To her Faust is a godless impious man, who covets their hut and grove, only pretends to be a good neighbor, but actually is arrogant and domineering. When Philemon again objects to her account by mentioning Faust's offer of exchange, she expresses her suspicion of the lowlands wrested from the sea and her faith in her old heights.

What has not been in the least perceived is that Baucis is interpreting the whole course of events not in terms of firsthand observation but in terms of the superstitious folklore that has always surrounded every great work, every great construction of man exceeding normal bounds. Even the construction of one of the great houses of God, one of the medieval cathedrals, was usually and typically interpreted by the folk as involving diabolic assistance, with a consequent toll of human sacrifice. Various of the famous cathedrals, whether at Cologne, Vienna, or elsewhere, have associated with them folk tales about a master builder receiving aid from the devil, usually at a tragic price that is only occasionally evaded. Baucis' account follows this stereotype from the well-worn introductory cliché about the uncanny nature of it all, through the claim of magically swift, overnight accomplishment amid cries of anguish and sinister human sacrifice, with the final picture of a godless tyrant who wishes to deprive them of their land. Philemon's corrective interjections fall on deaf ears, and she rigidly maintains the status quo in refusing to exchange their dune, hut, and grove for a beautiful property on the new land (11137–38):

> Traue nicht dem Wasserboden,
> Halt auf deiner Höhe stand!
>
> *Trust no ground that once was water,*
> *On your own height keep your stand.*

If we look about in Goethe's other works, we find that Baucis had made an earlier appearance as a superstitious old crone in "Was wir bringen," a little curtain raiser that he wrote for the opening of the new theatre at Lauchstädt in 1802. Here Mutter Marthe's stubborn clinging to the status quo and refusing to budge under similar circumstances is brought out even more plainly. Quite aside from this parallel, of course, a simple reading of the Faustian text should make it clear that Baucis can hardly be considered the reliable witness that she has been assumed to be. Actually, she is one of a long line of unreliable narrators that occur as an ironic motif in imaginative writings from early times to the present. Aside from this, however, there is no difficulty about joining the consensus on the old couple. Philemon's last words bring the whole scene into clear focus again, as the good, benign, simple old couple and their guest go for vesper prayers to the little chapel (11141–42):

> Laßt uns läuten, knieen, beten
> Und dem alten Gott vertraun!
> *Let us ring and kneel in prayer,*
> *Trusting in our God of old.*

Before we go on to observe the strangely violent way in which old Faust overreacts to the sound of the vesper bell from the little chapel on the dune, we need to pause long enough to examine the larger symbolic intent of the poet in the creation of this scene, an intent that was obscured as long as the critical reaction to it was specific and sentimental. The situation of the simple isolated old couple, suddenly finding a new, alien, frightening, overwhelming way of life encroaching upon it, is not solely individual and specific, it is also general and symbolic. All this has happened before and was destined to continue to happen as long as there were vast stretches of land open to colonization, land only scantily populated by an indigenous folk living in primordial innocence with all the primitive virtues of simple faith, human kindness, and hospitality. The eighteenth century loved to interpret the life of the primitives in distant lands in these terms (and to disregard the somewhat more sordid realities), even as did the centuries before this, not only back to Las Casas in the sixteenth, but much farther back to the Romans and the Greeks, so that this vision of the aborigine was an established poetic and artistic tradition, and Goethe quite properly used the names of Philemon and Baucis from one of the charming stories of antiquity to indicate his more-than-specific intent.

For the sparse primitive folk of any region that is being settled by a more powerful, technically more advanced, better organized people, the results are always tragic, not only when the advancing new people are thoughtlessly cruel and ruthless, but even when they strive to advance their ends in the most humane and equitable manner possible. The Indians of Pennsylvania were no less doomed under the benign encroachment of William Penn and his successors than were the Indians of certain other colonies that dealt less equitably with them, even though their doom was in part more quietly elegiac, and the treaty meetings of the eighteenth century left us an immortally eloquent literature of Indian orations.

For proper balance we must look at the other side of this process of colonization. Parallel to the best colonial projects in the real world stands Faust's great project of making a waste land fit for human habitation, and then establishing a society upon it that can make a new start, one not vitiated by the inherited factors of stifling tradition and entrenched corruption (satirized by Faust near the beginning of Act Four), a society moreover that, threatened by the always present peril of the elements, must remain ever alert and united in common purpose. Such a society is thereby insured against the fateful human weakness of declining into ease, security, decadence, disunity, corruption, inequality, injustice, and violence. It is not a perfectionist utopia, but a colonial project designed for normally fallible, corruptible, and indolent human beings, with a plan for helping them to avoid and overcome the worst consequences of their natural faults.

We have Philemon's word for it that the new lord strove earnestly to deal equitably with the old couple, and so it remains for us to examine carefully and strictly just how and why it came about that Faust in the end did *not* deal equitably and humanely with them but involved himself in a last grave guilt, a guilt for which he must fully and squarely bear the blame.

The key to understanding lies in the ringing of the vesper bell from the little chapel on the dune and in Faust's strangely resentful over-reaction to it. To understand him and his situation we can resort to a bit of folk wisdom that anticipates our modern psychological insights. When a person reacts with excessive emotion, anger or otherwise, to a situation or happening so minor that in itself it could not possibly call forth such a strong reaction, a discerning observer may try to bring him back to his senses by asking, "What's eating you?" Here is the truth of the matter: the turmoil lies within his own self, in a secret recess, and it is of a nature that he refuses to admit to himself, that he is ashamed to admit to himself. What is eating away at Faust inwardly is of a nature that he cannot face, that he pushes back into his subconscious. Suppressing the real cause of his disturbance, namely, a deep inner lack (as we shall see), he projects his lack upon an external "cause," an outer lack, one that even a casual scrutiny will reveal to be quite inadequate to the reaction it supposedly releases. Let us look closely at Faust's words, at the supposed "cause" of his violent reaction, at what his words unintentionally reveal about the true cause of his inner disturbance, and at the tragic course of events that finally brings him face to face with the real cause, and only then brings him to the ultimate insight that carries him on to his final creative vision.

At the end of Lynceus' paean to the beauty of the harbor sunset the little bell rings from the dunes and Faust is aroused to violent indignation, his first words in the last act being (11151–56):

Verdammtes Läuten! Allzuschändlich
Verwundet's, wie ein tückischer Schuß;
Vor Augen ist mein Reich unendlich,
Im Rücken neckt mich der Verdruß,
Erinnert mich durch neidische Laute:
Mein Hochbesitz, er ist nicht rein . . .

*Accursed bell! All too outrageously*
*It wounds me with a treacherous shock;*
*Before my eyes my realm's unending,*
*Yet at my back vexations mock,*
*Remind me through invidious ringing:*
*My high estate, it still is flawed . . .*

This covert mockery at the imperfection of his accomplishment is not the external and superficial one of his rationalization in his next words: that his sovereign realm is not purely his, that the linden grove, the brown hut, the decrepit chapel are not his, that he could not go there for recreation; it would be thorn to his eye, thorn to his soul. In the line (11160),

> Vor fremdem Schatten schaudert mir,
>
> *The alien shadow chills my heart,*

the subconscious wells up to partial view; it does so to full view in the last line of this speech (11162):

> O! wär' ich weit hinweg von hier!
>
> *Oh, would that I were far from here.*

He feels the strong need to escape from himself; he is unable to do so, but he is also unable to face his true self at this point. Since the Middle Ages the symbolism of the bells has been that of a reminder, a call to *Besinnung*, not only a *memento mori* but also a *memento vivere*, a call to remember where one came from, where one stands, where one is heading. Once earlier, near the close of the monodrama, the Easter bells fulfilled precisely this function for Faust, bringing him out of his linear, abstract decision for suicide by reawakening in him the full time-and-space perspective of his life back to his early youth and beyond that to the whole perspective of his civilization since Christ's resurrection—to the point where the past took control of the present and led to the sounder future that he announced in his concluding words, "The earth has hold of me again." In his later scene, by contrast, the call to *Besinnung*, to recollected perspective, is less welcome to Faust; indeed it is unendurable, and he tries to evade it, countering the dilemma of his deep inner lack by his fateful rationalization that it is only an outer lack, a gap in his possessions.

Unfortunately, this is the precise moment of the arrival of Mephistopheles and associates from their successful mercantile-piratic expedition. Faust, sunk in his subjective gloom, fails to welcome them, and Mephisto's reproach goes on to review the development of the glorious realm from its beginnings where palace and park now stand. His words "Von hier aus," "Forth from here" (11233) arouse Faust to another violent overreaction, one moreover that can leave no doubt about the nature of his inner turmoil (11233–34):

> Das verfluchte H i e r !
> Das eben, leidig lastet's mir.
>
> *That accursed here!*
> *That weighs upon me harsh and drear.*

Thus once more the unendurableness of the here and now, the urge to get away from it or to rid himself of it. But alas, his "solution" for ridding himself of it remains the outward one of removing the old couple from their dune, and he gives Mephistopheles the fateful order for their removal. Again there are impulsive phrases intervening that reveal his rationalization for what it is (11237–38):

Mir ist's unmöglich zu ertragen!
Und wie ich's sage, schäm' ich mich.

*It is impossible to bear it.*
*And as I say it, I'm ashamed.*

or (11251–52):

So sind am härtsten wir gequält,
Im Reichtum fühlend, was uns fehlt.

*Thus suffer we the cruelest rack,*
*Midst wealth perceiving what we lack.*

Or most revealingly (11255–58):

Des allgewaltigen Willens Kür
Bricht sich an diesem Sande hier.
Wie schaff' ich mir es vom Gemüte!
Das Glöcklein läutet, und ich wüte.

*The choice of my all-conquering will*
*Is broken on this sandy hill.*
*How shall I ever free my spirit?*
*The bell rings, and I rage to hear it.*

And then, with unconscious irony (11271–72):

Daß man, zu tiefer, grimmiger Pein,
Ermüden muß, gerecht zu sein.

*Till in deep furious pain one must*
*Grow tired at last of being just.*

Mephistopheles, of course, gleefully supports him in his rationalization, while his supporting words actually turn into a revealing parody of it.

To be sure, Faust's order of removal includes the clearly stated command to transport Philemon and Baucis to the beautiful little property he had chosen for them, and when Mephisto and his three sinister companions return after the fire that destroyed the whole property as well as the old couple and their guest, Faust curses the deed and puts the guilt on its perpetrators. Does that absolve him from the guilt? Of course not. After his many long years with Mephisto he could not fail to know the consistent pattern of response that always carried out his orders in the worst possible way, in a way that would involve him in guilt and wrongdoing. With such knowledge Faust could have given the executive order to Mephistopheles only in a moment of overwhelming emotional turmoil that temporarily blinded him to the consequences. Mephisto's intruding remark (11273–74):

Was willst du dich denn hier genieren?
Mußt du nicht längst kolonisieren?

> *Why then embarrassment evince?*
> *Have you not colonized long since?*

reminds us of the larger symbolic intent of this confrontation between
the indigenous inhabitants and the new settlers, and we think back in
the history of man to the tragedy that always occurred when whole
peoples were removed and uprooted for reasons of state. We can think
of the Cherokees in the 1830s or of the several peoples of the Caucasus a
century and more later, or of the subsequent ones, together with the
"tender mercies" of those in charge of the removals.

In sum, if we view this course of events symbolically, as the poet no
doubt intended us to, we perceive that Faust's guilt is of a kind that he
shares with more rulers and peoples in time and space than the critics
who have sat in judgment on him ever dreamed of. Rightly seen, these
events still toll down into our time as a warning bell from a crumbling
chapel on the dunes, and we are all together involved in Faust's guilt.
The great and vital difference between the tragic events in the drama
and the magnified parallels of our own decades is that Faust did not
continue to "cover up," to perpetuate the rationalizations of sancti-
monious historical hypocrisy, though he too had the all-too-human
impulse toward this end when he tried to push off the blame on Mephistopheles and his three bully boys. But this was only momentary; the turn
comes immediately in his next speech with his (11382):

> Geboten schnell, zu schnell getan!

> *Quick bidden, and too quickly done,*

and then when he honestly faces the issues as the Four Gray Women
approach with the smoke from the destroyed grove and hut. Before he is
confronted by the one who remains, Sorge (Care, Anxiety), he brings
out into the open the factor of the real lack, the real inner emptiness that
he earlier could not face and now has to face, with the tragedy he has
brought upon the old couple. This heedless, thoughtless, inhuman act
made him realize that he was less than human, that he had not yet
fought his way through to full humanity. Before he could give freedom
to the people of his own realm, he himself had to attain to freedom, and
this is the tenor of his next monologue when he has withdrawn into his
palace. He now states with clear full insight (11403–07):

> Noch hab' ich mich ins Freie nicht gekämpft.
> Könnt' ich Magie von meinem Pfad entfernen,
> Die Zaubersprüche ganz und gar verlernen,
> Stünd' ich, Natur, vor dir ein Mann allein,
> Da wär's der Mühe wert, ein Mensch zu sein.

> *My way to freedom I have not yet fought.*
> *Could I but break the spell, all magic spurning,*

*And clear my path, all sorceries unlearning,*
*Standing, O Nature, man alone, with thee,*
*Then were it worth the while a man to be.*

He sees that a deeply human principle is involved: with his besetting impetuousness he has gone beyond human means and human limitations to achieve his ends. However, this "going beyond," here expressed as the use of magic means, now no longer appears to him as an extension of his powers for the purpose of encompassing all human experience, but as an impairment of his freedom, an abridgment of his humanity. A moment later, in deepest peril, when he could turn back Anxiety with one magic word, he has a last quick flare-up of indignation, but he checks it, saying to himself (11423):

Nimm dich in acht und sprich kein Zauberwort.

*Be careful now and speak no magic word.*

Therewith he has won liberation from his own treacherous temper, from the treacherous outside forces he has employed, and from the insidious treachery of Sorge, Anxiety, who has been hovering in the background of his thoughts from the very first monologue onward. He does not emerge unscathed; the wound of his victory is a severe one, is blindness. But the victory, with glorious irony, reaches its highest height in his severest loss: out of his blindness comes his most exalted vision, his deepest insight into the realities of human life in society and the means to keep it free, active, and healthy, "tätig-frei zu wohnen."

And yet, we are stopped short by another consideration. Is this the proper way to acknowledge guilt for the crime just committed? Where is the confession, where is the remorse, where is the expiation? Can Faust be allowed to get off that easily, merely coming to new insights with regard to himself and then blandly going on to his grandiose new vision of the future?

The answer is: yes, he can. Although remorse and expiation are the generally approved way of atonement for a crime, there is another, less negative way that the poet chose, out of a deep conviction, a way that would bring a greater expiatory good to a greater number than any arid course of remorse and repentance. Goethe put the whole issue most succinctly in a verse aphorism:

Nichts taugt Ungeduld,
Noch weniger Reue;
Jene vermehrt die Schuld,
Diese schafft neue.

*No good in impatience,*
*Even less in remorse;*

> *One increases the guilt,*
> *The other's a new source.*

Impatience certainly was one of the ineradicable flaws of Faust's character, one that comes out within the first few minutes of his first monologue, soon after his display of another, related fault, that of exaggeration, of hyperbole. And more than once did his impatience increase his guilt or make it inevitable. However, the other defect condemned in the aphorism, that of remorse, was not central to his nature; instead of regretting the past that could not be remedied and lapsing into a paralyzing remorse that would only heap the further sins of omission upon the sins of commission, he went on to new activity with the intent and in the confidence that the active good that would result could more than compensate for the active wrong that had been done.

An extreme example of the opposite may serve to illustrate: if and when the main emphasis is put on the avoidance of wrongdoing, true consistency and consequentiality would demand that a person follow the example of the Tibetan monks of old who refrained from leaving their cells all summer long in order to avoid the grave wrong of crushing the life crawling beneath their feet. All human activity involves man in wrongdoing, inadvertently perhaps but also inevitably, and if he is at all sensitive, he has the bitter choice of refraining from all good doing, as well as all wrong doing, or else of making it the purpose of his life to create so great a good that it will far outweigh the guilt and wrongdoing that are the inevitable accompaniment of all human action.

Here the poets in the following of Goethe have shown a clearer, more sensitive understanding of the underlying ethical principles involved than have the critics, especially the philosophical critics. The latter go on repeating themselves to our day, even though an English poet more than a century ago used these scenes in symbolic extension within a poem of his own and gave his own fine formulation of their attitude when he indicated that the right use of past errors was "as stepping stones to higher things." Tennyson's artistic approach brought him this more direct and truer insight into Goethe's intent. For Faust the higher thing is an ultimate vision. He sees that the end result of his great creative act will be the furnishing of an environment and situation that would maintain in unfaltering activity a free people on a free soil. This will be a freedom that is a strengthening, deserved attainment rather than a corrupting, unearned gift (11575–76):

> Nur der verdient sich Freiheit wie das Leben,
> Der täglich sie erobern muß.

> *Of freedom and of life he only is deserving*
> *Who daily conquers them anew.*

Thus the simple goodness of the primordial couple could lead through tragedy over to the ultimate humanization of Faust and to the human dignity and freedom of a whole commonwealth. Verily, Tennyson's vision of the truly active creative ethical attitude contains the profounder comprehension of the Faustian intent.

In all three cases, that of Margarete, of Euphorion, of Philemon and Baucis, we have actually gained far more than we have lost when we have disposed once and for all of the soft soppy sentimentality with which we have surrounded these figures. Margarete in her tragic guilt is not only a profounder character, she is also a more intrinsic character for the whole drama, and her reappearance at the end is a more just and less superficial one, more truly a central factor in the ultimate symbolism. Euphorion, like Byron, in whose place he stands symbolically, tragically with the Faustian impetuousness and hyperbole, but without the Faustian balancing factors, is no less lovable and mournable and poetically valid for all his wrong-headedness. And his validity is increased by the contrasting illumination that comes from the remarkable, misunderstood, and underestimated figure of Homunculus. In the case of Philemon and Baucis we do not at all lose the dear old couple in the process of gaining great new symbolic vistas. Indeed, in retrospect, it would seem preposterous that where Ovid's story raises the two to higher symbolic life in the end, Goethe's story should leave them a mere helpless, pitiful, victimized pair, as the sentimentalists have tried to persuade us to believe through far too many decades. Depth and feeling are not lost when we cast our sentimentalities upon the rubbish heap of outworn critical attitudes.

# 3

# The Reductionists

OETHE ONCE TOLD US how he wanted his works to be read. This chapter tells how variously his works, specifically the *Faust*, can be misread, indeed have been misread through a disregard of his precepts. In a distich he described his favorite reader thus:

> Welchen Leser ich wünsche? Den unbefangensten, der mich,
> Sich und die Welt vergißt, und in dem Buche nur lebt.

> *Whom do I wish for a reader? The most ingenuous, forgetting*
> *Me, himself, and the world, living alone in the book.*

The undesired reader, then, is the one who cannot forget Goethe, himself, and the world and who subordinates the intrinsic work to such extraneous considerations. The first kind of undesired reader, the kind who cannot forget the poet, is the biographic, genetic, historical one. He will read Goethe's biography and philosophy into the *Faust* as though the drama were a piece of subjective self-expression. Or he will take the *Urfaust* as the established criterion, from which, alas, the completed *Faust* deviated, to its grave impairment. Or he will go back to the historical Faust or to the folk-book Faust (and Mephistopheles) and attempt to interpret the Goethean creation on these premises.

The second kind of undesired reader, the kind who cannot forget himself, is the self-concentrated one who projects himself into the *Faust* and interprets it from his own points of view and prejudices, personal, social, religious, aesthetic, or what not. For instance he does not like the Roman Catholic ending of the drama and never stops to observe why the work artistically could have had no other kind of ending. Or he does not approve of the way Faust translates the Bible, he disregards the context, and concludes gloomily that Faust has fallen into a dangerous anti-intellectual *Willensphilosophie*, a will to power. Conversely, he may approve of what he misreads into *Faust*, fancy himself a latter-day

"Faustian" man (or superman) exalted above ordinary mortals and the ethical imperatives that bind them. In the postwar period of the 1940s and '50s there were the catastrophists who gave negative values to Faust's final projects and plans that led to his vision of a free people on a free soil. These catastrophists, of course, were under the expert guidance of Mephisto, the frustrated false prophet of destruction; they were gullible enough to believe his final words about Faust's great work (11523–30, 11587–90) and indeed to cite them as "proof" of the rightness of their own dismal hangover mood. Therewith *Faust* interpretation again declined toward the naiveté of the post-1870s when one commentator sorrowfully regretted that Goethe had not lived on into Bismarckian Wilhelminian times under the inspiration of which he would have found a more worthy ending for his great poem.

With this we have already begun to describe the third kind of undesired reader, the kind who cannot forget the world, cannot simply live in the work itself, cannot look at it face to face, but must see it through the medium of whatever system of thought or intellectual fashion is current in the world or in his group or coterie. It is not the poem's own "Faustian" that counts, but Nietzsche's or Spengler's perversion of it that is forced upon the work. Or this dogmatic, anachronistic reader may be a Hegelian, or a Marxist, or a Freudian, or an existentialist, or a what-not-since-then, and perform equally gruesome though different mayhem as he forces a living poetic work into a schematic Procrustean bed.

More obviously amusing though actually no more absurd is another set of intellectual fanatics who have "improved" the work with their own subtleties. They range from the seemingly sensible and generally respectable internalists, whom we shall examine in the third part of this chapter, to the occultists, who regard the *Faust* as an occult text into which and out of which the whole "secret doctrine" can be read, alchemical, cabalistic, theosophic, or whatever. They set out to "solve" such mysteries as the witch's "one-times-one," and it is the extreme wing of them, the cryptogrammatists, who find all kinds of hidden messages tucked away in unexpected places. They have not yet developed the full ingenuity of the Baconian "researchers" into Shakespeare's works; they started later and their finest efforts will take a bit longer. The occultists do not realize that though Goethe was very knowledgeable in occult matters and made frequent use of occult motifs, he often did so ironically, or with puckish humor, and he always did so for primarily artistic reasons.

It may seem unjust to bundle together into one chapter the intellectually respectable Hegelians or existentialists with the far-out cabalists or cryptogrammatists. In another context it would be unjust. But in the context of the *Faust* we may behold in them a common error, one that is perhaps the most prevalent fallacy in *Faust* criticism: reductionism, the attempt to reduce a living artistic body to an abstract intellectual ghost. Equally reductionist, of course, are our first two groups, the biographic-genetic-historicist group and the egocentric-subjective group. *Faust* is a work of art whose dimensions extend far beyond its creator, his materials, and even his original intentions. It is, therefore, absurd for anyone to try to reduce it to his own personal dimensions or to the dimensions of any intellectual system, however great its pretensions to all-inclusiveness may be. The *Faust* is not an exemplification of any intellectual system. It is far more than that and lies far beyond any such approach. It is an artistic cosmos, to which the intellect alone affords only limited access, an artistic cosmos that will open up only to the re-creative artistic imagination of the unprejudiced, ingenuous, receptive reader who can forget the author, himself, and the world, and live alone in the book.

Let us examine, then, just what harm each of the reductionist approaches has done to our larger and fuller and truer understanding of the work. Not that I wish to take the reader on a full-scale voyage through this vast sea of errors, exposing every error in detail and documenting each as to authorship and origin. That would not only be wearisome, it would also be uncharitable. After all, an individual should not be blamed for having been subjected to an educational system that makes the extraction of an idea from a work of art a commendable achievement, or a system that urges him to express himself or to search for that which is relevant to himself or to the particular circumstances of his time and place in the world, or a system that stresses the genetic historical approach. All of these have validity, great validity. The fallacy lies in attributing to them exclusive validity, or highest validity, in not realizing that our educational system should give (but has failed to give) primacy to a fourth approach when it is a work of art that is under consideration. This fourth approach, the intrinsically artistic symbolic one, is the subject matter of the second, larger part of this book. The present chapter deals only with the impairments in understanding that come from its omission and from the substitution of the more limited approaches. Since good men and serious men have striven to encompass the *Faust* with these more limited means, it would be unfair to single out for censure or ridicule any particular individual who has lapsed into these fallacies when there are so many others who have done no better. It is only the fallacies that interest us, not their perpetrators, and in the exceptional cases where these, albeit unnamed, must be alluded to, no specific personal censure is intended.

1

Most pardonable, perhaps, are the fallacies that result from the biographical, genetic, historical approaches. Indeed, they can sometimes be transformed from fallacies into positive contributions to a broader and deeper understanding of *Faust* if they can be separated from the false basic assumptions that usually accompany them. Naturally, a poet puts himself into his work, and from one point of view Goethe's works, including the *Faust*, are, as he himself put it, "fragments of a great confession." The fallacy, however, consists in making this point of view the primary one, making it determining over Goethe's artistic intent in the creation of his masterpiece. We will be spared many a lapse in judgment if we simply keep in mind that Goethe also wrote the *Wilhelm Meister*. This is his masterpiece in the art of understatement, even as the *Faust* is his masterpiece in the art of poetic hyperbole. Until this critical insight penetrates more deeply into the fabric of Goethe exegesis, we shall continue to be afflicted with the contradictory nonsense that tells us on one page that Faust is Goethe and on another page that Wilhelm Meister is Goethe. When these two statements are brought together on one page and in one sentence, they become mutually self-destructive and open the way for the study of each basically different masterpiece on its own terms.

Naturally, in the second place, a work of art of such dimensions undergoes a commensurably long evolutionary process. Even though the original artistic vision may have been a sound and lasting one, the means found for realizing it in highest potency will probably change through the years, leaving many discards along the way, many reroutings even of the way itself. The fallacy, therefore, consists in an affection for, an atavistic bias toward the details and particulars of the earlier drafts, a bias against the later shifts and changes as though they introduced discrepancies and disharmonies. It is always dangerous to underrate the artistic discernment and overall perspective of a great artist, and in the end it is Zoilus the critic who will appear foolish for the complacent way in which he presumes to discover flaws and inconsistencies in the work. Actually, it is the genetic approach itself, the remembrance of earlier versions, that accounts for many a seeming discrepancy in the final version. What Goethe does frequently is to take over a passage from an earlier version and, by putting it into a different context, quite change its meaning. The geneticist's fallacy is to retain the old meaning in the new context and thus impose on the work a confusion that is wholly his own.

In the third place, also, the Goethean *Faust* is not a thing totally apart from the historical Faust or the legendary Faust; even less is it apart from the general era and the particular attitudes that the Faust figure came to exemplify. Goethe's fascinated study of the era, his use of symbolic, characteristic features of it in his work, precludes such a possibility. The fallacy here would consist in reading into the Goethean work traditional features that the poet clearly excluded or modified.

Examples would be: continuing to think of Mephistopheles as *the* devil or as a folk-book devil, continuing to think of a quid-pro-quo compact between him and Faust, continuing to think of Faust as a seeker after pleasure. The endless confusion that the critics continue to perpetrate on the pseudo problem of pact and wager is quite unnecessary; the Goethean text itself is perfectly clear if it is read with care, in sequence and context, free from all the assumptions inherited from the pre- and post-Goethean Fausts. The critical confusion has obviously been caused by the compulsive remembrance that the legendary Faust made a pact with the devil and the failure to realize fully that Goethe for his Faust supplanted pact by wager. As we have seen, the critics, one and all, have therewith failed to observe the crucial blunder Mephistopheles makes at this point, a blunder that costs him a firm compact and forces him to settle for a wager. Even more thoroughly disruptive to an understanding of the Goethean work on its own terms is the tendency of the historically minded to retain the factors of sin, guilt, self-indulgence as centrally ethical determinants and to pass judgment on the work, its protagonist, and his fate on the basis of these assumptions. Even though there is a formal recognition of the fact that a quite different set of ethical determinants is announced in the "Prologue in Heaven" and in the final scenes, there remains the unconscious tendency to brush these aside and relapse into the old extraneous moral judgments.

It may help to clarify issues, in summary (and partly in paraphrase from the Introduction), if we draw to the full the negative conclusions from the false basic premises cherished by the biographic-genetic-historical schools. Here they are in frank, bald statement:

1. Since, as they assume, Goethe was primarily using his *Faust* as a vehicle of self-expression, the only unity that the work can have is an autobiographical one. This would mean that the concluding scenes, written by a man of about eighty, are in contrast to rather than in continuity of the initial scenes written by a man in his early twenties.

Only an intrinsic analysis of the whole drama, one that establishes the tightly controlled unity and sequentiality prevailing throughout, will help us avoid this insult to the poet's artistic intelligence.

2. Since the *Faust*, as we finally have it and as Goethe intended us to have it, differs in important points from the more-or-less primordial fragment of the poet's youth that a court lady's copy preserved for us, it is assumed that what we have ultimately is a badly corrupted *Faust* that shows all too sadly the vicissitudes of the years and decades through which it was slowly and uncertainly brought to its conclusion, or at least its arbitrary termination. We have not only the *Urfaust*, but also the first printed *Fragment* of the 1790s and then the varied plans, outlines, and fragments of the subsequent decades, all of which together show that the poet had no clear notion of ultimate intent or of means to attain this

end, and that the final results are a matter of whim and accident, jerry-built of inconsistencies and inconsequences, with the seams showing patchily and painfully where *Fragment* was joined to *Urfaust*, Part One to *Fragment*, and Part Two to Part One. For silly, prissy reasons the poet put the Valentin scene before instead of after the Cathedral scene (part of it even earlier), and for sentimental reasons added at the end of the prison scene the assurance of the voice from above that Gretchen was saved.

The critical arrogance alone of such assumptions is stunning and indicates, as has been suggested, that *Faust* criticism is at about the stage of Shakespeare criticism around 1750. There is a surprise in store for critic and reader when they come to examine the final *Faust* text more carefully, more purely, and more exclusively, as well as in full context: they will discover that the final version is the artistically coherent and sequential one, that Goethe showed good judgment when he abandoned or changed earlier plans and sequences, and that if he had followed the wishes and precepts of the geneticists, he would have shown bad judgment. It is a matter of common agreement, of general consensus, that when a discrepancy, an inconsistency is found, it must be Goethe's fault in execution, it cannot be the critics' lack of understanding. There is good reason, sound artistic reason, for reversing the charges in favor of the author.

3. Since, as is further assumed, the Goethean *Faust* differs radically from the traditional Fausts, it is hardly to be considered a valid work of art. It should, therefore, be replaced by a Faust that conforms better to tradition and to the taste of the critics. This conviction brought forth a whole series of further Fausts—all of them stillborn, alas. Thus, vexatiously, Goethe the inept proved to be the superior poet who made every succeeding Faust, so much better conceived, appear sad and shabby by comparison. The next step, therefore, was to attack the Goethean *Faust* boldly and vigorously, force it to conform to the traditional consensus, even to "revise" it for stage and film, and make it serve the approved ends—with what results we have seen by way of one chief example in our study of the perversion of the Mephistopheles role.

From such a triple attack (Faust is merely Goethe, *Faust* is a confused botchery, *Faust* is un-Faustian), relentlessly propounded in the commentaries and critical expositions, the real *Faust*, as Goethe intended it and left it, has small chance of emerging and showing itself in its true shape and intrinsic form. Only if we reverse positions, if we put the horse before the cart and allow it to draw the whole load of *potentially* useful learning that has been accumulated about the author, about the genesis and development of the work, about the metamorphosis of a great tradition, about the poetic formation, transformation up to the final version—only then, when our knowledge is made subservient to artistic interpretation, will the proper sense of wonder overcome us at the superbly right artistic judgment that lies behind every scene, every sequence, and the ultimate composition of the whole. Objective judgment, that approaches this composition the way an art historian or a musicologist approaches a great composition in his field, with purely artistic criteria, liberated from all intellectual or genetic criteria, will invariably come to the conclusion that Goethe was a great artist who knew exactly what he was doing, from the smallest detail to the coherence of the whole and the ultimate perspectives.

On a less elevated level, the range of blunders that can come from a biographic-genetic-historical approach to *Faust* is multifarious, and hilarious. Again and again one hears it asserted that "Goethe said" this or that quotable statement such as (2171–72):

> Mein Leipzig lob' ich mir!
> Es ist ein klein Paris, und bildet seine Leute.
>
> *My Leipzig I do praise.*
> *It is a little Paris, shapes its people.*

Actually, of course, this is said by drunken Frosch in "Auerbach's Cellar," and the state of his *Bildung*, the shape he is in, can give us some notion of the irony intended when the poet put this statement in his mouth. Even worse, to attribute the various quotable sentiments of Mephistopheles to Goethe cannot help but block the way to any understanding of the intent and form of *Faust*. We shall see, for instance, how Mephistopheles' perversion of the concept of macrocosm and microcosm ("die große und die kleine Welt," "the large and the small world") has been accepted as the poet's positive and earnest intent, even recently, and how, consequently, his real, ironic intent has been totally overlooked. Gravest of all is where Mephisto's bitter negativism is accepted as Goethe's own attitude—to the misapprehension of the poetic intent of the whole.

Equally bad, possibly even worse results can come out of the genetic approach that assumes the primacy of the first or an early version. There is lament, for instance, that Goethe did not carry the "Walpurgis Night" through to the climax at the peak of the Brocken, despite the brilliant fragments of this scene that he had sketched, and instead weakly let the scene die out in a vapid "Walpurgis Night's Dream." There are further laments at the omission of the scene in which Faust confronts Persephone, a scene that would have risen to the heights of dramatic eloquence, as Goethe himself once, at an earlier stage, indicated. Only gradually does the insight come that if either scene were present, it would result in a heavy accent at the wrong place, it would be at the expense of the artistic whole. Indeed, Goethe showed deep poetic understanding when he refrained from carrying out either scene with the magnificent potentialities that stood at his command.

Another flaw of the geneticists, a strangely self-contradictory one, is their silent basic assumption of a rigidly immutable state that allows for no change or development in the protagonist, not even a perfectly natural and expectable change of mood between the two study scenes, the night before and the morning after. If Faust's relationship to the Earth Spirit in his first scene is catastrophically bad, then his good relations to him, his prayer of thanksgiving to him in "Forest and Cavern" must be censured as one of the many inconsistencies and carelessnesses that the poet perpetrated during the long slow course of his work on the poem. The opposite, truly genetic insight is nowhere clearly stated: that Faust learned from his failures. Out of his wrong notion and false approach to the Earth Spirit grew his better insight into his nature and into the gradual, natural, nonviolent approach to him. Similarly in Part Two Faust's rash and deluded attempt to come into possession of Helena and its crashing failure led to a more slow, patient, gradual approach to her true realm and person, this symbolized by the twice visualized enactment of the genesis of Helen in the meeting of Leda and the swan.

Goethe's deviation from history and tradition has always been a cross that some critics have found hard to bear, and they variously reproached him for it from the days of the romantics onward. Not being able to write a better *Faust*, they concentrated on re-forming Goethe's to suit their taste. In recent decades the attempts at the perversion have ranged all the way from the traditional diabolistic to the Plutonic atomic, all of this with the horrendously naive imputation that it was somehow authentically Goethean. Anachronisms to right of him, anachronisms to left of him, poor Goethe and his work in between disappear amid these belching fulminations.

## 2

If this relatively solid and responsible biographical-genetic-historical approach can lead to such aberrations, what must the personal (what's in it for me?) approach lead to? Part of the answer has already been given, for the former approach was, as we have seen, often used as a handy vehicle for the conveyance of subjective personal reactions of every variety. The combination resulted in artistic chaos.

Goethe, unfortunately, rubbed most of the people of the nineteenth century the wrong way (he still does that to a number of throwbacks and mossbacks of our own day). Even early in the century he came to realize that he did so, and he spared himself the annoyance of their uninformed subjective reactions by sealing his *Faust II* and reserving it for posthumous publication. After his death the vilifications began and, irrationally enough, they have continued to our day even though, in essentials, we stand opposed to the nineteenth century in just those particulars that aroused their anti-Goethean hostility. And, tragically, it was often the brilliant minds that were most perverse—Friedrich Theodor Vischer with his misbegotten third part of *Faust*; Nietzsche, with his naively wrong-headed acceptance of the prevailing sentimental misinterpretation of the "eternal-womanly," "das Ewig-Weibliche," and his imputation of this misconception to Goethe himself. To this day the critics, especially the popular and the general ones, are continuing this game of first grossly misinterpreting what the *Faust* contains and then passing off this travesty on a gullible public as Goethe's own botchery.

This is not to say that the subjective approach is always and inevitably reprehensible. Quite the opposite can occasionally be the case, as with a young student who reads *Faust* for the first time, naively, openly, receptively, sees a whole new world open up before him, and finds himself marvelling that this piece out of a remote time and place can mean so much to him in the here and now. On the surface, this would seem to be just another "What's in it for me?" reaction, a young student discovering a great masterpiece for the first time and discovering that it was doing things to him, changing him in unexpected ways. There is nothing wrong about that, everything right about it. It is the expansion of the self that can come to an individual from a great work of art. With such a good start he will eventually be able to raise himself to an understanding of the work of art on its own terms and then come to the insight that there is much of value in this world that goes beyond any personal measure he can apply. Then he will be able to change the question from "What's in it for me?" to "What's in me for it?"

With this comes a better insight into the true implications of the concept of relevance, going beyond the narrow negative spirit of implying that anything should be discarded if it cannot be proved to be subject to immediate use and understanding. In larger perspective such an attitude is in itself irrelevant, especially when the matter in question is a great work of art or any other prime human achievement. True perspective demands that we ask: Who, what, where, and when are we, we contemporaries, to pass judgment? We are living in a tiny slot of time, usually far less than a century, sometimes less than a quarter century long. We are living within a relatively narrow environment, of confined horizon, with limited experience for reaching beyond it. What right do we have to demand that a work of genius meant for the ages, ranging with widest perspectives over time and space and beyond, should be reduced to our present low and narrow level or be discarded? This is reductionism in its most arrogant and foolish form. The really relevant question that the thoughtful person will come to is, "Am I relevant?" or, more practically, "How can I make myself relevant, how can I raise my insights and outlooks to the point where I can see relevances that are at present beyond me?"

That can be a normal course of development for the young, provided their elders do not divert them from such a course. To be sure, the danger of diversion remains, for there are just too many for whom the subjective approach, critical narcissism, has become a way of life and a career: no interest in the artist's intent, deep fascination with their own internal reactions, satisfaction and relief at the delivery of their own critical judgment. The whole process can be put in the form of a fable, perhaps the briefest of all fables, entitled "Aesthetic Relevancy" or better:

### Critical Judgment

"There," said the fly, "I've settled that," as he left his speck on the Hermes of Praxiteles.

### 3

If it is so difficult to subordinate the author or one's own self to the intrinsic work, it is even more difficult to subordinate the leading course of thought, the prevailing intellectual climate, either in its new or in its traditional features, to the intrinsic work. The young especially will have difficulties, for, with their lack of experience, the temptation to succumb to an ideological scheme that promises to be a solve-all, a cure-all, becomes almost irresistible. But the older and more experienced are not spared since they have been subjected throughout their waking life to one ideological nostrum after the other and know no way out except the submission to still another, or else a pretended submission, in order to appear to go along with the fashion. In the 1950s a cynical professor of literature at a European university told me that esteemed colleagues in the field were continuing to use their same old lecture notes, except that they now on every page, once, twice, or thrice, would insert the word "existentially" with portentous emphasis. In the 1960s and 70s their kind made and make do with further weighty words, in remorseless succession, as yesterday's ideological key is thrown on today's scrap heap.

Granted, there is the work of literature, often an estimable one, that can be, even needs to be, approached intellectually, simply because its course of development is predetermined by an ideology. It is artfully contrived to illustrate that ideology. Such a work that has as its center ideas whose demonstration is foreordained may seem attractive at first sight, but it will not long hold a reader in its ban because its implications, its potentialities are soon exhausted. The opposite kind of work, however, one in which the leading themes have to be discovered and pursued through their often subtle and labyrinthine development, continues to increase in interest and fascination, leaves the reader with food for thought, and induces him to probe its further depths and implications. This latter kind of work *can* also be approached ideologically, can be approached through six or a dozen discrepant ideologies, if only the proper Procrustean instrumentalities are ruthlessly applied.

It is only a matter of course that such a work as *Faust* cannot escape such compulsive, indeed fashionable attention. The would-be leaders in literary criticism will stamp the newly molded stereotypes upon it, and their followers among the young and naive will admire the new and profound critical approach that finally unlocks the work and renders all earlier approaches obsolete. And so the winds of critical fashion continue to sweep through the *Faust* and in the end leave no trace but the echo of the rustle of their dead leaves. The new and current soon become the obsolete and the forgotten.

Thus there is really no need to detail the aberrations in *Faust* criticism that have grown out of the latest philosophical and critical fads. They all suffer from the same fallacy of putting the rocket in the nose cone, of pulverizing the work of art instead of propelling it into the space where it can show its own shape and perform its own function. Thereby they also have a built-in system of self-destruction that clears them out of the way just as a new fad is beginning to prove irresistibly attractive. Any details I could give here would be out of date before this could reach print, or would be soon thereafter.

Despite such continuing failure and rapid obsolescence, why is there this stubborn persistence in the misbegotten attempts to use the intellectual approaches to that which is accessible only to the symbolic-pictorial imagination? It would seem that the training of the exegetes is such that they know of no other approaches than the intellectual, that they are merely bewildered by Goethe's repeated warnings that the *Faust* is inaccessible to such an approach, that it is a symbolic work. They say yes, yes, of course; they use some of the symbolic-pictorial vocabulary, but under the cover of it they lapse right back into their compulsively abstracting, categorizing, reductionist practices. With every new philosophical and critical fashion that comes along they force the work into each successive ideological shape and admire the gruesome results during the five or ten years until the next type of intellectual straight jacket is developed to subject the work to yet another kind of critical mayhem.

A few intellectual fads and fashions have been more persistent; for some faithful souls a Hegel, or a Nietzsche, or a Freud, or an X, offers an incantatory, ritualistic logomageia that will unlock everything, including

*Faust*, and they cannot understand how anyone would presume to talk about the work without first enshrouding it in the winding sheet of their mortuary terminology. It might be useful as well as entertaining to preserve for the future a few characteristic statements about the work from each such ideological sect, if only the prose in which nearly all are composed were not so utterly abracadabra-cadaverous.

A generally better prose makes the efforts of the internalists more attractive, and they are also more impressive in their obvious profundities. They have expended a vast amount of ingenuity on such subtly psychologizing speculations as whether Mephistopheles is simply the alter ego of Faust, and also whether all the strange and supernatural events of Part Two are only the subjective dream projections of Faust— who thus would be sleeping through most of the drama and merely talking to himself during the crucial scenes with Mephisto. Quite aside from the fact that a careful scrutiny of the internal evidence of the drama, of the text itself, clearly precludes either possibility, there is an appalling lack of artistic tact and sensitivity in introducing such anachronistic and inappropriate considerations. Would anyone who reads "Sleeping Beauty" feel it necessary to seek a psychosomatic cause for her long sleep and be convinced that his modern medical jargon was essential for the understanding of the story? Or would he feel that he has no right to read "Cinderella" as a pure work of the imagination transpiring in the world of wonder, but would have to compel himself to narrow it down to socio-psychological terms as the escapist fantasy of an underprivileged adolescent?

With *Faust*, as with works of the imagination in general, we would do well to heed Goethe's own attitude as he variously expressed it, most succinctly perhaps in a general remark in "Die heiligen drei Könige," his critical essay on a fifteenth-century manuscript on the Magi:

> If an ancient myth, or a genuine poem developed directly out of it, affords adequate freedom to the imagination for developing the improbable, the impossible itself, then the listener is satisfied and the rhapsodist can boldly stride forward.

Thus with *Faust* also; we have no right to restrict its imaginative scope within the narrow confines of what we consider allowable. We should take it the way Goethe gave it to us, without forcing it into any pet scheme or theory of our own. Only when we let it talk to us directly, without such interference, will we hear what it has to say, and this will be far more profound and subtle than anything our overheated and misdirected ingenuity will be able to invent. When Faust was conversing with the Earth Spirit, Wagner on the other side of the door thought he was practicing his elocution and the twentieth-century scholiast thinks he is practicing his psychic projections. Is there all that much difference between these two commentators? Goethe, by contrast, tells us to take it as it is and for what it is: Mephisto is on his own, is his own particular self; Faust is unconscious and in a dream state only near the end of one scene in Part One and through one scene of Part Two.

From these internalists we can proceed to certain truly long-lived and persisting attitudes or systems of thought that are widely believed to be fundamental and yet run contrary to the spirit and the basic assumptions prevailing in the *Faust*. Long since and several times I was able to demonstrate that reading Platonic trains of thought into the work would usually lead to grave misunderstandings, since the intellectual aspects of the work, where they exist, are more likely to be anti-Platonic than Platonic. More recently, in *The Mothers in Faust: The Myth of Time and Creativity*, I showed that the realm of images in the scene of the Mothers, far from being the superior, the primary, the ultimate realm of reality, according to Platonic assumption, was instead simply the realm of forms, of models, mere schemata of whatever had once been or was still to come into the realm of reality. Goethe, who here made the realm of images subordinate to, less complete than the realm of material reality, was in agreement with those Renaissance poets who before him had imaginatively projected similar realms. The intellectual background for this, and for so much more in *Faust*, must, as I have shown, be sought outside the realm of Platonism, most prominently in the natural philosophy of the Middle Stoa, about which one can find little of pertinence in the handbooks of philosophy, but a great deal, and most elegantly, in certain of Cicero's philosophical dialogues, which Goethe and his poetic predecessors read and which the Goethe critics have failed to read.

But there is an even greater source of error in another persisting intellectual attitude, that of a dualism too generally and imprecisely attributed to the *Faust*. This dualistic fallacy has led not only to a misunderstanding of one of the drama's prevailing symbolic complexes, but also, and in consequence, to the obscuring of an essential feature of its form and structure. Before we turn then to our main task of studying the form of *Faust*, we must clear away this false intellectual barrier to our understanding, thinking of it, to be sure, not as a singular instance, but as a typical instance of a foreign body intruding upon the line of our artistic vision.

When the symbolism of the *Faust* drama is discussed, it has frequently, and correctly, been observed that the light symbolism is thoroughgoing and of highest importance. Unfortunately, this *correct observation* has been accompanied by a *false assumption* derived from an alien ideological attitude prevailing outside the drama, among the critics and interpreters, but with only a small and occasional place within the drama itself. Quite unwarrantedly the critics have imposed upon the drama the assumption of a dualistic struggle between evil, earth, matter, on the one hand, and good, heaven, spirit, on the other. Such an assumption may be correct for other Fausts or other Christian dramas, but it is quite contrary to the text of the Goethean *Faust*. The poet has his protagonist affirm and reaffirm repeatedly his commitment to life and experience on this material earth, from the very first scenes in which he appears on to the very last. The earth, far from being considered evil, is considered to be the proper sphere of man in which he can carry on his microcosmic creative tasks that will bring him closer to the divine. Contextually also the song of the archangels in the "Prologue in Heaven" harmonizes with such an attitude and is discrepant with the attitude of a dualistic hostility; equally so the song of the angels near the end (11958–65).

Let us look at the characteristic passages that confirm such a non-hostile, nonantithetical attitude, that go as far as a benediction on man living on this turbulent earth (as the archangels express it) whirling about in light *and* darkness through God's everlasting day.

In Faust's first monologue his vision of the sign of the Earth Spirit leads to the first of the recurring statements of affirmation of life on earth, whatever its impairments (464–67):

> Ich fühle Mut, mich in die Welt zu wagen,
> Der Erde Weh, der Erde Glück zu tragen,
> Mit Stürmen mich herumzuschlagen
> Und in des Schiffbruchs Knirschen nicht zu zagen.

> *I feel the courage through the world to fare,*
> *The woe of earth, the bliss of earth to bear,*
> *To battle with the tempest's roar and glare,*
> *And in the crunch of shipwreck not despair.*

After his wager with Mephistopheles he reaffirms his resolution to experience the whole of life on earth, even to ultimate shipwreck (1770–75):

> Und was der ganzen Menschheit zugeteilt ist,
> Will ich in meinem innern Selbst genießen,
> Mit meinem Geist das Höchst' und Tiefste greifen,
> Ihr Wohl und Weh auf meinen Busen häufen,
> Und so mein eigen Selbst zu ihrem Selbst erweitern,
> Und, wie sie selbst, am End' auch ich zerscheitern.

> *And whatsoe'er to all mankind is portioned*
> *In mine own inner self will I enjoy,*
> *Grasp with my mind the summit and abyss,*
> *Heap on my breast their troubles and their bliss,*
> *And so my self to all their selves extend,*
> *And like them perish shattered in the end.*

In the first scene of Part Two comes his renewed affirmation of life on earth, in metaphorical form abjuring the transcendent (4715),

> So bleibe denn die Sonne mir im Rücken!
>
> *And therefore let the sun remain behind me,*

and confirming the immanent (4727),

> Am farbigen Abglanz haben wir das Leben.
>
> *We have our life in many-hued reflection.*

At the time of his first vision of his last creative task he again rejects transcendence (this time sarcastically suggested by Mephistopheles) and confirms the earth as the proper sphere of man (10181–82):

> Mit nichten! dieser Erdenkreis
> Gewährt noch Raum zu großen Taten.
>
> *Not in the least. The sphere of earth*
> *Still offers room for mighty deeds.*

And during the last hour of his life on earth comes his strongest affirmation of man's life on earth and condemnation of transcendental yearnings (11441–52):

> Der Erdenkreis ist mir genug bekannt,
> Nach drüben ist die Aussicht uns verrannt;
> Tor, wer dorthin die Augen blinzelnd richtet,
> Sich über Wolken seinesgleichen dichtet!
> Er stehe fest und sehe hier sich um;
> Dem Tüchtigen ist diese Welt nicht stumm.
> Was braucht er in die Ewigkeit zu schweifen!
> Was er erkennt, läßt sich ergreifen.
> Er wandle so den Erdentag entlang;
> Wenn Geister spuken, geh' er seinen Gang,
> Im Weiterschreiten find' er Qual und Glück,
> Er, unbefriedigt jeden Augenblick!
>
> *I know enough the sphere of earth and men,*
> *The view beyond is barred from mortal ken.*
> *Fool, who would yonder turn his blinking eyes,*
> *Imagine his own kind within the skies.*
> *Let him stand firm, the prospect round him scan,*
> *The world's not mute unto a worthy man.*
> *Why need he soar through all eternity?*
> *Here he can grasp whate'er he knows to be.*
> *So let him wander through his earthly day,*
> *When spirits haunt, let him pursue his way,*
> *Through joy and torment let him onward stride,*
> *He, every moment still unsatisfied.*

Not only in the "Prologue in Heaven" is the condition of man on earth given ultimate approval by the Lord, but in the Easter Choruses also, at the end of Faust's first great scene, is this life on earth confirmed as the proper sphere of man in the devout immanence of human service (801–07):

Tätig ihn Preisenden,
Liebe Beweisenden,
Brüderlich Speisenden,
Predigend Reisenden,
Wonne Verheißenden
Euch ist der Meister nah,
Euch ist er da!

All the translations are sadly inadequate. Here is another attempt:

*Praising Him fervently,*
*Loving concernedly,*
*Sharing fraternally,*
*Preaching sojournally,*
*Pledging felicity:*
*For you the Lord is near,*
*The Lord is here.*

This promise of Divine immanence comes from the angels in reply to and correction of the disciples' vain yearning for transcendence, as voiced in the preceding stanza. And Faust himself here shows that he well understood the import of Christ's resurrection, of his resumption of his earthly body. In strong contrast to the false yearning for transcendence that had just previously brought him to the verge of suicide, he here declares with quiet finality (784):

die Erde hat mich wieder!

*the earth has hold of me again.*

To these last words in his first scene, to this commitment to earth, he remains faithful to his last hour, as we have observed. Thus, in conclusion, we can say about the false intrusion of hostile dualistic attitudes into the drama that this philosophical blinding of clear perception, this general disregard of the drama's plain statement of attitude, in single texts and total contexts, is bound to lead to misconceptions of its form also. Conversely, a tactful avoidance of the intrusion of alien points of view into the drama will not only allow such ideological patterns as do exist to emerge in their natural form and validity, such an avoidance will also give full room and scope for the emergence and full development of the symbolic complexes that, after all, do establish the continuity of the work and harmonize with its ultimate form.

# II

## Goethe's *Faust* Intrinsically

# 4

# The Four Corners and
# the Three Beginnings

HE LIGHT SYMBOLISM OF THE DRAMA, so generally observed, so
generally misunderstood, has now been freed from false ideological associations and thus can be observed in relation to the
larger formal aspects that are intrinsic to the drama. The earth
is the proper sphere of man, approved as such by the Lord in the Prologue
and given the promise of sanctification by the chorus of angels on Easter
morn. At the beginning of the "Prologue in Heaven" the archangels describe the earth, emphasizing, especially in the words of Gabriel, that it
is characterized by light *and* darkness, not light versus darkness (251–54):

> Und schnell und unbegreiflich schnelle
> Dreht sich umher der Erde Pracht;
> Es wechselt Paradieseshelle
> Mit tiefer, schauervoller Nacht.

> *And swift, past understanding swift*
> *The splendor of the earth turns round,*
> *From radiant paradise a shift*
> *To awe-inspiring night profound.*

Mephistopheles also, in one of his rare moments of truthfulness (the
reasons for which we examined in Chapter One), and in his own different way, offers a similar report on man's ambiguous position (1782–84):

> Er findet sich in einem ew'gen Glanze,
> Uns hat er in die Finsternis gebracht,
> Und euch taugt einzig Tag und Nacht.

> *Eternal radiance is his existence,*
> *Us he has brought unto an utter night,*
> *And fit for you alone are dark and light.*

With the essential and intrinsic background thus established, we can proceed effortlessly to an observation of the light symbolism in its broadest formal perspectives, an observation that, truly simple though it is, has hitherto escaped attention because of the false intellectual barriers impairing the view of it.

The earthly action of Part One begins at night, "Nacht," in a "high-vaulted, narrow Gothic chamber," which Faust promptly calls a "prison," a "Kerker," and continues past midnight to the first announcement of the new Easter morn. Part One ends in the darkness before dawn with the scene entitled "Prison," "Kerker." Part Two begins with a scene entitled "Anmutige Gegend," a pleasant region that is promptly shown to be in the mountains at night before dawn and at sunrise (with Faust again confirming the validity of life on earth, whatever its limitations, conceding the pure full light to the superhuman realms and contenting himself with the play of light on darkness in the beautiful colors of the rainbow over the waterfall). Part Two ends, not at midnight with the death of Faust, but on the way upward through the mountain defiles, the "Bergschluchten," past the holy anchorites of ever higher and wider perspectives, when the angels carry the immortal parts of Faust, to which, as they observe, there still persistently clings a remnant of the earthly, "ein Erdenrest" (11954, 11961–63):

> Kein Engel trennte
> Geeinte Zwienatur
> Der innigen beiden.
>
> *No angel could part*
> *The joined twin nature*
> *Of the intimate twain.*

Only with the Doctor Marianus do we have the transition out of the earthly to the heavenly.

In sum, Part One is encompassed by confinement, cut off from perspective, albeit in each case with the prospect of the light to come. Part Two is encompassed by mountain vistas, by widening perspectives, by the advent of the full surge of light. Only at the end, after a full earthly life and widest perspectives can come the transition, the transcendence to higher spheres.

What is of especial interest to us for the formal structure of the work is that at the beginning and end of each part, at all four points, we have a darkness before dawn, a "death" before a "resurrection."

1. In the first Faustian scene (which we shall come to call the monodrama) Faust's monologue, after Wagner leaves, tends toward suicide for the purpose of forcible transcendence beyond the vexatious human limitations that are the chief plaint of the protagonist. But just as he raises the cup of poison to his lips, the chorus of angels sings the

message of Christ's resurrection from death. Faust's heart is melted at the message; even though the faith of his youth is not restored, the whole meaning of his youthful faith comes over him so powerfully that his past takes control of his present and his future. His urge toward transcendence by an act of violence now seems presumptuous when the message comes to him of Christ's loving immanence, of his return to his human body in his resurrection. In unwonted humility and gentleness Faust abjures the superhuman spheres (767),

> Zu jenen Sphären wag' ich nicht zu streben,
>
> *To yonder spheres I do not dare to strive,*

and concludes with quiet finality (784),

> die Erde hat mich wieder.
>
> *the earth has hold of me again.*

2. Near the end of Part One, even as near the end of Part Two, Mephistopheles presumes to deliver the final verdict on what has happened. In each case his verdict is canceled out by a superior verdict. When Margarete turns to the Heavenly Father and away from Faust, Mephistopheles declares (4611), "Sie ist gerichtet!" "She is sentenced," and a voice from above counters with "Ist gerettet!" "Is saved."

The geneticists and fragmentists long since observed that in the *Urfaust* the voice from above was not yet present, and then they supplied the typical narrow or extraneous explication that Goethe added the voice from above for conciliatory or sentimental reasons—dear, gentle Goethe, who had no sense for the tragic and no will toward the tragic, who wanted to add this bit of consolation for the next ladies' sewing circle that might be weeping over the Gretchen tragedy. It never dawned on a single one of them that the careful, planning, forming artist Goethe added the voice from above for compelling artistic reasons after he had his great vision of the totality of the *Faust* near the turn of the century, some intimation of which can still come to us from what is left of his numbered plan of scenes. (Needless to say, the ingenious recent attempts to reconstruct the whole scenario from the preserved fragments are still subject to improvement on the basis of a closer regard for Goethe's artistic intent.)

3. Faust's complete collapse after the harrowing tragedy of Gretchen is indicated clearly by the words of Ariel at the beginning of Part Two. However, we must be careful to see their symbolic intent and especially not to take the "four watches of the night" literally. Like Timoleon and many another predecessor, Faust was here healed from overwhelming guilt and tragedy only by the long passage of time. Ariel

tells what such a passage of time can do to a deeply wounded and heavily laden soul (4623–33):

> Besänftiget des Herzens grimmen Strauß,
> Entfernt des Vorwurfs glühend bittre Pfeile,
> Sein Innres reinigt von erlebtem Graus.
> Vier sind die Pausen nächtiger Weile,
> Nun ohne Säumen füllt sie freundlich aus.
> Erst senkt sein Haupt aufs kühle Polster nieder,
> Dann badet ihn im Tau aus Lethes Flut;
> Gelenk sind bald die krampferstarrten Glieder,
> Wenn er gestärkt dem Tag entgegenruht;
> Vollbringt der Elfen schönste Pflicht,
> Gebt ihn zurück dem heiligen Licht.

> *Assuage the cruel conflict of his heart,*
> *Remove the burning arrows of remorse,*
> *Let suffered horror from his soul depart.*
> *Four vigils has the night upon its course,*
> *Now fill them promptly with your kindly art.*
> *Here first his head on a cool pillow lay,*
> *Then bathe him in the dew from Lethe's stream;*
> *His limbs, cramp-stiffened, then will smoothly play*
> *When he rests strengthened toward the day's new beam.*
> *Accomplish, elves, your fairest duty,*
> *Restore him to light's sacred beauty.*

So here again a "death" and a resurrection, a restoration to light after coming out of darkness. It is the mitigated light of earth, to be sure, that he finally faces, with glad consent (4727):

> Am farbigen Abglanz haben wir das Leben.

> *We have our life in many-hued reflection.*

4. At the end, when Faust has had his final great vision of a free people on a free soil, remaining ever alert and creative, when he agrees that with such a future realization he would rest content, when he then calls this vision of the future his highest, most exalted moment, and when he thereupon dies, Mephistopheles declares in bitter contradiction that this was instead Faust's last, bad, empty moment, "Den letzten, schlechten, leeren Augenblick" (11589). The voice from above does not here immediately cancel out his verdict (except very subtly in the "vorbei" of the chorus that outrages Mephistopheles so intensely). The voice from above comes later, but then in full clarity (11934–37):

> Gerettet ist das edle Glied
> Der Geistewelt vom Bösen,
> Wer immer strebend sich bemüht,
> Den können wir erlösen.

*A fellow spirit saved, this one,*
*From evil machination;*
*Whoever striving labors on,*
*For him there is salvation.*

So for the fourth time, most plainly and fully realized, there is a death and resurrection, an end situation followed by a promise of continuity. In four as in two there is a denial followed by an approval, a condemnation followed by a vindication.

This is our first and simplest observation of the form of *Faust*. We behold Goethe, the literary artist, carefully coordinating beginning and end of each part and of both parts together, decisively developing point one and changing point two for this purpose. The fact that the double motif of darkness and light (as well as of death and resurrection) is strongly developed at each of the four bounding parts of the Faust action, should be kept clearly in mind and related to the first announcement of the double motif by the archangels in the "Prologue in Heaven." However, we must take care not to give too great an emphasis to this first observation of essential, of intrinsic form. Important and encompassing though it may be, there are others of equal importance and as central to our understanding of form and structure.

Before we go on to further observations, there is one more preliminary factor of form about which there must be complete clarity if we are to avoid the confusions of the past and prevent them from distracting us later when we face more complicated issues. When we examine the first edition of Part One (Tübingen, 1808), the first thing we see is the title: *Faust. Eine Tragödie*. The next leaf is a so-called half-title containing only the word "Zueignung," the title of the first preliminary part, the "Dedication," the text of which then follows on the third leaf. The second and third preliminary parts, the "Prelude in the Theater" and the "Prologue in Heaven," are also preceded by half-titles with blank versos before the text proper. Then before Faust's first monologue comes another half-title: "Der Tragödie Erster Theil." In addition to the first three scenes, there is only one further scene that is provided with a half-title, namely, the "Walpurgis Night's Dream." All the other scenes have mere title headings in much smaller type. This arrangement was maintained in all further editions of Part One issued under Goethe's supervision, including the one in volume twelve of the final collected works (Tübingen, 1828), where the smaller format and more economical printing practice might have called for the elimination of half-titles and blank versos. That they did not may be an indication that this was a formal arrangement that it was important to preserve. For Part Two, issued posthumously in 1832, the title reads: *Faust. Der Tragödie zweyter Theil in fünf Acten*.

That brings three points up for consideration: first why Goethe

called *Faust* a tragedy, then why the three preliminary scenes are set off
by half-titles, and finally why of all the other scenes only the "Walpurgis
Night's Dream," this "Intermezzo," as Goethe goes on to call it, has such
a half-title with blank verso. After the brief though essential consideration of point one, we shall proceed to a closer examination of the three
preliminary scenes that will make it clear why they are set off as they
are. Then in the next chapter we shall take up the fourth scene so
treated, the little "Intermezzo" coming after the "Walpurgis Night"
proper. Only then will we be fully aware of the poet's intent and will
realize to what an extent our understanding of the form of *Faust* has
been impaired by the fact that most (nearly all) modern editors have
eliminated the half-titles and blank versos. The merely intellectual critic
may feel that he can disregard this visual disposition and formal arrangement. However, the critic who is interested in *Faust* as a work of
art must face the facts and phenomena: this is the way Goethe wanted
it; any abridgment of his intent is a falsification of the text and an
impairment of our understanding of its form.

First on *Faust. A Tragedy*. Goethe would not, of course, have included the word tragedy if he had not wanted us to think of the drama
as a tragedy, from the first. But what is a tragedy? What does he mean
by tragedy? Here at the very beginning we have our first object lesson in
the importance of understanding a word in its own context and not
according to some definition or assumption brought into it from without.
Once we are acquainted with the drama, we know that it ends in a great
conciliatory act, on earth and in heaven. Goethe, however, does not
thereby do violence even to the classic meaning of the word tragedy. If
we look back at the Greek dramatists, we see that final disaster is not an
integral and inevitable part of a tragedy. Aeschylus' great *Oresteia*
trilogy ends in a solemn conciliatory religious act; other ancient trag-
edies, extant and lost, also had conciliatory endings.

Final catastrophe, therefore, is not an essential ingredient of a
tragedy. The essentials are these: a tragedy is a serious and imperiled
action concerned with the ultimate questions of man living on earth,
with himself, with his fellow men, and with God.

However, there is further internal evidence of the work's tragic
design in the immediately previous consideration of this chapter,
namely, in the prominence given to the motifs of darkness and light,
death and resurrection at the beginning and end of each part of the
drama. Furthermore, the two Dionysiac scenes at the end of Act Two
and Act Three of Part Two are likewise quite explicitly concerned with
the mystery of death and resurrection, Homunculus making the transition from artificial enclosure to organic embodiment, the girls of the
chorus dissolving into the four elements and being reunited again in the

coming together of the four in the wine, and in it being elevated to the fifth, the quint-essence.

In these Dionysiacs the poet symbolically indicates the connection of his tragedy to ancient tragedy and its origin in the perilous exhilarating Dionysiac rites. Furthermore, the vital center of the Eleusinian Mysteries and, so far as we know, of other ancient mysteries was a symbolic act of revelation that brought home to the participants, experientially, the comprehension of the mystery of death and resurrection. Even in modern times the rites of initiation into the Masonic and other secret societies involve the symbolic death of the old dissociated self and the awakening to life of the new consociated self.

In ancient tragedy the death of the protagonist often brings with it, implicitly or explicitly, the end of an era and the dawn of a new one. In the conclusion of the *Oresteia* there is such an end of one era and the announcement of a new one; though this does not involve the physical death of the hero, it most clearly does open up to him the prospects of a new life.

In sum, the text and context of *Faust* is that of a tragedy in the true and primordial sense of the word.

Apart from these larger vistas and from the point of view of personal fate alone, the outcome for the protagonist is tragic: Faust dies at the moment of his final vision of a free people on a free soil and cannot fulfill his ultimate wish of living among them as an equal. Like Moses (and unlike Timoleon) he is only allowed a view of the promised land but cannot enter into it. Faust cannot fulfill his life during his lifetime, and in this respect he is strangely like the Blessed Boys of the last scene, though in experience at opposite poles from them. With his wish for the full human experience, unobtainable within the normal human limits of time, range, and power, he resorted to Mephisto's magic to overcome all limitations. The tragic irony is, as he finally realizes, that this course deprived him of true human freedom and brought him to the grievous peril of dehumanization. Only after he has made himself free again by abjuring magic can he have his culminating creative vision of a larger human freedom, of the true course of human development in the understanding of man's place on earth.

Turning now to the three preliminary scenes and examining them for what they can tell us about the poet's intent, we can at once observe that an essential, indeed determining factor of form receives its first statement, quite properly, at the very beginning of the drama, with the lyric "Zueignung." It is generally assumed that this "Dedication" is not an integral part of the whole, though everyone readily concedes the beauty of these four stanzas of *ottava rima* in which the poet speaks with his own voice and tells us of his own attitude toward his creation. Aside from such words of praise the "Dedication" is usually dismissed with a few words of comment that have never called attention to the dominant themes announced in it. Just how futile has been the effort to construct a literary-symbolic interpretation of Part Two alone, separate from Part One, will become apparent as we analyze the symbolic content of these first lines of the whole drama. At this point, preliminarily, we need only be mindful of our basic principle of granting that Goethe was a good artist, that he knew what he was doing, and that the "Dedication" also stands in the service of the whole, is an integral part of the total form. We therefore think of it not as a supernumerary bit preceding the "Prelude in the Theater" and the "Prologue in Heaven" (these by some editors counted as scenes one and two), but as properly and significantly the very first scene, and a determining one.

If we examine what the poet says here, we shall find his precept for symbolic drama already met: "an important action that points to an even more important one," "eine wichtige Handlung, die auf eine noch wichtigere deutet." The poet is about to resume his work on the drama. Years have elapsed since he began it. Many of the dear friends of his youth among whom and for whom he first wrote it have departed or are now widely scattered. Those who will hear its continuation are later comers, strangers, whose very applause is frightening.

And yet, as the poet begins to speak, the wavering forms of his youthful creation rise up before him once more. They come from so remotely in the past that he doubts whether he can continue with the task of giving them poetic realization. But at once he sees that it is not up to him to decide whether or not he will continue. They take possession of him (5):

> Ihr drängt euch zu! nun gut, so mögt ihr walten,
>
> *You press on me. So be it, you may govern,*

and he feels himself transported out of the present back into his youth.

Then, in conclusion, he notices that something wondrously strange is happening to him: with the invasion of his present by his remote past (something that will happen to Faust also, near the end of his first scene, the monodrama), with the emotion that this engenders in him, with the breaking down of the barriers it achieves, his sense of present presence is lost. That which he is and has seems remote and unreal; that which has long since disappeared becomes reality:

> Was ich besitze, seh' ich wie im Weiten,
> Und was verschwand, wird mir zu Wirklichkeiten.
>
> *What I possess, I see afar off lying,*
> *What disappeared, grows real and undying.*

The chief poetic motifs in the "Dedication," then, are: the mystery of creativity, the mystery of time, the mystery of place, the mystery of memory, the mystery of the different kinds of reality, the mystery of the creative individual whose "real" environmental configuration can be made unreal by an imaginative, mentally created and projected configuration. This, once brought into being, has a life of its own and can at any time, unsummoned, rise up out of the past and demand its creative due.

Therewith we have, at the very beginning, a first statement of the dominant motifs that run through the whole of *Faust*, give it symbolic coherence and continuity. Again and again, in ever varying form and action and situation, we shall find the poet exploring the great mysteries of time, of place, of creativity, of the reality and unreality of man's life on earth between birth and death, and beyond in that arc of the cycle that lies outside his ken. If we notice these recurrences and developments of primary themes as we progress through the work, we shall be better prepared, for instance, to understand the great voyage through time and place that becomes all-encompassing in the second and third acts of Part Two. Especially shall we be better prepared to understand the great prelude to all this, Faust's entrance into the realm of memory and creativity, symbolized by the Mothers. Greek myth tells us significantly that the Muses were daughters of Mnemosyne. Memory is the mother of the Muses; there is no art without recollection. And when we traverse the multifarious scenes with their different kinds of reality, in some of which the characters themselves are perplexed about their reality-unreality (as we are ourselves at times in the course of our earthly existence), we must take care to avoid an either-orish decision as to the poetic intent and see any such character and scene in the context of the whole, ever mindful especially of the primary "Dedication" and its thematic complex.

For his Italian journey Goethe recorded at Rome on March 1, 1788, the beginning of this return to his old *Faust* creation. For our present purposes the pertinent passages are the following, and we can note here also how these motifs of time, memory, creativity, reality-unreality are intertwined, how the past can invade the present and poetically displace it:

> This was a bountiful week that in recollection seems like a month.—
> First the plan for *Faust* was made, and I hope the undertaking may prove
> successful. . . . Since through long rest and solitude I have been brought
> back entirely to the level of my own proper being, it is surprising to note
> how much I resemble myself and how little of my own inner self has
> been impaired by years and circumstances. The old manuscript some-
> times gives cause for reflection when I see it before me. It is still the
> first, in the main scenes indeed written down directly without previous

draft. Now it is yellowed with age, worn from handling (the quires were never stitched), so brittle and frayed at the margins that it really looks like the fragment of an old codex. Thus, just as I formerly by contemplation and intuition transported myself back into an earlier world, so now I have to transport myself back again into an age I myself lived through.

This creative symbolic relationship of poet to work remained constant through the years, recurring poetically in the "Dedication," written nearly a decade later (probably on June 24, 1797), and finding expression again at the time of the separate publication of the Helena act. Significantly, Goethe wrote as follows to Nees von Esenbeck, May 25, 1827:

> The way I quietly and patiently proceed, you will see in my three-thousand-year "Helena," whom I have been pursuing through some sixty years in order somehow to derive some advantage from her. . . . From long years ago such diverse concepts lie before me, concepts that I myself must esteem because they originate from a time that will not return; actually all they need is a certain inspired redaction. . . . Thus last year with a mighty spurt I finally brought the "Helena" to harmonious life. How variously has this work been formed and transformed through long, scarcely measurable years. Now finally it may come to rest, crystallized in the world of time.

It would be an overstatement to maintain that the chief theme of *Faust*, especially of the crucial scenes of *Faust*, is creativity, the mystery of creativity. But it would be a pardonable overstatement. Here, at any rate, is the place where the poet's own chief concern, at the middle period of his fashioning of *Faust*, coincided with the (or a) chief concern of the drama itself. Here is the point where poet and work meet. However much of himself Goethe put into the work, it must be recognized that beyond this tangential point, the work is a world of its own; it can and should be explicated out of itself.

We are prevented from going on into even more solemn reflections by the second preliminary scene, the "Prelude in the Theater," "Vorspiel auf dem Theater," where the poet varies the handling of the great primary themes to the point of making a jest about them. The dialogue moves along so lightly and pleasantly that the jest may be at the expense of the viewer or critic if he is not alert to it. And if he is alert to it, the temptation would be to think of it not as a jest intended by Goethe, but as a blunder, an oversight of his, in accordance with the old compulsive critical platitude of "Hier irrt Goethe." To my knowledge, only one critic both noticed the discrepancy and offered a defense of it, but only the idealistic defense that time in poetry essentially demands internal, not external causality. That Goethe's intent in this jest was more subtle and far-reaching, we shall see.

In this scene the director, the comedian, and the poet are talking together, as the spectators are filing in and some of them are already seated. And what are they talking about? About the play that is to be presented. The director wants a good box-office success; he represents showmanship. The comedian wants a good acting vehicle; he represents entertainment. And the poet uncompromisingly insists on making it a literary work of art; he represents creativity. So entertaining is the dialogue, so eloquent the poet's declaration of the integrity of the work of art and the nature of the creative process, that only in the end do we realize with a slight shock that, though the audience is assembled, the drama is not yet written, far less rehearsed and staged, and yet the director, unperturbed, puts an end to the discussion, commands the poet to commandeer his poetry, the stagehands to produce their most splendid effects, and the actor by his magic to transmute the stage of boards into the stage of the world.

In the first place, this is an intentional anachronism. The theme of the mystery of time, announced in the "Dedication," is here played with in a light and jesting manner. At a number of points the poet deliberately introduces anachronisms (and also anachorisms), with humorous intent on the surface, though with larger intent in the thematic continuity of the whole. By the time we reach the second part, particularly the second act, and then the third, we shall know what all this jocoserious play with time is leading to.

In the second place, however, what the poet intends to convey also reaches over to another level. This intent is suggested by the old metaphor, here once more expressed, that the magic of art can transmute the stage of boards into the stage of the world, that "all the world's a stage." The right answer to the poet's intent comes easily once we know how to ask the right question: we need merely inquire just where it does happen that the spectators are assembled before the play they are to see is written, rehearsed, and staged, then we readily come to the answer and the poet's point. This happens continuingly on the stage of the world where the spectators watch an action for which no one, whether actor or manager or playwright, knows the exact course of the outcome, and where only the set traditional conventions of the political *commedia dell' arte* can lend some semblance of form. The dramatist writes the action before it is staged; the historian writes the action after it has happened.

Here is one of Goethe's most pleasant and profound creative acts: he has turned an old metaphor around, endowed it with a new meaning, and opened up new vistas, ironic ones, of life as a comment on literature over against literature as a comment on life. Furthermore, in this second preludial part, as in the first, there is a profounder relation to the main action than has been realized: Faust, like mankind in general, is unable to perceive the full meaning of the unwritten drama in which he has to participate until it draws near its end. Analogously, to come down to the

level of specific details, the *Faust* drama contains many seemingly episodic passages and such long stretches of supposedly mere pageantry as
the carnival scene and the "Classical Walpurgis Night." Thus the very
tight form and carefully calculated structure of the drama are successfully hidden and only slowly and late emerge to view. Here too,
psychologically, in the spectator as in the actor, cosmos only gradually
emerges out of chaos.

If we come back to the surface level of this particular scene (also a
valid level, most certainly), we may note that the stage has always been
in a perpetual state of unreadiness and improvisation, with every par-
ticipant contributing his own share to it from his own different and often
conflicting point of view, so that in the end it is something of a miracle
when integrated sense and effect, and even art, come out of it—particularly in view of the deplorably low tastes and tyrannous demands of the
theater-going public that must be catered to. All the world is a stage and
creation rises from chaos. This sequence, of cosmos arising out of chaos,
will be found in later scenes, such as the "Witch's Kitchen," as we shall
see.

There is yet a third preliminary part, the "Prologue in Heaven,"
"Prolog im Himmel," (this in the opinion of many a critic the actual
beginning of the drama). Here we leave these single and limited and
conflicting points of view of the *theatrum mundi* to see the drama and its
show place, the earth, *sub specie aeternitatis*, first in the song of the
archangels, and then more specifically directed toward Faust in the
words of the Lord, with the dissenting reedy voice of Mephistopheles in
comic contrast to the heavenly harmonies. The great theme of the scene,
raised to an ultimate beyond the limitations of place and time, is announced by the archangels at the beginning and confirmed by the Lord
in his last words. It is the theme of creativity, continuing creativity as the
ultimate meaning of the universe, embracing all in its divine purpose,
even Mephistopheles who has an unintentionally creative function in
spurring man on to constant striving, constant overcoming of past errors,
constant rising to higher things. We are thus early prepared for Faust, at
the last, choosing a life of creativity (under the oldest and most persistent symbol of creativity: that of separating the land from the waters),
and for the angels at the end restating the intent of the whole
(11936–37):

> Wer immer strebend sich bemüht,
> Den können wir erlösen.
>
> *Whoever striving labors on,*
> *For him there is salvation.*

—with love coming down from above to welcome him.

There is also something else of great importance that the poet wishes to convey to us by implication in the course of these preliminary scenes. This becomes all the clearer when we turn to the next scene, find Faust himself telling us his attitude toward his own and the human dilemma. We suddenly or gradually realize that what Goethe has been giving us is a series of quite different points of view of the action that is to follow: first the poet's own, then the director's, the dramatist's, the actor's, then the archangels', the Lord's, and Mephistopheles', with each of them, except the poet's and the Lord's, limited in its perspective, true so far as it goes, but incapable of comprehending the whole. Here Goethe establishes for the drama the principle of *multiple points of view*, each of them more or less important but only all of them together leading to a comprehension of the total intent. Mephisto, in the "Prologue" and so often thereafter, is "right," brilliantly and wittily right (as well as obtuse and blundering at crucial moments), but his rightness is of a lower order than Faust's and, more especially, than the Lord's. Faust's assistant, Wagner, is also "right," in his limited way, so is the Earth Spirit, or Margarete, or the Emperor, or Thales, or Anaxagoras, or Homunculus, or Euphorion. To each his due, no more than his due, no one alone will lead to the play's full meaning or the author's full intent. Only in the combination of them all, only in their multiplicity (intended to stand for and poetically reflect the rich variety and bewildering diversity of life itself) do we come to some approximation of the ultimate meaning, and to an understanding of the "important action that points to a still more important one."

Even this, all together, does not exhaust the formal import of these three preliminary parts. Indeed, we behold here furthermore a formal principle established that is maintained throughout the rest of the *Faust* drama, not simplistically or mechanically, of course not, but thoroughgoingly, so that it becomes one of the characteristic organizational features of the whole drama. This is to be the concern of the next chapter, and by the end of it there can remain little doubt that this formal principle of the drama, like those examined in the present chapter, can be overlooked only at the peril of basic misunderstanding.

# 5

# Symmetrical and Progressive Sequences: The Principle of the Interlude

 T IS CLEAR THAT the three preliminary parts establish the perspective and the main thematic structure of the drama, so decisively indeed that any study of symbols, themes, attitudes, or structures in later parts of the drama is doomed at least to partial failure if it does not give full attention to the matter and manner of these three prologues. The formal guidance they afford appears even more impressive if we take one further careful look at them, viewing them together, as we did for the purpose of establishing the principle of multiple points of view. What do we see when we view them in their succession? We see a lighter, more relaxed, even comic scene between two intense and serious scenes. If we go on, what do we find between the two first great monologues of Faust? We find the lighter, more relaxed, comic Wagner interlude (with Faust, like the poet of the "Prelude," remaining in an eloquent state of high seriousness).

Let us go on. Between this double monologue of Faust and the two study scenes to follow, what do we have? The lighter, gayer, more relaxed scene, "Outside the City Gate," of Faust's and Wagner's Easter walk amid the festive populace, with Faust again turning serious and here making one of the profound thematic statements about himself and the condition of man, in the middle of which stand his reflections on the "two souls," reflections that, by the way, have been constantly misinterpreted, not only with regard to context but even with regard to a small though crucial point of grammar. Again and again we must observe how the poet's words are made to suffer when they get in the way of a critical attitude, here the dualistic bias.

And so the interludes continue to occur. After the study scenes comes the double interlude of "Auerbach's Cellar" and the "Witch's Kitchen," one closing the previous action, the other opening the coming action, but also serving deeper dramatic purposes, the former a more profound one than would seem possible under a separatist, fragmentist reading, as we shall see in the next chapter. Having two scenes here tying a larger group of scenes, before and after, warns us that we cannot simply speak of a tripartite sequence, as we might be tempted to do from the first instances. We had better speak more generally of the principle of the interlude, and indeed as we go through the *Faust*, we shall see that this is one of the chief compositional means in the drama, bringing together not only scenes, but even the two parts of the work.

As far back as 1952 I pointed out that the "Walpurgis Night's Dream," actually called an "Intermezzo" by Goethe, can artistically be an interlude only between Part One and Part Two of the drama. The carrying over of themes, motifs, and actors from the framework of the scene to the first scene of Part Two would appear to confirm this observation. And when we find the motifs of the enclosed satiric review in the "Dream" reappear in Part Two, the political satire conspicuously in Acts One and Four, then the transitional function of the playlet seems obvious. However, objections to such an interpretation could well rest upon the fact that between this intermezzo and the beginning of Part Two there are the three scenes that conclude the Gretchen tragedy and Part One. This playlet would thus seem to be in the wrong place for an interlude. At the time I offered only as much of the internal evidence as seemed necessary since my interest was concentrated more on other important structural matters: just why artistic considerations called for elves on the Brocken at this point, and especially why artistic considerations forbade the carrying out of the "Walpurgis Night" to its conclusion in the satanic rites, even as they forbade the carrying out of a Persephone scene in Part Two.

Now, in the larger context, we can more readily perceive that Goethe's use of the principle of the interlude was always functional and not mechanical. Therefore it was at this point, and not later, that Goethe had to indicate that the end of the Gretchen tragedy was not the end of the drama, and it was properly here that the interlude would have to be placed. Further confirmatory evidence comes from the text itself—not the text as the modern editors present it to us, but the text as Goethe originally intended and presented it. Modern editorial practice in *Faust* confronts us with a sad paradox: although every slightest verbal shift of *e* and apostrophe, of *m* and *n* is solemnly weighed, there is a bland disregard of the scene headings and even the scene divisions, without any thought that these may have been of artistic significance to the author. The verbal intellectual bias has again obscured the artistic, the

visual, the spatial factors. In Part Two editorial interference has at several points resulted in a serious disturbance of the intended scenic
balance, and at one point it has even, as we shall see in Chapter Eleven,
imposed an embarrassing error of judgment and an anachorism on the
Goethean text.

Here, for Part One, it would be well for every critic to take in hand
the first complete edition of 1808 and carefully examine its typographical
disposition. As we have noted in the preceding chapter, there are separate title pages (so-called half-titles), with following blank pages, for
each of the three preliminary parts, the "Dedication," the "Prelude in the
Theater," and the "Prologue in Heaven." Then follows another half-title
for the "First Part of the Tragedy." Then come the separate scenes, each
of them, from the first Faust monologue onward, with only a title heading and stage directions in small type. Each new scene begins on a new
page, but there are no blank pages in order to have a new scene begin
on a right-hand page. This continues to be the case through the "Walpurgis Night," which has its title in the usual small type. But then, after
the end of this scene, there comes a blank left-hand page, then facing it
a special title page inscribed in large type:

Walpurgis Night's Dream

or

Oberon and Titania's Golden Wedding

———

Intermezzo

The verso of this is blank again, and then only, on a right-hand page,
does there follow the text of the interlude. The ensuing last three scenes
have simple title headings once more, in small type. Goethe's final edition of Part One in his collected works, despite its greater typographical
economy, does not save space at the expense of such a disposition but
carefully preserves the half-titles and blank versos of the first edition.
Among the dozens of editions now generally available only the Weimar
edition of 1887 and the more recent one of the Berlin Academy of 1958,
to my knowledge, pay due regard to Goethe's artistic will in this matter,
though without any noticeable effect on *Faust* criticism.

The merely intellectual critic may feel that he can disregard this
visual disposition and formal arrangement. However, the critic who is
interested in *Faust* as a work of art must face the facts and phenomena:
the first three preludial parts have separate title pages; the only other
scene of Part One that is brought into visual correlation with them is the
"Walpurgis Night's Dream." The answer can only be that this scene
likewise performs a preludial function. Goethe no doubt took delight in
the fact that it also parodistically suggested a theatrical placard; if it had

been intended merely to suggest that, the arrangement would have been a different one without such a close coordination to the first three scenes. The close internal relationship of the intermezzo to Part Two that we have observed can leave no doubt about its function as the connecting interlude to what is to come after the Gretchen tragedy.

For a larger group of scenes connected and divided by an interlude, let us look at this Gretchen tragedy as it is developed up to the "Walpurgis Night," that is, from the scene "Street" where Faust first sees Margarete through the scene "Cathedral" where she finally collapses in tragic misery. The middle scene is the serious interlude "Forest and Cavern." Its pivotal position has always been recognized, easily recognized, although its relation to the six scenes immediately before it and the six scenes immediately after it has never been examined. No one has even so much as counted them or noticed the fine balance that exists. Here we shall perceive something artistically remarkable: a tightening of the composition, the establishment of a beautiful symmetry that raises the final version far above the level of the *Urfaust*, though there, to be sure, it is already adumbrated. Let us look at this group of scenes.

In the first scene, "Street," Margarete comes from church, from confession, innocent and absolved from her small sins. In the last scene, "Cathedral," she is again in church, laden with guilt, with the dreadful "Dies Irae" resounding and the voice of the "Evil Spirit" driving her to despair and collapse.

In the second scene, "Evening. A Small Neat Room," we find her in the serenity and security of her own home and room, with this serenity and security for the first time invaded by Faust and Mephistopheles. In the second from last scene, "Night. Street before Gretchen's Door," we find her at home, all serenity and security shattered, with the last remaining relative, her brother, turned against her, and even he killed by a last invasion of Faust and Mephisto.

In the third scene, "Promenade," we have the comic episode, as narrated by Mephistopheles, of the official external church taking unto itself the jewels of Margarete, naturally for her own good. In the scene third from last, the "Keep," before the image of the Mater Dolorosa, we see her turning, in her tragic agony, to the true spiritual church as her last and best refuge.

In the fourth scene, "The Neighbor's House," we meet the fitting feminine instrument through which Mephistopheles can attain Faust's desire in the worst way, namely, Martha, an exemplar of the negative corruptive feminine. Another example of the negative corruptive feminine comes in the scene fourth from last, "At the Well," with Lieschen's gossip about Bärbelchen and a report of the vicious actions against her. Gretchen sadly reflects on her earlier consent to such conventional cruelty before she herself was stricken, even as she earlier had taken the

second gift of jewels to Martha, well knowing that from her she would
get desired rather than good advice.

In the fifth scene, another "Street," with dialogue between Faust
and Mephistopheles, Faust hears that all is arranged for him to meet
Margarete if he will only bear witness to Martha on the death of her
husband in Padua. He at first rejects this device as obliging him to bear
false witness, but then with the haste of impatience succumbs to
Mephisto's evil design (3072),

> Denn du hast recht, vorzüglich weil ich muß.
> *For you are right, especially since I must.*

In the scene "Martha's Garden," fifth from last, Margarete, deeply trou-
bled, especially by the presence of his sinister companion, probes Faust
on the state of his religion. Faust is evasive on specifics and veils himself
behind an eloquent statement on the universality of the worship of the
Divine. The witness he bears, although it is not false, is disingenuous. He
is also evasive about Mephisto, and all the time he has with him the
sleeping potion that he persuades Margarete to administer to her
mother, a potion that by Mephisto's evil design is something more
deadly.

The sixth scene, "Garden," (with the appended "Garden Pavilion")
leads to Margarete's first acknowledgment of love. The scene sixth from
last, "Gretchen's Room" ("Meine Ruh' ist hin," "My peace is gone"),
gives lyric expression to Gretchen's surrender to love.

The pivotal scene in the midst of this symmetrically spreading sequence, this rising and falling action, the "Forest and Cavern," also
makes the transition from the bright to the dark side, from Faust's
prayer of thanksgiving to the exalted spirit who has brought him to
harmony with nature and all its living creatures, an imperiled harmony,
as he adds with the thought of his malefic associate who fans his emotions to a consuming fire. Mephisto on his arrival finds it relatively easy
to plunge Faust back into his emotional turmoil, back on the course he
realizes helplessly will lead to destruction.

We stand in astonishment before this perfect pyramid of tragic
consecution, already partly envisaged in the *Urfaust*, though not brought
to measured calculated perfection until the final version that Goethe
intended for us. In the final version we not only have the interlude
placed in its pivotal position, we also have a crucial rearrangement of
the last two scenes in the falling action, a shift on which much critical
ink has been expended, without even a suggestion of the artistic as well
as dramatic reasons lying behind it. Can this be the work of the irregular
genius we are told about who in the rage of inspiration flung forth the
scenes of the *Urfaust* in splendid disorder and then later for the completed Part One left so many loose ends and discrepancies to distress the

superior critic? If this symmetrical sequence stood isolated within an otherwise haphazardly arranged drama, it would, to be sure, only confirm the convictions of the fragmentalists by being a foreign body distressing in its regularity amid a more natural and casual distribution of scenes. But the opposite is the case: in both Parts One and Two there appears, on closer and more careful examination, an articulation of scenes into groups, sometimes, as here, centering about a point, at other times in series of various kinds, never mechanical or routinely repetitive, never forcing a symmetry, always the work of a presiding genius for whom form is the direct outcome and expression of function.

In Part Two, for instance, the placement and function of the interludes in the first act are quite different from those in the second act. In the first the seven scenes alternate regularly between a serious or symbolically weighty scene and a lighter more comic scene. Once we observe that all the scenes are concerned with various aspects of the realm of forms and appearances, we can readily go on to observe that the interludial scenes (that is, the even-numbered ones, two, four, and six) are concerned with the false or deceptive forms: In scene two, the throne room, a false show of power and glory poorly cloaks the bankruptcy and chaos of misrule and nonrule. Scene four offers an illusory solution for the ills of the realm in the new solvency of the paper money, from which only the poor banneret and the fool derive lasting benefit, whereas the disintegration of the realm will only be speeded by the forces of inflation. Scene six, in the brightly lit halls, shows the false culture and self-indulgence of the courtly society that continues voicing its shallow opinions even amid the classic visions of the next scene.

The four odd-numbered scenes enclosing these explore the larger aspects of the realm of forms. The opening scene appropriately begins just before sunrise and continues as the shadowy and vague gradually assume more and more definite form and the protagonist contemplates the growing splendor of the mountain scenery, the sunrise, and the rainbow over the waterfall. The long third scene, the carnival, makes use of mask and masquerade as instruments that serve less to conceal than to reveal, so that the whole human pageant passes before us in allegoric and symbolic forms. The fifth scene is that of Faust's perilous voyage beyond place and time to the realm of the Mothers, the presiding goddesses in the ultimate realm of forms and transformations. In the seventh and last scene he returns from this realm with the power to bring back to vision the forms of Paris and Helen, so vividly indeed that he mistakes the forms for realities and impetuously brings the act to its catastrophic conclusion.

The second act, also with seven scenes (in the original disposition, before the inept tinkering of the modern editors), has an entirely different interrelation of scenes, an interrelation that easily comes to view

once we observe that the whole act is concerned with varied aspects of
the realm of origins. Indicating this in the very beginning is the fact that
Mephistopheles in his perplexity brings the unconscious Faust back to
origins, in his and his father's old study, this unchanged since the beginning of the drama except for the dust and disintegration of time. However, the action of this first scene is a comic contrastive one in the
reappearance of the naive freshman of Part One as the superb sophisticated Bachelor of Arts. Mephisto's earlier advice to choose a medical
career (for all the wrong reasons) has been defeated by the superior
temptations of the transcendental subjective philosophy. The Bachelor
declares himself autonomous, free of all origins outside himself, with
even the world around him nonexistent until he willed to create it within
his sovereign mind. Here is the self-created "Original" about whom
Goethe wrote in one of his humorous verse epigrams:

> Ein Quidam sagt: "Ich bin von keiner Schule;
> Kein Meister lebt, mit dem ich buhle;
> Auch bin ich weit davon entfernt,
> Daß ich von Toten was gelernt."
> Das heißt, wenn ich ihn recht verstand:
> "Ich bin ein Narr auf eigne Hand."

> *A someone says: "I am from no man's school,*
> *And I concede no living master's rule.*
> *Likewise I'm far from being led*
> *By any influence from the dead."*
> *This means, if I correctly understand it:*
> *"I am a fool and that first-handed."*

After this comic scene of the denial of all origins outside one's own
autonomous self, of all time before one's own, there follow the scenes
that take up the various kinds of origin. The next takes up the artificial
origin of a manikin, a Homunculus, in the alchemical laboratory of
Wagner, Faust's former research assistant and present successor. However, the first intimation of Homunculus' discontent with his artificial
existence comes with his reading of the dream of the unconscious Faust,
concerned as it is with the organic origin of Helen in the meeting of
Leda and the swan. Amid ridicule of Mephisto's helplessness, Homunculus arranges for Faust's transfer to classic soil, and it is here, moving
forth from the Pharsalian Fields, that the five scenes of the "Classical
Walpurgis Night" transpire. In the original Goethean disposition, before
the disruptive intrusions of the modern editors, these five scenes are
arranged symmetrically, with two scenes of natural origin and genesis
coming before, and two coming after a comic scene of monstrous and
grotesque origins and transformations. It all proceeds amid much humor
and whimsy in all the range from simplest punning to subtlest allusion,

as Faust, Mephisto, and Homunculus in turn arrive at their diverse destinations, the middle figure only after a series of further humiliations.

We first enter the Greek world of the time of its primordial origins amid the wondrous forms of griffins, sphinxes, and other creatures. In the second scene one of the last of these composite creatures to survive, namely, the centaur Chiron, leads over into the age of the heroes and thus into the age of Helen. Here at the headwaters of the Peneios (not at its lower reaches) Faust sees the reenactment of the genesis of Helen that had earlier been the subject of his dream, after which Chiron, the tutor of the heroes, takes Faust swiftly from the upper to the lower Peneios, to Manto, who will guide him onward to the attainment of his supreme desire. The next scene, back at the upper Peneios, stands in comic contrast to the two before and the two after, as successive monstrous and grotesque origins and transformations take place. In a fivefold action (after the Sirens foretell the transition to the coming scenes at the seashore) we observe Seismos raising a sudden mountain up out of the plain, second a group of primordial little folk busily populating the mountain until they are destroyed by the next sensational event, third Mephisto, further upset and totally dislocated, seeking consolation and finding only further humiliation in his flirtation with the wierdly changeful Lamias, fourth Homunculus expressing his desire to leave his glass vial and enter into real organic life (7831):

Und möchte gern im besten Sinn entstehn,

*I'd like in the best sense to come to be,*

but finding this a poor place for it, and seeking the advice of the two disputing philosophers, and fifth Mephisto, that "queer son of chaos" finally achieving his union with this strange old world at the edge of chaos where he finds the daughters of Phorkyas and becomes one like them. The scenes along the seashore are two (not one) in number, the first concerned with metamorphosis and evolution as introduced by Nereus and his daughters and exemplified by the Cabiri and particularly by Proteus. The final scene, culminating in the great sea pageant of the triumphal procession of Galatea, celebrates the origin of organic life in the littoral sea, under the inspiration of an all-encompassing Eros and ends with a paean of praise to the life-giving union of the four elements.

The third act, concerned with human continuities in tradition and the arts, has a simple though mist-enshrouded transition from the classic Hellenic to the romantic Germanic, and then to a fusion of the two in the idyllic Arcadian, with the middle member, in its brave show and playful pageantry, forming the festive interlude between the more serious beginning and ending, overshadowed as they are by threat and tragedy.

The fourth act is more complex again, with the first scene constituting the transition from Faust's traversal of the three thousand years of his (and our) civilization, in its traditions and artistic manifestations, to his first vision of a new world of active fashioning and creating under the oldest symbol of creativity, of turning chaos into cosmos: in the separation of the land from the waters. Both the dissolution of the divine feminine form of antiquity and the reintegration of the form of his first love also help to indicate that this is one of the great pivotal scenes of the drama. Before Faust's new creative activity can develop in the next act, he is witness to a former grand integration being destroyed, a political cosmos disintegrating into chaos, with the Emperor after his victory prodigally squandering all the power and treasure he would need for any reintegration. The action in Act Four also literally descends from the perspective of the high mountains, to the foothills of the battle with its confusions and illusions, down to the tent of the rival emperor, with the looters succeeded by the squanderers who fail to see the irony of their celebration of power and glory. However, the passing mention of the seashore granted to Faust, unencumbered by the dead hand of the past, does take up the motif of the first scene of the act, suggests the transition back again from chaos to cosmos, and leads over to the main movement and vision of the last act.

Act Five begins with the brief idyll of the primordial, of the indigenous inhabitants of a once lonely land impinged upon by the new order of a prosperous and teeming civilization. From idyllic hut, tiny garden and chapel we make the transition to the palace, ornamental garden, and canal, with the discontents and frustrations of his present being imputed by Faust (in tragic psychic error) to an outer lack, the small property that is not his own, rather than to an inner lack that he cannot honestly face until tragedy has ensued. The next, brief scene, significantly entitled "Deep Night," is the pivotal scene, a grave one, in conformity with the continuity of the action. It has not been noticed that its structure stands in remarkable parallel to that other grave pivotal scene in Part One, the "Forest and Cavern." Here as there, the scene begins with a hymn of thanksgiving to the beauties of nature and the blessedness of life on earth in the midst of its beauties. Here as there, such serenity is brief and transitory, in each case interrupted by Mephisto and his evil machinations, previously leading to disaster, here consummating the disaster in the conflagration and death on the dune. The next scene shows Faust courageously drawing the conclusions and coming to the insights that he had earlier blindly refused to face. The new inner light more than compensates for the new outer blindness, and he proceeds in the next scene, his last on earth, to develop his vision of a free people on a free soil, remaining united in their struggle against the elements and thus also freed from the degenerative curse of ease and security.

The great comic satyr drama comes in the next scene, the "Burial," where Mephisto decides his own fate. This we have already examined at the close of the first chapter. Then comes the last scene of all, another wandering scene, rising upward from the mountain defiles to ever clearer and brighter regions unto the final vision of the Divine Mother in Glory and the concluding Chorus Mysticus.

This is the last scene, a postlude in heaven parallel to the "Prologue in Heaven," but it leaves us with the problem of the absence of the other two postludial scenes that Goethe at a much earlier stage had planned to add in symmetrical counterbalance to the other two preludial scenes at the beginning of the drama. Although Goethe had actually begun to write these, his final decision was to omit them, for the entirely cogent artistic reasons that we shall more appropriately examine near the end of Chapter Eight.

# 6

# The Context of Patterns and Motifs

𝔄 S WE HAVE SEEN, the interludial type of structure, in all its different forms and functions, runs through the whole drama. So does a variety of further structural devices that we shall examine in this and the two following chapters. In this chapter we shall be concerned with various repeat patterns and leitmotifs, most of them small in size, some of them of greater significance than would appear likely from their size or from the poet's seemingly casual use of them. The next chapter will take up a remarkable higher development of the repeat patterns in one of the characteristic technical devices of the drama, hitherto observed only in isolated instances and without any larger awareness of their general nature and recollective function. In Chapter Eight we observe a still higher level of formal integration when we examine the structure of the initial Faust monodrama and find that, to a remarkable degree, it anticipates the larger general structure of the whole drama, even as it is in concord with the closing Faust monodrama. Let us first look at the context of patterns and motifs that, small though they be, do call the listener's attention to continuities and nodal points that he must not fail to observe if he is to understand the main sequence and import.

The recurrent patterns woven into the texture of *Faust* are of a richness, intricacy, and interdependence that call for a contextual approach to the work and make an isolated interpretation of its parts a dubious undertaking. There is many a speech, scene, or sequence in the drama that, taken by itself, is ambiguous, that can be and has been interpreted equally well in a number of different and conflicting ways. As long as the isolated piecemeal interpretation of the work continues to prevail (and it still does), almost any idea, attitude, ideological position and conviction can be read into or out of one or the other part of

*Faust*—and has been, in bewildering multiplicity, to the point where a general impression prevails that this is indeed a heterogeneous and disparate work.

However, the moment we examine any one of the ambiguous scenes or episodes in its larger context of recurring motifs or patterns, before and after, the number of possible ways of interpreting it decreases remarkably, to the point where we are usually left with only one interpretation that will satisfy the conditions of the total complex. These considerations, then, establish the need for ascertaining the primary motifs and patterns that run through the whole of *Faust*, come up at crucial points in it, and in their repetition with variation prove mutually enlightening.

Among these patterns there are several of genuine importance, and it is not a little disconcerting to discover that even some of these have been overlooked in the process of the piecemeal interpretation that has prevailed in the past. The closely knit unity between Parts One and Two seems ever more impressive the more carefully we study the continuity of patterns and motifs through the whole drama. Other patterns and motifs, though significant and pervasive, are not of the same degree of decisiveness and seriousness. They may establish lesser connections and continuities contributing to the coherence and interrelation of the whole. Or they may serve a less serious purpose than mutual enlightenment and regulative connotation, being there, like some recurrent flourish in music, simply to delight and to keep the listener pleasantly aware that all is continuing according to plan. The number of little motifs that keep bubbling up throughout the drama, often with a charmingly witty or comic effect, can be a delight to the perceptive reader—legitimately so, for Goethe had great joy (as well as agony) in writing the drama, as familiar letters to friends indicate again and again, and he certainly hoped that this joy would pass on to his readers. The reader to whom this pleasure is most likely to come is the one Goethe described in his aphorism: "the most ingenuous, forgetting me, himself, and the world, living alone in the book." And such a reader is best served by the undogmatic critic and interpreter who is able to make him aware of the varied patterns and designs and stimulate him to find others on his own. Such a critic is delighted when a reader does find further continuities that he himself has not mentioned and may even have overlooked. Certainly he is in a more relaxed as well as valid position than is the theoretical dogmatic critic who first has to impose his will on the work and then, joyless and anxious, has to impose his will on his disciples to prevent all deviation.

One of the most important motifs to run through the whole of the drama is that of creativity, both in its masculine and in its feminine aspects. The creatively masculine is the vital center of the Faust theme;

it would long since have been recognized as such if it had not been obscured by extraneous moralistic or idealistic considerations arbitrarily forced upon the work. With the factor of creativity so prominent in the three preludial parts, as we have seen, its varied occurrence in the first Faust monologue is only to be expected. There is the "Wirkenskraft und Samen," "the effective power and seed" (384), that the protagonist is seeking to behold. In the sign of the macrocosm he sees revealed "die Kräfte der Natur," "die wirkende Natur," "the powers of nature," "effective nature" (438, 441). Thereupon the Earth Spirit describes his creative role in fashioning the "living garment of God" (509). After Faust is rejected by him and interrupted by Wagner, he wavers between despairful negation of his creative role (620) and delusive prospects of transcending to its attainment (705) until his psychic balance is restored by the Easter Choruses, in the midst of which he recalls his youthful intimations of creativity: "Fühlt' ich mir eine Welt entstehn," "I felt a world unfold within me" (778).

Thus we could go on examining in detail the many and varied recurrences of the theme, obvious or more subtly allusive. For present purposes, however, it would be more profitable to turn instead to Faust's first close examination of this matter. It occurs when Faust has returned to his study after his Easter afternoon "Outside the City Gate." To keep up the mood of exaltation he has brought back from his walk, he seeks revelation by beginning a translation of the New Testament. Significantly, he does not begin at the beginning with the Gospel according to Matthew but with the fourth Gospel, that according to John. And if we ask why he does so, the answer need not be long in coming. This Gospel begins with a clear and obvious symbolic extension to the very beginning of the whole Bible, in Genesis: "In the beginning God created the heaven and the earth," and with potent allusion in the third verse of John to the third verse in Genesis that God's word then uttered led to manifest creation: "And God said, 'Let there be light'; and there was light"—and so on through the rest of the creative words that became creative acts. Faust translates only the first verse in John: "In the beginning was the Word," but he translates it in full awareness of the larger context, specifically the statement about the divine creative *Logos* in the third verse: "All things were made by him; and without him was not any thing made that was made." Thus Faust deduces that the *logos* cannot be a mere *word*, it must have *meaning*, significance; beyond that it must have the potentiality, the *power*, to lead over to the divine *act* of creation. In sum, Faust's course of translation, far from being heretical or subjectively voluntaristic, was entirely orthodox and reverently seeking understanding of the nature of divine creativity, so that it could, however humbly and imperfectly, be followed by man in his own quest for highest human validity in a creative life on earth—this latter consequence variously alluded to during the course of the drama and coming to full clarity in Faust's last undertaking.

As far back as 1951, and with further perspectives in my second *Euphorion* article of 1954, I was able to indicate the intrinsic intent and complete orthodoxy of Faust's development of the *logos* concept (*Wort, Sinn, Kraft, Tat*; "word," "meaning," "power," "act"), and, beyond that, its full agreement with the evolution of the concept of the *logos* as we find it in the Early and Middle Stoa. Beyond that I was able to show that young Goethe had as early as 1775 employed this same sequence, had even done so in connection with the specific Stoic terminology of the "seed power," the *logos spermatikos*, in order to describe the human act of artistic creation in microcosmic analogy to God's macrocosmic creation. What Faust was concerned with here was not a subjective willful justification of his own uncontrolled impulses but simply an analysis of the course of the creative process. For the scene itself as well as for the drama as a whole this makes better sense than does the conventional critical consensus on this passage, and our enlarged understanding quite obviously affects our interpretation of Faust's character and Goethe's poetic intent. I was of course delighted that in 1970 another Goethe scholar came to a similar conclusion, albeit as a new revelation, from a more exalted philosophical eminence, though with less adequate background knowledge. Possibly this is the beginning of a new critical consensus.

The theme of creativity is so pervasive in the work, so much a part of the whole drama that it was bound to come up in various connections in earlier chapters of this study and will continue to recur in subsequent ones. For present purposes only two further matters need to be mentioned. First of all, there is the opposing motif as exemplified by Mephistopheles. He is the anticreative negativist, so well characterized by the Lord in the "Prologue" (338–343) and so frankly by himself (1338–41):

> Ich bin der Geist, der stets verneint!
> Und das mit Recht; denn alles, was entsteht,
> Ist wert, daß es zugrunde geht;
> Drum besser wär's, daß nichts entstünde.

> *I am the spirit that e'er denies,*
> *And justly so, for all that is created*
> *Is fit to be annihilated.*
> *'Twere better then that nothing came to be.*

His preceding and following words add all the necessary background and details on his anticreative role.

We have already touched upon the second matter and need only to carry it a bit further at this point. Man's microcosmic role is most fully realized when he rises to creativity and, with all his human limitations, endeavors to turn at least one small corner of chaos into cosmos. Thus the theory of artistic creativity, when it comes to be formulated, revolves around the precept that the artist, the poet, must be like God, creating a universe within himself, within the work. James Joyce subscribed to that, quite explicitly, and he was not the last to do so. For the final creative act of Faust Goethe used the oldest symbol of creativity, of cosmos arising out of chaos, namely, the separation of the land from the waters, first formulated by the divine act of Genesis, confirmed in poetic tradition, notably by Milton, and developed by Faust to his ultimate vision of gaining a new land for a new start of a free people on a free soil.

Counterbalancing the motif of the creatively masculine is the motif of the creatively feminine. As far back as 1953 I published a first study of this motif, later developing it in connection with its central symbolic manifestation in *The Mothers in Faust; The Myth of Time and Creativity* (1969). This motif runs from the first monologue of Faust through the whole of the drama to the final words of the Chorus Mysticus on the "Eternal Womanly." It is the ultimate deep symbol of motherhood raised to the universal and cosmic, the creative continuity of life, birth and rebirth in constantly renewed forms, the ultimate resolution of death, destruction, and tragedy in new cycles of life, constructive activity, and fulfillment. It is the abundantly fruitful, eternally replenished matrix of the fullness and recurrence of life, out of which the purposeful and constructive, conscious and active personality could arise and, with his task accomplished, return again to be reborn once more on a higher level. The persisting sentimental-idealistic (and woefully shallow) misinterpretation of the last statement in *Faust* could come about only through the intrusion of extraneous attitudes and the disregard of the continuity of the motif. When, as here, a profound ultimate statement is reduced to a sentimental banality, we have a classic example of the fact that the interpretation of any text in the drama can reasonably hope to be valid only if it takes into consideration the total relevant context.

On a less encompassing though still important level is the recurring motif of *Erdensohn*, "son of earth." The failure to observe this motif, both in its development and in its full contextuality, has led to a misinterpretation of the last scene in which it explicitly occurs, the scene of Faust's son, Euphorion, who is warned by his parents that he is a son of earth and warned against denying earth and seeking to leave it. Strange how the plain speaking of the drama at this point has been disregarded by the majority of the interpreters who intrude their contrary transcendental convictions to the point of perverting the poet's clearly stated intent. In Chapter Two, where we observed the way the sentimentalists have succeeded in damaging the form of the *Faust*, this particular aspect has been examined in more detail.

There is another sequence, however, another repeat pattern that is even more instructive in showing the contrast between the poet's intent and the critics' comprehension. It is the recurrent motif of *macrocosm* and *microcosm*, sometimes clearly expressed, sometimes obscurely or indirectly, sometimes with the twist and perversion that Mephistopheles in his special animosity can give to the terms, using all the resources of his wit and sarcasm to debase them or make them appear ludicrous. Where the modern critic fails is in not realizing that the term *microcosm*, small world, usually had a single specific meaning on through the age of Goethe and that the vaguer usage of "small world," any kind of small world, is generally of later origin when the traditional symbolic complex was forgotten or disregarded.

For the *Faust*, as for the centuries before it, the one central meaning of the word *microcosm* is *man*. The concept of the microcosm is built on the old postulate that man's increasing understanding of the macrocosm, the universe and its phenomena, implies a development of man's inner self toward a harmonious correspondence to the whole of nature. Only man, of all creatures, has this microcosmic potentiality; out of this, his unique position, flows the concept of the dignity of man. The implications are already in the Old Testament, and Faust reechoes them almost literally in his "I, image of the Godhead," and "I, more than cherub" (614 and 618), though the full development of the concept, with its implied theory of knowledge and the corollary theory of creativity, begins with the Middle Stoa and culminates in the Renaissance, most conspicuously in Pico della Mirandola. However, we do not actually need this outside information; Faust's words on viewing the sign of the macrocosm (430–53) suffice to introduce us to this creative view of harmonious correspondence. The whole concept irritates and outrages Mephistopheles, particularly because the creativity of man is so clearly implicit in it, and from the "Prologue" onward he continues his perversion and mockery of it (281 ff.): "the little god of the world" with his "gleam of celestial light" that he calls "reason." And again (1347): "Man, that little booby world," or more at length in mockery of Faust's aspirations to encompass all human experience (1789–92, 1801–02):

> Assoziiert Euch mit einem Poeten,
> Laßt den Herrn in Gedanken schweifen,
> Und alle edlen Qualitäten
> Auf Euren Ehrenscheitel häufen.
> . . . . . . . . . . . . .
> Möchte selbst solch einen Herren kennen,
> Würd' ihn Herrn Mikrokosmus nennen.
>
> *Take to yourself one of the poet guild,*
> *And let this gentleman's thoughts, far-sweeping,*
> *With all the noblest traits be filled,*

*These then upon your honored head a-heaping.*
. . . . . . . . . . . . . . . . . . . .
*I'd like to meet that man of fame,*
*Sir Microcosm would be his name.*

These are the more obvious of his references to man as a microcosm, although, repeatedly through the rest of the drama, his more or less veiled scorn of man's higher pretensions conveys his hostility. However, his real perversion of the term, a perversion anticipating modern usage (and thus escaping modern attention) comes near the end of the last study scene, after the new student has left and Faust returns ready for departure. To Faust's question, "Where do we go to now?" Mephistopheles answers (2051–54):

> Wohin es dir gefällt.
> Wir sehn die kleine, dann die große Welt.
> Mit welcher Freude, welchem Nutzen
> Wirst du den Cursum durchschmarutzen!

> *That's up to you.*
> *We'll see the small, and then the great world too.*
> *What joy, what profit yours perforce,*
> *As we munch onward through this course.*

By isolating the first two lines from their context it has been possible to arrive at a critical consensus, unquestioned to this day, that Mephistopheles is here outlining the future course of the drama: from the "small world" of the Gretchen tragedy to the "great world" of the imperial court and of Faust's realm. But whose faith in this consensus can remain unshaken in the context of the decidedly scurrilous "durchschmarutzen"? No, the old rascal is not serving as a convenient mouthpiece for the poet to announce the program of the play, he is serving his own ends, announcing a program indeed, but a more specific and immediate one, for the next two scenes, as we shall see.

Our misgivings are more than confirmed by his other conspicuous use of these terms in their German form. Here again in the commentaries and interpretations two lines are cited in isolation, the larger connotations and implications are not recognized, and the point is missed. Again there is the prime fallacy and its associated fallacies that Mephisto is serving as a mouthpiece to convey Goethe's philosophical reflections or dramatic intentions, that he is playing no tricks, and that the passage can be interpreted outside its relevant context and environment. Then profound meanings are extracted from this isolated couplet, for one on the various "worlds" in Faust, for another on its revelation of the meaning of the following scene. In isolation this could pass; in context, however, faith in such an interpretation would require an innocence more becoming to a Gretchen than to a critic. For, embarrassingly enough, what we actually have at this point is one of Mephisto's obscene jests, not one of his wittiest, but quite appropriate here in connection with the very next two lines (4046–47) which in their turn are a prelude to the most obscene episode in the whole of *Faust* (4124–43). Let us first examine the passage in its immediate context. It comes at that point in the "Walpurgis Night" where Mephistopheles diverts Faust from the mainstream of devotees, who are surging up to the great scene of satanic worship, over to some interesting "side shows" along the way, with Faust objecting because he wants to press onward in order to explore the mystery of iniquity (4030–47):

FAUST
> Du Geist des Widerspruchs! Nur zu! du magst mich führen.
> Ich denke doch, das war recht klug gemacht:
> Zum Brocken wandeln wir in der Walpurgisnacht,
> Um uns beliebig nun hieselbst zu isolieren.

MEPHISTOPHELES
> Da sieh nur welche bunten Flammen!
> Es ist ein muntrer Klub beisammen.
> Im Kleinen ist man nicht allein.

FAUST
> Doch droben möcht' ich lieber sein!
> Schon seh' ich Glut und Wirbelrauch.
> Dort strömt die Menge zu dem Bösen;
> Da muß sich manches Rätsel lösen.

MEPHISTOPHELES
> Doch manches Rätsel knüpft sich auch.
> Laß du die große Welt nur sausen,
> Wir wollen hier im Stillen hausen.
> Es ist doch lange hergebracht,
> Daß in der großen Welt man kleine Welten macht.
> Da seh' ich junge Hexchen nackt und bloß,
> Und alte, die sich klug verhüllen.

The translation of the key words must be an accurate and not an approximate one:

FAUST
> *Spirit of contradiction, go! I'll follow straight.*
> *Forsooth, I say, your plan is very bright!*
> *We travel to the Brocken on Walpurgis Night*
> *Only to choose this place, ourselves to isolate.*

MEPHISTOPHELES
> *Just see those flames, their motley glare.*
> *A merry club's assembled there.*
> *In a small group one's not alone.*

FAUST

> *I'd rather be up there, I own.*
> *Already glow and eddying smoke I view.*
> *On toward Evil the surging crowd has traveled;*
> *There many a riddle surely'll be unraveled.*

MEPHISTOPHELES

> *And many a riddle will be knotted too.*
> *Just let the great world rock and riot,*
> *We'll live it up here where it's quiet.*
> *It is a custom long relayed*
> *That in the great world little worlds are made.*
> *I see young witches there stark naked all,*
> *And old ones wise enough to cover up.*

When Mephisto dampens the ardor of Faust's quest after the mystery of iniquity, where many a riddle must be solved, with the wry remark that many a riddle will also be knotted, his chief intent is not the innocently pedagogical one of making sure that Faust sees the metaphysical point. His chief intent is diversionary: it would go gravely counter to his purpose and interest if Faust were to turn the Walpurgis expedition into a quest to fathom this mystery, and so he does the best he can to discourage him from such a course. His purpose and interest were exactly what he had outlined in an earlier monologue, to lead Faust through "flache Unbedeutenheit" (1861); and these separate tableaus on the Blocksberg are just such "shallow inconsequentialities." How badly he miscalculated, here and in the last study scene, needs to be seen more clearly.

As for Mephisto's quip that it has long been customary in the large world to make small worlds, it should be clear that the tone of voice, the context, and the speaker quite preclude any such pseudo profundities as at least a few of the critics have tried to read into it. I have no wish to indulge in personal censure, so I shall merely quote from one unnamed English critic, adding only that I could just as well have quoted from a German critic:

> Through exploration of the expansion and development of this one cell, the word *world*, we gain intimate knowledge of the movement and growth of the whole vast organism—so that when we light again on Mephisto's words,
>> It's something that has long been done
>> To fashion little worlds within the bigger one.
> it strikes us with new resonance and is pregnant with our experience of all the "worlds" we have encountered whether in the poetry or the dramatic action.

The usual, more sober explanation of the lines, that in the large world of society and affairs the continuing formation of cliques is an old tradition, would be satisfactory enough if the next two lines were not there. Their presence, however, and, even more, the larger contexts and perspectives compel us to note that: (1) Mephisto everywhere else uses the term and concept of microcosm maliciously; (2) frequently, almost at every good opportunity, he likes to twist a remark or a situation into an obscenity; and (3) in the jesting talk of Goethe's day and since "Kinder machen" was a common euphemism for the sexual act, often with implications of illegitimacy. Such considerations would at least make it likely that what Mephisto is implying here is that the typical goings-on of the world of high society have through the ages resulted in the production of micro-cosmic little bastards.

Be that as it may, the degradation of the microcosmic terminology is obvious in each case when even the slightly larger context is considered. But what is Mephisto's purpose and program in this verbal perversion at the end of the last study scene? Here again a relatively clear and simple observation will help, if added to the sensible precept of interpreting each text within its larger context. In an earlier study, a structural analy-sis of Goethe's lyric "An den Mond," I noted as a feature of the poet's formal mastery that at the end of one stanza or group of stanzas he announced the theme of the next following, though sometimes in the most casual and unobtrusive manner. I went on to observe that Goethe employed this same principle in the main divisions of his longer com-positions, citing the instance of *Wilhelm Meister's Apprenticeship*. In later studies I gave specific examples of this technique of his from the *Apprenticeship* and the *Faust*. Here in our present instance we are deal-ing with this same formal technique: Mephisto by his perversion of the terms announces the perversion of the concept of microcosm that we are to witness in the next two scenes, the "Auerbach's Cellar in Leipzig" and the "Witch's Kitchen."

His perversion of the concept of the dignity of man, man as a microcosm, is developed in its full destructive negativism in these two scenes where he is master of ceremonies. The potentiality of man, indi-cated in the "Prologue" and in the whole implicit view of man rising upward toward divinity ("higher than the angels"), has its necessary complement in the potentiality of man to sink lower than the animals. Such are the implications of man's freedom, man's freedom of choice. Just as the dignity of man is a potential state, so the indignity of man is equally potential, equally possible.

In "Auerbach's Cellar" we meet a group of four boon companions who have exercised this freedom of choice. Their God-given intellects and their education to reason they have chosen to befuddle in drink. Through all their self-stultification they retain the illusion that they are still in brilliant possession of their wits; the "witticisms" they exchange seem to them the acme of scintillating social intercourse, and their "humorous" social song about the passionate poisoned rat indicates that they have reached their proper level, a level on which the newly entered Lord of the Flies joins them in his "Song of the Flea," a favorite basso aria to our day.

In this ominously unfunny scene the funniest thing is the sentimental nostalgia with which some commentators regard it, the way they explicate the Rippach "witticism" and quote with innocent approval drunken Frosch's eulogy of Leipzig as a little Paris. Here again, Goethe's alteration of the scene to the point of making Faust a nonparticipant was in the service of his larger purpose.

The "Witch's Kitchen" is Goethe's virtuoso piece of surrealism, Brueghelesque in its cast and setting, almost unprecedented in its conceptual calisthenics, its verbal virtuosities, where sense glides over into nonsense and fluctuates indeterminately between the two, with free association and every other kind of nonsensical continuity substituting for coherent sequence. This goes on, depth beyond depth, to the culminating nonsense of the witch's "one-times-one," in which the crowning irony is that the occultists have tried to explicate it by magic square or cabalistic calculation, without any contribution to our understanding, whereas there is a simple arithmetical solution of no profundity at all that does add to our understanding, is integral to the proceedings, and is indeed the cream of the jest. More on this later.

However, it is the monkeys in this scene that are the ultimate symbolic repositories of the triumph of un-reason and non-sense. They can verbalize, quite free of any brain control, with rhyme taking the place of reason, and free association that of responsible con-sequence. In places sense seems to emerge, but it is topsy-turvy sense, as in the male monkey's formula for getting rich, with its displacement of cause and effect, or as in the play with the globe where rhyme and set phrase determine the "order," though in the crown sequence the rhyme does accidentally lead to the sensible statement that rhyme can sometimes accidentally lead to sense (2458–60):

> Und wenn es uns glückt,
> Und wenn es sich schickt,
> So sind es Gedanken!

> *If good luck attend*
> *And things fit and blend,*
> *Then thoughts will emerge.*

If Mephisto had been right in his monologue in counting on Faust to abandon reason and knowledge, he might have been able to draw him into this chaos of unreason and word wandering. Being a "son of chaos," Mephisto is in his element. But Faust, being a "servant" of the Lord, remains in full control of his reason and of his critical detachment from unreason, as his first words clearly indicate and later words repeatedly confirm. But even more than that, he goes on to exercise his microcosmic potentiality in creatively making cosmos emerge out of chaos. In the midst of this subhuman, scurrilous parody of human activity and speech he has the image of womankind perfected emerge from the magic mirror.

Earlier, in Chapter One, we observed in a number of instances how dangerous it is to trust Mephisto's interpretation of any feature or happening in the drama, but also how often just that has been done, and how generally this lapse in judgment has been the source of misinterpretations, past and present. So here. Even a moderately careful examination of Faust's description of his creative projection of the vision in the magic mirror, but especially an awareness of the imagery in relation to the imagery of those other passages throughout the drama where the principle of the feminine, the womanly creative, comes to the fore, makes it clear that we must take this vision on Faust's terms and not on those of Mephisto as expressed immediately thereafter and then at the conclusion of the scene. Furthermore, there is the factor of poetic expression and language level, toward which the critic can be insensitive only at his own peril. Here, as in the case of the "great world" and "little world," Mephisto's tone is decidedly scurrilous and in striking contrast to his tone when he is under obligation to tell the truth.

Son of earth, microcosm, the creatively masculine, the creatively feminine, these variously interrelated and constantly recurring signs and figures would suffice as exemplification of the continuity and interweaving of the primary themes and motifs in the drama. They will serve, furthermore, to make it abundantly clear that we cannot hope to see the full import of these themes and motifs, together with their accompanying symbolic network, unless we see them in the context of the whole drama, beginning with and including the "Dedication." The motifs of the mystery of place and time here announced rise to a point of highest importance in the second and third acts of Part Two. The bewilderment of the critics at the complex time factor in these two acts would be readily alleviated if these acts were studied not separately as hitherto but in the context of the whole drama. This is to be our task in Chapter Ten.

However, aside from the main motifs that bind the drama together in their larger coherences and make clear the separate parts by the process of mutual reflection, of contextuality, there is also a variety, a multiplicity of smaller continuities that help clarify the lesser texts and contexts and help keep the abundant fullness of life in this drama in proper perspective and clear articulation. It would be the task of a separate study of some size to tabulate and trace them in their full scope and variety. Here a few characteristic examples of the different kinds of continuities will suffice to show how the poet uses this formal principle variously in his drama, sometimes in a not-at-all serious manner.

Among the nonserious repeat patterns those surrounding Mephistopheles are perhaps the most amusing, though they do at the same time aid in defining this character's true status and limitations. If these patterns had been observed more clearly in the past, many of the misconceptions about his role and scope could have been avoided. The largest such pattern connects his first scene with Faust to his last scene in the drama. The first, to be sure, does not have the broader and deeper implications that we found in the last scene when we examined it more closely at the conclusion of Chapter One. If it did, it could be included among the echo structures to be examined in Chapter Seven. Even so, through reflection back from the last scene, the intent of the first more readily becomes clear, and we understand better why the poet felt it necessary to devote two study scenes to the Faust-Mephisto preliminaries rather than one, as would normally be expected. In the first scene Mephisto makes small progress because he has blundered in the time and manner of his entrance and has to devote his main attention to recovering from his predicament.

Indeed, what connects the first scene to the last is the fact that in both Mephistopheles is in deep trouble and has to neglect his designs against Faust in order to save himself. In the last scene, as we have observed, he came dangerously near to being saved by the grace of God when the fiery roses of heavenly love penetrated deep into him and he barely managed to fend off salvation by a master stroke of his perverted genius when he converted this consuming love into a hopeless pederastic passion for the boyish angels. In the process of doing so he quite neglected to watch for Faust's soul emerging from his body, and the angels take it upward while he is still triumphing in his own "salvation" from salvation. In the first scene no such ultimate issues are at stake, but there is an annoying dilemma for Mephisto because in his poodle guise he has not only failed to foresee Faust's mood of exaltation that turned him to translating the beginning of the Gospel of John and fathoming the mystery of creativity. What was more serious for himself, he had as a poodle heedlessly leaped over the threshold and the carelessly drawn open outer point of the pentagram. That made him a prisoner in Faust's study, forced him to postpone his plans over against Faust, and to concentrate his ingenuity on freeing himself, as he successfully did, though only with the help of spirit chorus and rat's tooth. Such a first scene is naturally intended to alert us to the old rascal's limitations and lapses in judgment, as they become so glaringly manifest in the next study scene.

Further indications of his limitations can be found in the fact that he is mocked and humiliated successively by the aerial spirits, by Homunculus, by the sphinxes, and especially by the Lamias, and can only enter the classical world in the most ungainly fashion by assuming the grotesque guise of the weird Phorkyadic sisters at the edge of chaos. He had to enter the classical world in order to continue to serve Faust and carry out his orders. Here again he tries to cover up his ignominy by pretending in the Helena scenes to be not merely the stagehand but the *magister ludi*. He is so very clever about it that he could hoodwink most anyone who is not alert to every detail of text, context, and the psychological dynamics of the unfolding action.

Less important, though likewise indicative, is the way the poet brings Mephisto down to the level of Wagner by having him paraphrase a smug remark of the pedant (601 and 1582) and repeat the old Hippocratic chestnut (558–9 and 1787) about art being long and life short. There are also the further clichés into which this mentally limited old rascal lapses from time to time. His lack of firm personal definition is indicated by his hermaphroditic manifestations in the carnival scene, the "Classical Walpurgis Night," and the Helena act.

In the drama as a whole another large area of repeat patterns is concerned with various aspects of the interplay of reality and illusion, with some delightful mockery aimed at the super-acute intellect of the Bachelor of Arts (and an occasional critic) who reveres an illusion as the only reality. Within this complex perhaps the most persistent repeat pattern in both parts of the drama is that of buried treasure and (usually) Mephisto's relation to it. Beginning with the two sets of jewels left for Gretchen and her succumbing to their lure, this motif becomes even more fateful when Faust is so abstracted by his vision of buried treasure (3664–75) and his desire to take another present to his beloved that he is quite unprepared for the rapid succession of events that lead to his killing Valentin in a duel (a symbolic extension from the Iago-Cassio episode, of course). The subterranean vaults and veins of Mammon's palace are appropriately illuminated for the Walpurgis Night (3914–34).

But the motif attains its full dimensions in Part Two when Mephistopheles suggests to the Emperor (4890 ff.) that the financial difficulties of the realm could easily be resolved by the recovery of the treasure buried throughout the empire during the turbulent course of the centuries. In the carnival Faust appears as Plutus, god of wealth, along with the Boy Charioteer as the spirit of poetry and prodigality and Mephisto in the mask of hermaphroditic Avaritia-Geiz. The jewels that the boy flings forth are illusions that the crowd takes for reality, even as is the chest full of molten treasure that is lifted down from Plutus' chariot. At the arrival of the Emperor, as the great god Pan, the whole scene ends in an equally illusory conflagration. Only the next morning does the Emperor realize that he had in the midst of the carnival commotion signed the document authorizing the issuing of paper money, the buried treasure of the realm serving as "security." Therewith comes the illusory solution of the financial woes of the empire, the beginning of a galloping inflation, clearly suggested this early, and the other prerequisites tending toward civil war. At the end of Act Four the Emperor, really victorious through magic illusion, standing in the midst of the partly looted treasure of the rival emperor's tent, proceeds to fling away all that he has gained. Before that, in the third act, Lynceus lays the treasure gathered during the Great Migrations at the feet of Helen, as part of the pageantry at her reception, and Faust, carrying on the splendid gesture, dismisses him with the remark that everything in the castle already belongs to her.

This play between treasure and phantom, value and show, reality and illusion recurs in varied form throughout. Of some significance is the incident in which Anaxagoras assumes that the newly arisen mountain (this also connected with the motif of buried and mined treasure) is a lasting reality and advises Homunculus to establish his realm there. The significance comes in the dramatic contrast to the realm Homunculus actually chooses, under the advice of Thales and Proteus: the truly permanent yet ever changeful sea, the realm of formation, transformation, where organic life originates and in constant mutation yet changeless lawfulness develops to higher forms. More on the larger aspects of the Thales-Anaxagoras dispute in the next chapter.

Twice in the drama the reality of the representative man or the hero, and the role of the poet in relation to him, is put to question by the corrosive wit of Mephistopheles, who relegates man's achievements to the imagination of the panegyric poet, thus degrading them to an illusion and a deluder. There is the instance in the last study scene, after the wager, when Faust tries vainly to make Mephisto understand what his real purpose in life is: not self-indulgence, but the experience of everything human, in weal or woe, the expansion of his own self to that of an all-inclusive representative man (1770–75). Mephisto's sarcastic rejoinder is that Faust should hire a poet who could assemble all the desired qualities in an imaginative composition and exalt him into a Mr. Microcosm. And again, a short distance into Act Four, when Faust tells Mephisto about his vision of a great creative act on earth, maintaining that "the deed is everything, nothing the fame" (10188), Mephisto counters with the remark that poets will arise nevertheless to proclaim Faust's glory to the future world and thus ignite folly through folly (10189–91). Peripheral to all this, yet related, are Mephisto-Phorkyas' remarks near the end of the previous act in the reflections on the poetic garments Euphorion left behind. The contrast to his sarcastic derogation of human validity and poetic veracity comes in Act Two near the beginning of Faust's conversation with Chiron when he commends this noble pedagogue who raised a heroic people, the circle of the Argonauts "and all who established the world of the poet" (7340). Furthermore, there is the whole drama itself and its poetic reality, which the critic can interpret from Mephisto's illusionistic, nihilistic point of view, with the natural consequences that will come to anyone who puts his trust in this spirit of denial.

The ultimate triumph of illusion over reality is achieved not by Mephistopheles but by the Bachelor of Arts in a mental tumbling act that leaves even that hard-shelled old reprobate momentarily speechless, though he quickly recovers in recollecting that even this folly of self-apotheosis has a long human history behind it. It is neatly ironic that the Bachelor's last words, "Brightness before me, darkness at my back" (6806), are in direct contrast to Faust's words at the sunrise near the beginning of Part Two: "Then let the sun remain behind me" (4715), neatly ironic because it is the moment when Faust comes to the reality of reflected earthly light and the Bachelor to the illusion of self-engendered transcendent light.

Varied in nature and intent are such other smaller repeat patterns as the trivializing audience of the "Prelude in the Theater" and the one in the last two scenes of the first act before and during the appearance of the images of Paris and Helen. Then there are the aerial voyages on the mantle (2065 ff., 6983 ff.), and there is the numerological play first in the witch's one-times-one (2540–52) and then at the appearance of the Cabiri (8186 ff.). There are many more such patterns of lesser importance, and also a number that call attention to central relationships and continuities between Part One and Part Two. Faust's words at the time of the wager about the clock stopping (1705 f.) are paraphrased by Mephistopheles immediately after Faust's death (11593–94). Margarete's prayer to the Mater Dolorosa in the depth of her despair (3587 ff.) is recalled through the similar beginning of her joyful prayer to the Mater Gloriosa (12069 ff.). And the Lord's words of assurance about Faust's continued striving (308–09, 317, 328–29) find their fulfillment in the song of the angels taking Faust's soul heavenward (11936–37). Let us go on now from these briefer connecting patterns to the larger dimensions of the echo structures.

# 7

# Echo Structures

FURTHER AND HIGHER DEVELOPMENT of Goethe's technique of recurrent themes and unifying patterns is to be found in certain larger structures and continuities, the character and extent of which have till now not been assessed, even though an occasional example has been observed in isolation. There is good reason for this oversight, for by their very nature they are elusive and difficult to perceive, particularly where there is a scene or sequence apparently quite different in essentials of content or context from a preceding one that is nevertheless formally or typically in parallel relation to it. Not having been discerned, they have also not been named, and I have ventured to call them echo structures. Let us examine a series of examples of them, of varied nature, extent, and importance, and therewith attempt to appraise their scope, function, and implications.

We can begin with the initial poem, "Dedication." If we regard it from the traditional points of view, there can be no possible parallel between it and the concluding section of the monodrama: in the one the poet tells of his attitude toward, his vision of his creation; in the other the Easter bells induce Faust to refrain from suicide. However, when we look more carefully at the inner processes as they develop step by step, the motifs that preside over this development, then the parallels appear so striking that we can truly speak of the second as structurally an echo of the first. The dominant theme is that of time, inward human time. In the "Dedication" the poet notices that something strange is happening to him: with the invasion of his present by his remote past, with the emotions that this engenders in him, with the breaking down of the barriers that it achieves, his sense of present presence is lost. That which he is and has seems remote and unreal; that which has long since disappeared becomes reality.

118

If we apply these same words to the concluding sections of the mono-drama, we should have to modify them hardly at all to make them fit. Here too the past invades the present and becomes decisive for the future. The first slight counter-current to Faust's decision for suicide comes with the crystal goblet that summons up the images of a happy childhood and youth, the fond memory of the festive board of his father. This helps open up his soul to the deeper perspectives of the past, to the Christian tradition in which he had grown up, and even though he is now far removed from his youth and its associations (as is the poet of the "Dedication"), the Easter message and its implications come through in full decisive force for him. The past deprives the present of its power over the future. Without memory and its perspective man is one-dimensional, a point in time. With an assimilated past man becomes three-dimensional and acquires a creative power in the fashioning of time.

The Easter Choruses, however, add a factor that goes beyond the three aspects of time: the factor of transcendence and immanence. From the choruses Faust learns to see the folly of the transcendence he yearned for and the rightness of the immanence exemplified in Christ's return to life on earth. He recognizes the earth as the proper sphere of man, and the final chorus of angels tells of the kind of life on earth that will make the transcendent immanent. The final chorus here anticipates the final chorus of the whole drama, with the contrast only in the point of view: here the heavenly coming down to earth, there the earthly, the transitory, the inadequate as a parable of the heavenly, merely a parable, yet truly one. At the beginning of Part Two the conclusion of Faust's mono-logue conveys the same spirit and intent: the light of heaven is too strong for man, but its reflection on the beautiful earth is his joy and glory (4727). Even on the way to the empyrian, after the last of the earthly has been removed from him, like a chrysalis from a psyche (11981–88), the heavenly light is at first too strong for him (12093).

The echoes from the monodrama continued in the second part with the contrast between Faust and Euphorion: the son, having no past to draw on, heedless of the warnings of father and mother, commits the act of dissociative transcendence that carries him not to higher spheres of purer activity but to the darksome shadows of the underworld. He could have become the more lasting embodiment of the spirit of poetry; instead, the "aureole" separates from him, rises on high, whereas his body falls to earth and his soul descends to the nether realms. He had been that mere point of time, without past, without future, a brilliant meteoric flash.

Thus the "Dedication," in inner psychological motivation and continuity, as well as in basic motifs, is related to the main course of the drama, and this intrinsically. Poetic creativity and human destiny thus come into close parallel. In the second of the preliminary scenes, the

"Prelude in the Theater," the motif of solitude, of "Einsamkeit," is brought into closest association with the creative activity of the poet, though the word itself does not occur here except in paraphrase, "quiet heavenly nook" (63). In the carnival scene, near the beginning of Part Two, Plutus-Faust dismisses the Boy Charioteer, the freely spending spirit of poetry, with these words (5696):

> Zur Einsamkeit!—Da schaffe deine Welt.
>
> *To solitude!—And there create your world.*

The motif of solitude, however, rises to its highest potency two scenes later, in the "Dark Gallery," where the way to the Mothers is described with a solemn, intense insistence on its timeless, placeless, desolate nature (6213 ff.). There are graphic descriptions of known solitudes, none of which can compare to this utter solitude. The best and most sensitive of the critics have for some time agreed in equating this realm of the Mothers with the realm of memory and creativity and in adding an impressive exposition of the mortal peril of this realm. If they are right, and it seems clear that they are, then the motif of solitude builds up from slighter stages to this highest symbolic stage, and then goes on to Faust's last human creative act and its necessary preliminary, the standing alone by abjuring magic (11406–07, 11499–500):

> Stünd ich, Natur, vor dir ein Mensch allein,
> Da wär's der Mühe wert, ein Mensch zu sein.
>
> . . . . . . . . . . . . . . . . .
>
> Die Nacht scheint tiefer tief hereinzudringen,
> Allein im Innern leuchtet helles Licht.
>
> *Stood I, O Nature, man alone, with thee,*
> *Then were it worth the while a man to be.*
>
> . . . . . . . . . . . . . . . . .
>
> *Still deep and deeper yet night seems to enter,*
> *And yet within me all is radiant light.*

Here also a further echo from the past when Faust in "Forest and Cavern" did stand before nature as a man alone. The second "allein" does not mean "alone," of course, but it does serve to reecho the first.

Quite different is the close structural parallel that unites the succession of events in the first monologue, in the Bible-translation scene, in "Forest and Cavern," and in Lynceus' song and ensuing report. Even the reader who has them clearly in mind may find it difficult to see them as structural analogues until he comes to think of the succession of events in general terms; in each case, after a vision, an insight, or a contemplation of luminous clarity, there follows an ominous, a threatening demonic intrusion. First, after the contemplation of the sign of the macrocosm there follows the turmoil of the four elements and the emergence of the overwhelming apparition of the Earth Spirit. Second, after the thrilling intellectual insight into the inner meaning of the *logos* in St. John (a fully traditional and orthodox insight, as we saw in the preceding chapter), there comes the conjuration, the monstrous apparition, and then, to be sure, the anticlimax in the appearance of Mephistopheles in the guise of a wandering scholar. Third, after the prayer of thanksgiving to the sublime spirit for granting him all he had prayed for in his harmonious union with nature, Faust senses the advent of the negative demon who wrecks every perfection and stirs up the wild destructive fires within him, and then Mephistopheles appears and turns Faust back on his course toward tragedy. Fourth, after Lynceus' beautiful song of praise to the loveliness of this earth there follows his horrified description of the conflagration on the dune that brings to an end the primordial idyll of Philemon and Baucis. A somewhat more tenuous fifth analogue would come in Arcadia, where the demon of self-will enters to bring the idyllic union of Faust and Helen to a tragic end.

Impressive in their poetic development are the Dionysiac celebrations that mark several culminating or concluding stages in the dramatic action. Most fully developed and clearly discernible are the lyric dramatic conclusions of the second and third acts of Part Two, but they have their briefer, equally lyric celebratory analogue in the first song of the spirits in Part One. This first lyric is of an entrancing, hypnotic character, quite in agreement with its evident purpose of lulling Faust to sleep. But its content and continuity accomplish much more than that and thus early provide a bridge over to the larger symbolic actions to come.

The sensuous sound of the lyric seems to have been effectual in veiling its sense, but if we follow the spatial contours of the poem in their dreamlike blending (1447–1505), we behold a vast arc from the heavens down through the ether, clouds, and air to the arbors that enclose pensive lovers and furnish the pendant grape that from the press flows down over jeweled pebbles to lakes of wine, providing ecstasy to wild fowl that fly upward toward the sun, outward toward the blessed isles, where one can hear the choruses rejoicing, behold the dancers on the meadows, see them dispersing, upward, onward, outward, all toward life, toward the blessed grace of the stars.

The arc of movement, the union of the four elements in fruitful nature, the celebration of life, the entrancement and the ecstasy—all come together again a second and then a third time in a splendid Dionysiac hymn of praise to the glory and joy of life on this earth. The death-and-rebirth, the "stirb-und-werde" union of Homunculus with the organic life of the sea, in an effulgence at the foot of Galatea's throne, evokes the concluding hymn of celebrant praise (8480–87):

Heil dem Meere! Heil den Wogen,
Von dem heiligen Feuer umzogen!
Heil dem Wasser! Heil dem Feuer!
Heil dem seltnen Abenteuer!

Heil den mildgewogenen Lüften!
Heil geheimnisreichen Grüften!
Hochgefeiert seid allhier,
Element' ihr alle vier!

*Hail the ocean, hail the waves,*
*Round which holy fire laves.*
*Hail the water, hail the fire,*
*Strange event we hail in choir.*

*Hail the gently flowing breeze,*
*Hail earth's caverned mysteries.*
*Highly praised here evermore*
*Be ye elements all four.*

The echo structure near the conclusion of the third act comes with
the chorus of captive Trojan maidens who refuse to follow Panthalis to
the underworld to continue to serve Helen; they want to remain in the
glorious light of day on the surface of the beautiful earth. Lack of
individuality and loyalty means loss of personality and dissolution into
the elements, they are told (9982); and as they divide into four groups,
they sing their hymn of dissolution, not tragically but joyfully, since at
the culmination the elements are united once more in the Dionysiac
creation of the wine, in the process of the natural alchemy that raises
them once more into the realm of spirit. The first part, the Dryadic,
describes the activities in the element of air, the second, the Oreadic, in
continuing variant as echo, gently in field and stream, thunderously in
the storm shaking the earth in its threefold, tenfold reechoing. Here, of
course, water is already introduced and the fire of the storm suggested,
although the explicit rise to flame is reserved for later. The third part of
the chorus, the Naiadic, praises the living quickening waters, and the
fourth part, the Oenodic or Bacchantic, the fertile slope of earth on
which the vine is planted, laved by the waters, caressed by the air, and
the grape ripens under the light and warmth of the sun god (10022–23).
Then with all the elements united comes the vintage and the celebratory
Dionysian orgy.

In Chapter Four we observed the relation of these Dionysiacs to the
"stirb und werde," the dying and becoming that dominate the earthly
beginning and ending of each part. Quite different is the celebratory
ending of the carnival scene, with Pan rather than Dionysus leading the
wild sylvan crew. Earth and air are here, and the other elements come in
the magic conflagration quenched by the magic rain. In the next scene
Mephisto employs the configuration of the four elements in a courtly

panegyric to the Emperor. There is a kind of anticipatory parody of a
Dionysiac near the end of "Auerbach's Cellar" (2316–19), a halucina-
tion induced by Mephisto. Such faint echoes are hardly echo structures.

The four elements also occur in the drama in other, usually unre-
lated settings, for instance, at the appearance of the Earth Spirit and at
Faust's first vain attempt at exorcism before he finds the right way to
make Mephistopheles appear. The separate elements or combinations of
them also occur. Among the many there are a few of some significance as
echo structures. It is interesting to observe, for example, that Faust's
rejuvenation took place amid the fire and occult nonsense of the "Witch's
Kitchen," and that the origin of Homunculus occurred amid the fire and
occult nonsense of Wagner's alchemical laboratory, with Mephisto on
both occasions in a comic supporting role. The chaotic nonsense in the
one finds its creative contrast in Faust's vision of the reclining figure of a
beautiful woman in the magic mirror; in the other it goes over to
Homunculus' observation of Faust's dream vision of the conception of
Helen by Leda.

When we trace the further implications and consequences of these
two analogous scenes, the total interrelated complex turns out to be of
somewhat greater significance. In the first place, Homunculus comes to
be involved in a strange kind of contention of the elements of fire and
water when he joins the two disputing philosophers and seeks advice on
how he can "come to being in the true sense of the word." Anaxagoras is
the catastrophist who sees fire and turbulence as the factors of origin; he
gives Homunculus advice that the latter fortunately does not take.
Thales is the gradualist and evolutionist who sees the seashore as the
place of origin and endless mutation upward to higher forms, and it is
he, along with Proteus, who guides Homunculus on to his entrance into
organic life. Where both philosophers are wrong, of course, is in their
either-orishness, their mutual exclusion of each other's insights, their
inability even to conceive of a both-and attitude. And so they add
their two voices to the multiple points of view prevailing through the
drama. In this case, where Homunculus and organic origins are concerned,
Thales does have the superior truth and errs only in believing that he has
the exclusive truth and must reject every conflicting insight.

The fascinating analogue to this (previously observed by others, but
without awareness of its full contextuality or of its status among the
varied echo structures) comes soon after the beginning of Act Four
when Mephistopheles joins Faust in the high mountain regions and explains to him in demonomorphic terms how these mountains were once
the pit of Hell and counters Faust's gradualist convictions with a: You
just think so, but I was there and I know. Here again it is not a matter of
wrong versus right, but a matter of putting the emphasis on the violent,
destructive, death-dealing forces, as is quite proper to Mephisto's will

and attitude, or of putting the emphasis on the gentle, gradual, continuous, life-giving forces, as is proper to Faust's striving, creative nature.

However, the implications of this echo structure go significantly further. Anaxagoras offers Homunculus prestige and honor; Faust has found these wanting; so does Homunculus. Thales offers striving for greater and higher development, and this corresponds to Faust's intent. Faust is thus brought into closer analogy to Thales, and Homunculus by committing himself to their way of life becomes, in a sense, the future Faust, with Galatea taking the role of mediatrix on his entrance into the new and truer life, this an instance of the "eternal womanly," the maternal principle in the process of birth and rebirth. At his transition, his "stirb und werde," Homunculus disappears in a glory of light and song; so does Faust later at his death and entrance into a new life. As he does so, Homunculus shatters his confining glass and enters into a new life, in his case an organic one; the Blessed Boys strip off the last earthly vestiges restricting Faust from growing and developing into his new life that comes after the completion of the earthly. It should be added that there is in the drama another voice of approval or exhortation toward the creative life, the life of striving on earth, this beyond the voice of the Lord in the "Prologue" or of the angels at the conclusion, or Faust's own repeatedly, or the voices of Thales, Proteus, and Homunculus together. It comes at the crucial point in the scene of the wager, after Faust's great curse, when the aerial spirits (most inopportunely for Mephisto) call upon the protagonist to begin a new life of reconstruction and creativity. Such a harmonious relation to those other crucially important voices cannot lightly be dismissed in favor of a noncontextual interpretation.

The vision of the beautiful reclining woman in the magic mirror reminds us of the fact that Margarete and Helen appear both as dramatic realities and as images or visions. The relation between the two, however, is as much a matter of contrast as of analogy. Because of still prevailing confusions it may be well to examine the whole matter more closely and exactly, from the initial mirror image onward. Of course, we cannot for a moment trust Mephisto's interpretation at the close of the "Witch's Kitchen." Tone of voice and choice of words alone assure us that he is up to his old tricks again, and we should be very naive if we fell for his suggestion that the witch's potion was more strictly an aphrodisiac and that with this under his belt Faust would view any woman as a Helen. Examination of the text shows that Faust at no point offers the slightest indication that he regards Gretchen as a Helen; conversely, Mephisto's words alone cannot convince us that the mirror image is that of a Helen. Faust's own ecstatic words in the scene tend rather to bring the image into relationship to a Titian or Giorgione Venus, as several of the commentators inferred long ago. The observed parallel to the first Homunculus scene would suggest a Leda and thus, to

be sure, a Helen. Much later Faust does once again mention this image
in the mirror. This was in the "Hall of the Knights" when he had brought
back the images of Paris and Helen from the realm of the Mothers; and
even here, when he speaks of the image in the magic mirror that once
enchanted him, he calls it a mere foam-phantom ("Schaumbild," 6497)
of the supernal beauty now before his gaze. In other words, Faust here
did see an analogy between the two images, even though the one was
only a faint anticipation of the other. Faust, however, in his enthusiasm
commits the error of mistaking the image of Helen from the realm of the
Mothers for the real Helen whom he later more aptly seeks in the realm
of Persephone. It should be noted that such an image, in the magic
mirror, or on the Brocken, or in the hall of the knights, is always mute
and unapproachable, quite in contrast to the real Helen or the real
Gretchen.

Faust's first encounter with Gretchen, by contrast, was with the real
Gretchen of the drama, and it is only later, when she is nearing her
tragic end, that he sees a vision of her in the "Walpurgis Night." The
images of both Helen and Gretchen appear before him at the beginning
of the fourth act, and yet with such different implications. As the
garment-cloud drifts on, it assumes the shape of a beautiful reclining
woman, thus like that in the magic mirror, but heroic in proportions and
godlike: a Juno, a Leda, a Helen, in other words, not specifically Helen.
And when it loses form, that is the last we hear of Helen. By contrast,
the smaller cloudlet takes more definite, more specific shape and retains
the image of the soul beauty of his first and lasting love, this in symbolic
anticipation of the final reunion intimated at the end of the drama. The
two women are brought in closest parallel to one another as each sadly
contemplates the tragic fate that resulted from her beauty. First
Gretchen (4434):

Schön war ich auch, und das war mein Verderben.

*Fair was I too, and that was my undoing.*

And Helen concludes (9940):

Daß Glück und Schönheit dauerhaft sich nicht vereint.

*That happiness and beauty form no lasting bond.*

Let us conclude with just one more example of an echo structure,
this quite different again, and furthermore of central significance for
the understanding of the protagonist. It is the echo structure that unites
a supreme effort of his in Part One to a supreme effort in Part Two.
When Faust first summoned the Earth Spirit by an impetuous act of
ultimate, passionate magic will, he was poorly prepared to understand
him. After this wild attempt and crashing failure he then, much later,

found a gentler, more gradual, more harmonious approach to him in the union with nature and its living creatures in "Forest and Cavern." Near the end of his sojourn there he is able to thank the sublime spirit for giving him all he prayed for. Analogously, Faust's first attempt to attain Helen was equally wild, impetuous, and ill considered, and it ended in an equally crashing failure with still graver consequences. And yet, even before the voyage back to Greek time and place, his dream vision of the conception of Helen by Leda indicates the more gradual, genetic approach he will take toward the recovery of Helen, going back to primordial origins, making himself fit to enter her world and to bring her into his world. Impetuousness, failure, reconsideration of the proper means to the desired end, and eventual success—this is the pattern of Faust's stormy, humanly fallible progress through the world, a pattern that is repeated in the last act also, where his tragic failure over against Philemon and Baucis, which was at the same time a tragic failure of insight, as we saw in Chapter Two, leads to the realization that the extension of his human range through magic was also an alienation from humankind, a dehumanization, and this insight in turn leads consequentially to his last great creative vision of a free people on a free soil and to his understanding of the ultimate meaning of his creative life.

This will suffice to indicate that the echo structures play an important part in the construction of the Faust drama. A fuller understanding of them, going beyond the few isolated and dissociated *aperçus* of the past, will lead inevitably to a fuller and deeper understanding of the form of *Faust*. They take their place above the multifarious variety of small motifs and recurrent patterns that add meaningful richness at so many points. And they lead onward, they form the transition to the great thoroughgoing themes and motifs of the drama and especially to the main architectonic structures of the drama that we shall examine in the next chapter. If we attain to the ability of seeing the patterns and contexts of the *Faust* at these varied levels of scope and importance, then the wondrous poetic richness of the whole will no longer be bewildering and confusing, but will instead be comprehended in the carefully articulated structure that runs from the smallest features to the ultimate great form.

# 8

# Monodrama and Polydrama

$\mathfrak{A}$ STRUCTURAL FEATURE of central importance in the drama must now engage our attention. Despite its size and significance it cannot even be perceived unless the total drama is seen as a coherent continuous whole. That means it has not been perceived, least of all by those who have tried to study the formal aspects of Part Two as a separate entity apart from the whole.

If we look carefully at the first monologue of Faust, see what is actually there, the larger formal import of the scene will also become clear. It is meaningful that in the first great sequence of scenes in which Faust himself appears the theme of time should be announced in the title, "Night," and the theme of place in the first stage directions. The time, the action, and Faust's own attitude proceed from the late despairful Sauday night of Eastertide, under the sign of death, past the mortal crisis at midnight, to the joyful announcement of the angelic choir that Christ has arisen from the dead—an arc of development through which Faust himself passes and which he himself in the next scene of the Easter Walk extends symbolically to the whole populace, and the whole earth (921–22 and ff.).

The place is indicated as follows: "In a high-vaulted, narrow Gothic chamber, Faust restless in his chair at the desk." The room dates from the past, his father's past, as we soon hear. It is spacious upward but narrow, confining around him. The way is open to transcendence but not to immanence, and Faust himself in the same passage of the Easter Walk confirms the parallel of the liberation of Christ from the grave, of spring from the icy bonds of winter, of mankind from its confining chambers, and of himself in sympathetic relationship to this general Easter spirit of rejoicing, liberation, and human fellowship.

Before he reaches this point, however, he has a perilous arc of darkness to traverse. Here actually in these first few hundred lines of the Faust action we have in prefiguration and epitome the greater arc of the total drama from the dark night of despair, through first insights, relating past with future, to the ultimate vision of the meaning of man's life on earth and beyond. We can, therefore, with some justice think of this initial section as a kind of monodrama with interludes.

We need not review the whole of this familiar scene but we do need to look more closely at the concluding parts of it. And we do need to repeat certain details that we have previously considered in other contexts. After magic has failed him, Faust embarks upon a second perilous adventure, the venture that seeks forcible release from earthly limitations and attainment of pure intellectual insight by means of suicide. He is already tending that way when he develops the theme of "image of God" by splitting the divinity from its incorporation: first the exaltation of feeling oneself "more than cherub" (618)—a cherub after all is only a specialized power rather than a microcosm—then quickly the depression at being hurled back into the realm of human incertitude (629).

As he continues, the mention of his father and his heritage establishes the first still tenuous, still disparaged link to his own past that is to furnish the gradually emerging counter-theme to his new bold venture into the unrevealed future. The vial with the potent poison also comes by inheritance and suggests a way over uncharted seas to a new shore, or (with heightened imagery) on a chariot of fire to new spheres of purer activity. With that he is ready to turn his back on the earthly sun (how differently he does so later) and courageously venture through that darksome portal before which most men quail—even at the risk of dissolving into nothingness.

The crystal cup he takes down is also a heritage, but the images it summons up in him are those remembered from a happy childhood and youth when the cup filled with wine went from guest to guest about his father's festive table: the guests before they could drink had to improvise the appropriate verses to go with the emblems engraved upon it. Faust pours into the cup the more potent drink from the vial and raises it in festive greeting to the new morn.

But this is not only the new morning through the portals to death, it is also the old traditional morning from the tomb back through the portals to the new life in Christ's ressurection. And at once, after this last moment of dead midnight Saturday, the first moments of Easter morning are announced by the sound of bells and the song of the angels, "Christ is arisen."

The musical beauty of these Easter Choruses must not cause us to overlook their content and intent. They meaningfully accompany the successive closing stages of Faust's monologue. This first chorus of angels tells us that Christ's resurrection brings joy to mortal man who is surrounded by his heritage of destructive insidious shortcomings. Faust's own heritage of recollected Easter morns from childhood onward is a force strong enough to draw the cup away from his lips. The first conscious associations Easter summons up in him, questioningly, are those of consolation, of assurance of a new covenant.

The choir of women tells of the preparation of Christ's body for the tomb that he has now left and the choir of angels confirms the glad tidings of Christ's great love that carried him victorious through these sorrow- and bliss-filled trials. Faust's heart is melted at the message; even though the faith of his youth is not restored, the whole meaning of his youthful faith comes over him so powerfully that his past takes control of his present and his future. His urge toward transcendence by an act of violence now seems incongruous when the message comes to him of Christ's loving immanence, of his resumption of his human body in his resurrection. In unwonted humility and gentleness Faust abjures the superhuman spheres (767) and concludes with quiet finality (784): "die Erde hat mich wieder," "earth has hold of me again," "I belong to earth again."

The final choruses reecho this deep human conflict between the urge to transcendence and the realization that the sphere of man's activity is on earth. After the joy of Christ's resurrection comes sadness for his disciples in his ascension to higher spheres of creative joy, comes the feeling of being forsaken amid the sorrow and yearning of earth. The final chorus of angels brings the resolution of the conflict: that man's creative activity on earth, in praise of God, in love and help to his fellow man, in spreading of the gospel of promise over the earth, will bring the Master to dwell among them and make his presence near. Christ again becomes immanent through the Pentecostal experience.

It conforms to the design of the whole that this brief monodrama should, like the great drama as a whole, end with an angelic choir proclaiming the validity of the earthly, transitory, and human as a symbol, a parable of the great divine creativity, however grave the earthly and human shortcomings may be, however shadowy their anticipations of heavenly glory. And it is significant that in both instances Faust's commitment to earth should be the necessary prelude to the transcendence to higher spheres. In the next scene Faust again, though only in passing, yields to the yearning for transcendence (1074–99) but then proceeds in the passage on his two souls to counterbalance this yearning with the affirmation of his strong earthly urge and inclination (1112–17). Much later in the drama we come upon an equally strong will to transcendence in Faust's son, Euphorion, though here, tragically, not counterbalanced by the perspectives of heritage and experience, so that Euphorion commits the act of violence from which Faust refrained.

This small arc of the monodrama, though it prefigures the great arc of the polydrama to come, is hardly an epitome of its content in the same sense that it is an outline of its form and forces. Some of the main events and decisive crises are not here even in faintest suggestion (unless one burdens the text with meanings that go beyond what it can reasonably bear). Still and all, we do know, by anticipation, the dynamics and the destiny of the whole drama and can allow the rich succession of events to unfold panoramically before us without fear that we shall more than momentarily or in detail lose our sense of direction or falter in our understanding of the poet's larger intent.

Thus once more we have an instance of a scene illuminating and being illuminated by the larger context. Through the decades critic after critic has objected to Goethe's ending of the whole drama with the angelic choruses of the Christian way to salvation, as though this were an ending that did not comport with the rest of the *Faust*, an old man's unfortunate whim that arose from a temporary impulse rather than from careful planning. However, when we see the close parallels that exist between the monodrama and the drama as a whole, particularly in the two endings with Faust's two commitments to earth and with the message then conveyed by the two sets of choruses, we must come to the conclusion that the ending of the whole is exactly the kind of ending the poet had planned at an early stage. At the very latest his writing of the Easter Choruses in the first years of the new century foreshadowed the ending he would give to the whole—inevitably, for no other kind of ending would have fitted into the structure of the whole.

We can, with caution, go a few steps further. Faust's last monologues in the scenes "Midnight" and "Great Forecourt of the Palace," proceeding undeterred first amid the oppressive negativism of Sorge (Anxiety) and then amid the grotesque negating activities of Mephistopheles and his Lemures, in a sense, also constitute a monodrama with interludes in which Faust once more and finally faces all the issues in parallel and contrast to the first monodrama. The early (377):

> Drum hab' ich mich der Magie ergeben,
>
> *Therefore I have turned to magic's sway,*

is here countered by (11404):

> Könnt ich Magie von meinem Pfad entfernen,
>
> *Could I but banish magic from my path.*

The early urge to life experience (464–65):

> Ich fühle Mut, mich in die Welt zu wagen,
> Der Erde Weh, der Erde Glück zu tragen,

*I feel the courage through the world to fare,*
*The woe of earth, the bliss of earth to bear,*

here finds its approval (11441, 11445–46):

Der Erdenkreis ist mir genug bekannt.
. . . . . . . . . . . . . . . .
Er stehe fest und sehe hier sich um;
Dem Tüchtigen ist diese Welt nicht stumm.

*I know enough the sphere of earth and men.*
. . . . . . . . . . . . . . . . . . .
*Let him stand firm, the prospect round him scan,*
*The world's not mute unto a worthy man.*

The early foolhardy urge to transcendence (703–05, 718–19):

Ich fühle mich bereit,
Auf neuer Bahn den Äther zu durchdringen,
Zu neuen Sphären reiner Tätigkeit.
. . . . . . . . . . . . . . .
Zu diesem Schritt sich heiter zu entschließen,
Und wär' es mit Gefahr, ins Nichts dahinzufließen.

*Ready I feel and free*
*On a new path to penetrate the ether,*
*Unto new spheres of pure activity.*
. . . . . . . . . . . .
*To take this step in buoyant resolution,*
*Despite the jeopardy of utter dissolution,*

is early countered by (784) "Die Erde hat mich wieder!" "The earth has
hold of me again," and near the end countered by (11442–45):

Nach drüben ist die Aussicht uns verrannt;
Tor, wer dorthin die Augen blinzelnd richtet,
Sich über Wolken seinesgleichen dichtet!
Er stehe fest und sehe hier sich um.

*The view beyond is barred from mortal ken;*
*Fool, who would yonder turn his blinking eyes,*
*Imagine his own kind within the skies.*
*Let him stand firm, the prospect round him scan.*

This earthly stand is confirmed in Faust's final words (11583–86):

Es kann die Spur von meinen Erdentagen
Nicht in Äonen untergehn.—
Im Vorgefühl von solchem hohen Glück
Genieß' ich jetzt den höchsten Augenblick.

*Nor can the traces of my earthly days*
*E'en in the course of aeons perish.—*

*Such a presentiment of lofty bliss*
*I now enjoy, my highest moment this.*

Thus we have a monodrama at the beginning of the earthly action
and a monodrama at the end of the earthly action, each of them with
discordant intrusions, each of them leading to the Christian choruses
conveying the message of resurrection, grace for those who strive, and
salvation. From this view it is as though we had two small arcs of action
flanking the great arc of action, epitomizing it in miniature and indicating its larger configurations. Before the earthly action and after the
earthly action the vistas lead from eternity to eternity, with the final
reflection of the Chorus Mysticus on the symbolic validity of earthly
endeavor, if this is in the service of the Lord under the aspect of the
humanly creative.

At mid-drama, if we can consider the beginning of Part Two as that,
comes another monologue of Faust that, in a sense, unites the beginning
monodrama with the end monodrama, stating several of the main motifs
of both in the form appropriate for the protagonist at mid-course. Significantly, the monologue begins and ends with a statement of Faust's
commitment to earth and the acceptance of earth's limitations as fitting
and appropriate to man. Faust begins (4679–85):

Des Lebens Pulse schlagen frisch lebendig,
Ätherische Dämmerung milde zu begrüßen;
Du, Erde, warst auch diese Nacht beständig
Und atmest neu erquickt zu meinen Füßen,
Beginnest schon, mit Lust mich zu umgeben,
Du regst und rührst ein kräftiges Beschließen,
Zum höchsten Dasein immerfort zu streben.

*Freshly revived, life's pulses beat anew*
*The mild ethereal dawning now to greet;*
*Thou, earth, this night hast kept thy constance too,*
*And now refreshed art breathing at my feet.*
*Beginnest now to gird me with delight,*
*To stir and move a mighty resolution,*
*Ever to strive toward being's sovereign height.*

And in conclusion he contemplates the mitigated light and the colors of
the rainbow, seeing it as a symbol of what is accessible to man, in
contrast to the unmitigated direct blinding light of the sun to which he
must turn his back (4715, 4721–22, 4725–27):

So bleibe denn die Sonne mir im Rücken!

. . . . . . . . . . . . . . . . . .

Allein wie herrlich, diesem Sturm ersprießend,
Wölbt sich des bunten Bogens Wechseldauer.

. . . . . . . . . . . . . . . . . .

D e r spiegelt ab das menschliche Bestreben.

Ihm sinne nach, und du begreifst genauer:
Am farbigen Abglanz haben wir das Leben.

*And therefore let the sun remain behind me.*

. . . . . . . . . . . . . . . . . .
*Behold how glorious arching o'er this tumult*
*The many-colored rainbow's changeful being.*

. . . . . . . . . . . . . . . . . . . .
*Man's striving mirrored in it to perfection.*
*Take thought, and you will understand more truly:*
*We have our life in many-hued reflection.*

In both this beginning and this end there is likewise the motif of striving
(4685 and 4725). In the intervening description of a mountain dawn
there is also an echo of "Forest and Cavern." More significant, however,
are Faust's reactions to the sunrise (4702–3):

> und, leider schon geblendet,
> Kehr' ich mich weg, vom Augenschmerz durchdrungen.

> *alas, already blinded,*
> *I turn away, my eyes with pain pervaded.*

For they anticipate his reactions to the celestial light near the very end
(12093):

Noch blendet ihn der neue Tag.

*The new born day, it blinds him still.*

In Faust's further reflections on the unendurable and overwhelming of
that for which he had fervently yearned there are echoes of his reaction
to the appearance of the Earth Spirit, in his exclamations (482, 485,
499): "Schreckliches Gesicht! . . . Weh! ich ertrag dich nicht! . . .
Flammenbildung." "Appalling apparition! . . . Woe, I can not endure
thee! . . . thing of flame." Here at mid course he reflects (4707–12):

Nun aber bricht aus jenen ewigen Gründen
Ein Flammenübermaß, wir stehn betroffen;
Des Lebens Fackeln wollten wir entzünden,
Ein Feuermeer umschlingt uns, welch ein Feuer!
Ist's Lieb'? ist's Haß? die glühend uns umwinden,
Mit Schmerz und Freuden wechselnd ungeheuer.

*Now from those everlasting depths doth burst*
*An overwhelming flame. We stand aghast;*
*The torch of life to kindle we were fain,*
*A fire flood—what a fire!—doth round us close.*
*Is it love, is it hate, with joy and pain*
*In alternation vast, that round us glows?*

Even if the forty-nine lines of this monologue are a somewhat slight
statement to serve as a central monodrama, they nevertheless do have

their place, and an important one, in carrying the reminder, at midpoint, of the monodramas that anticipate and recapitulate the polydrama.

But granted all this fine symmetry of monodramas flanking poly- drama, why then did Goethe not complete the symmetry by adding, after the final celestial scene, a "Postlude in the Theater" and a concluding lyric poem, as he had apparently once intended at an earlier stage of planning, even drafting some sets of verses toward this purpose? The answer is: for very sound and sufficient artistic reasons, just as sound as those that caused him to refrain from carrying out a Persephone scene and the conclusion of the "Walpurgis Night." One need only imagina- tively visualize such further parts at the end to realize how inappropriate they would have been: they would have established a merely contrived and mechanical symmetry and would have done so at the expense of the more relevant form that would be functional for the intended conclu- sion. After all, this drama does not circle back on itself and end where it began; it moves on, in the Lord's words, from the "darksome urge" to an emerging "consciousness of the right way," through a labyrinth of errors, to a final creative act. In our first observations of intrinsic form, in Chapter Four, we noticed the fourfold movement from an end to a new beginning. The movement at the conclusion must therefore be the ulti- mate carrying out of the direction of the beginning and of the two middle parts; if there were a reversal for the sake of symmetry, then the form would be discrepant with the content and therefore artistically bad. What we do have at the end is a threefold movement in the same direction as at the beginning: the poet's reflections at the beginning revolve around the themes of time, reality, and creativity; so do Faust's last reflections. There follows in the one case the comic variant on these themes in the "Prelude in the Theater," in the other case the grotesque comic interlude of the "Burial," just as paradoxical, as we discovered in Chapter One. Here too, as in the "Prelude," the poet provides a stage setting, this time a medieval one, when the comically terrible mouth of Hell is brought onto the scene by Mephisto's assistants, the fat devils with short straight horns and the thin devils with long crooked horns. And thirdly, in both cases, the scene of action rises beyond earthly time and place and looks upon them *sub specie aeternitatis*, with the words of the archangels, the Lord, and the Chorus Mysticus devoted to what remains on earth as it is in heaven, the striving toward creativity in the one and its accomplishment in the other.

On this spacious landscape, then, is constructed the great edifice of the Faust drama, with the arcs of the monodramas at beginning and end indicating to us and clarifying for us the vastly larger and more compli- cated structure of the whole, the polydrama. Miniature form anticipates total form; miniature form recapitulates total form.

# 9

# Configurations and Symbolic Metamorphoses

**W**HEN GOETHE IMPLICITLY INTRODUCED the principle of multiple points of view into his Faust drama, he did so within the context of the great critical age that first effectively called into question the normative criticism subjecting every work of art to preestablished critical standards and condemning those features of it that did not conform to the accepted rules. With the abolition of forced conformity to past models, however, the relation or relevance of the new work of art to the great continuity of literary tradition was not broken, was not even impaired in essentials. The impairment came with the critics of the nineteenth and twentieth centuries who did not understand the nature of the continuity. Once we understand it, much of the "busy work" of "source" hunting in which the earlier intervening age indulged and which the later intervening age scorned and condemned, becomes suddenly pertinent and useful, even though in a way that neither the "source hunters" nor the "priests of pure interpretation" could perceive or can understand. Thus here too, in critical method, the old compulsive "either-or" is supplanted by a third point of view (not to mention a fourth or a fifth or further ones), one that sees relations to past tradition from a far more complicated, non-simplistic, non-either-orish, that is, multiple point of view.

Instead of regarding "sources" as either determining or irrelevant, there is at least a third possibility, one that I suggested years ago: that of observing whether the creative artist intended an obviously or subtly introduced parallel from the past to serve as a symbolic extension, a device to increase the potency of the point or the position or the perspective that he was intent on presenting. For lack of critical precedents I

had to invent the term "symbolic extension," a term that others subsequently have also found useful. Such a symbolic extension often indeed
constitutes a vital part of a new poetic configuration. If a character or a
sequence is given symbolic extension by being made parallel to a comparable one from the past, then that character or sequence will have a
configurative relation with it and thus will acquire attributes and implications that need not even be stated in the new work of art. The new
configuration is defined as well as enhanced by the old one.

The old standard notion of "influence" thinks of the poet as making
a passive, dependent use of the past, whether unconsciously against his
will or knowledge, or consciously and weakly because he is unable to
proceed independently. By contrast, the implications of the poetic technique of symbolic extension are that the poet is active, deliberate, sovereign in his use of the past for the purpose of extending the vistas and
the relationships. What is more, he expects and hopes that the reader
will notice this use of the past, however subtly it may be woven into the
work, will experience the pleasure of recognition, and especially will
perceive the larger symbolic intent thus made manifest.

Poets past and present have made extensive use of this device.
However, it cannot be said that their use of it has always met with the
correct critical understanding, especially after the "source hunters" had
misinterpreted its presence as a sign not of sovereign intent but of weak
dependence, and the intrinsic textualists had succumbed to this misunderstanding and then disregarded the presence of the device as beneath their concern. Beyond all this Goethe had a special reason for
making the extensive use of this device that he did make in the drama.
The figure of Faust, in its original historical and then legendary form,
was far too small and narrow to include the full scale of implications and
consequences that the poet, from his first youthful vision onward, wished
to incorporate. In his search for ways and means to develop and expand
the figure of Faust to the full potentialities he envisaged, he enlarged
this old device, familiar to the poets, unanalyzed by the critics, to a
position of artistic importance that makes its understanding crucial for
the correct understanding of the drama as a whole.

It was Goethe's conscious plan and purpose to evoke the poetic past
not only to enrich his drama and enhance its protagonist, but also to
surround it and him with an aura of implications that would define his
larger purpose and the end toward which he was tending. It is less
surprising that this was his design and intent than that the critics have
failed to discern this design and intent. Far from being the first to use
such techniques, he could look back upon a long and continuous tradition. One of the early and very great practitioners was Vergil; indeed the
full, rich poetic texture of the *Aeneid* can be comprehended only by a
reader clearly aware of the symbolic extensions that reach out to the

*Odyssey* especially, but also to the *Iliad*, the *Argonautica*, Lucretius, Catullus, and others, not to mention the historic parallels implicit under the varied poetic guises. And so it goes on to Dante's Vergilian and other extensions, on and on through the continuing and cumulative extensions of the great tradition from the Renaissance and its sequels to our day.

Before we proceed to the main business of this chapter, to observe the ways and means that Goethe used to achieve the symbolic extension of the Faust figure into that of a representative man, it may be well to examine a more special and limited kind of symbolic extension. This is of a striking, indeed extreme kind, because it involves the taking over of a seemingly foreign body, a preformed artifact into the poet's own work. The degree of obviousness of this intrusion, naturally, depends not only upon the poet's way of communicating but also upon the reader's knowledge and understanding. In our first instance there is no special barrier to the normal reader's perception: the "source" is well known and obvious, the artifact is ostensibly taken over from Shakespeare. A closer, more exact, more thoughtful regard, however, modifies the situation.

Both Shakespeare and Goethe in succession made use of a "readymade," a preexistent artifact. Thereby they showed not their dependence on the past, their derivativeness, but quite the opposite, their originality, their sovereign poetic mastery, and beyond that their profound irony, their tragic view of man, Goethe no less than Shakespeare.

Here is what happened: there is an inferior and trivial poem by Thomas, Lord Vaux, in Tottel's *Miscellany* of 1557. Short of a half century later, about 1603, Shakespeare adapted it for the gravediggers' song in his *Hamlet*. More than two centuries thereafter, in 1831, Goethe in his turn (via Percy's *Reliques*) adapted it for his song of the Lemures at the digging of Faust's grave (11531–38). Naturally, both these authors possessed the necessary poetic powers to write gravediggers' songs of their own. Nevertheless (and this is the point), they chose not to do so, but chose instead to take over a preformed artifact. We can readily see why they did so if we will refrain from all prejudgments and be receptive to the phenomena themselves, proceeding in the simplest and most obvious manner, first taking in hand Richard Tottel's anthology and reading the poem in its original setting, from its title, "The aged louer renounceth loue," through all of its fourteen awkward doggerel stanzas, then read it as it stands in Act Five, scene one of *Hamlet*, then read it as it stands in Act Five, scene five of *Faust II*.

Textually the poem does undergo extensive change, most notably its sharp abridgment, then also the garbling for its intended new purpose. But the shock comes when we realize that these textual changes are only the superficial ones compared to the profound changes in meaning achieved by putting this old worn-out artifact successively into two new and entirely different contexts. This one poem with its three different sets of speakers and contexts turns out to be three essentially different poems of varied meaning and function. It is sheer virtuosity the way these two poets pull a silly jingle out of the dust heap of literature and simply by adaptation to the new context make it a work of art, or rather two different works of art. It only enhances the poetic effect that the poem both times reappears as a damaged, truncated fragment. As a new poem it had small merit; as an archeological relic from the past, thereby symbol of the transitory, it was transformed into a work of art. Its real creator was not Lord Vaux, it was Shakespeare, it was Goethe.

Another poem from *Hamlet* occurs early in *Faust* and in its new context undergoes a transformation, especially since it is Mephistopheles who uses the song of poor crazed Ophelia as a serenade in the "Street before Gretchen's Door" and mockingly directs it against the new victim, especially in the perversion of the refrain (3682–97). We, however, hear both songs together in both contexts, and thus Goethe was able to add a further symbolic significance that would be lacking if he had himself invented a new song for this occasion.

Turning now to the Faust figure itself and its symbolic extensions, we readily perceive that in Part One these extensions come primarily though not exclusively from the period of the Renaissance and that in Part Two they come predominantly from classical antiquity, though also from biblical antiquity, the Middle Ages, the Renaissance, and the eighteenth century—this quite in harmony with the structure of time that will be our concern in the next chapter.

In Part One, as we have seen, Faust twice announces his intent to become a representative man, embracing all experience within the range of man, quailing not even in the face of ultimate shipwreck (464–67, 1770–75). Mere statements of this kind would hardly carry the full power of conviction in the drama; the protagonist must also be shown actively demonstrating the situations, thoughts, words, and actions of such a representative man with a range far beyond that of the historical or legendary Faust. The device that Goethe used to attain this greater amplitude, these wider perspectives, was that of symbolic extension to the other, greater figures of the Renaissance who more fully incorporated its spirit and its vision.

The boy Goethe had already been introduced by a brilliant, wittily misanthropic old gentleman, Counselor Hüsgen, to that enigmatic, ironic, corrosive work of Henricus Cornelius Agrippa von Nettesheim, *On the Vanity and Incertitude of all the Arts and Sciences* (1530). And so at the very beginning of Faust's first monologue the shadow of Agrippa looms behind that of the protagonist. But earlier Agrippa had also written the great magic work of the Renaissance, the *Three Books of the Occult Philosophy*, first published completely in 1533 (the fourth book is a later forgery); and thus another aspect of this complex, ver-

satile personality presides over the immediately following second part of
the monologue from (377):

Drum hab' ich mich der Magie ergeben.

*Therefore I have turned to magic's sway.*

Yet this is not all: one reservation and two supplements must be
added. Even more relevant to the first section is the penetrating critical
skepticism of Conrad Mutianus Rufus, and behind him there is a tradition of the antiacademic that in Germany reaches back to the 1450s, in
Italy even further. As for the second, the magic stage, it must not be
forgotten that in his own time Johannes Trithemius, the Abbot of
Sponheim, was considered to be the archmagus. Further aspects of the
Faust figure show intentional reminiscences or parallels to Paracelsus
(less perhaps than has generally been believed), to Pico della Mirandola
(by contrast, more important than he may seem), and in a more limited
way to Tansillo and others. To this magic circle of Pico, Trithemius,
Reuchlin, Mutianus, Paracelsus, Agrippa, could be added the somewhat
later Nostradamus whose manuscript is in Faust's possession. Reminis-
cent of Agrippa's black poodle is the dog that accompanies Faust back
from his Easter Walk and is referred to in "Dreary Day. Field."

For certain special traits and episodes of the early scenes the symbolic extensions are obvious enough: suicide contemplated and refrained
from (Hamlet), Mephisto's role in the duel scene (Iago's manipulation
of Cassio), the Bible-translation scene (Erasmus, Luther), withdrawal
into the wilderness (Zoroaster, Merlin, various hermits). The recurrent
motif of flight has a rich background beyond the clearly indicated Elijah,
as, for instance, Simon Magus or Apollonius of Tyana. Among them the
Daedalus has a special extension to Faust's son who is mourned as
Icarus. The elixir of life, the restorative of youth, is at the center of the
Hermetic quest, and among the alchemists and their successors the ones
most closely associated with these aspects were Artephius the Jew, Nico-
las Flamel from the Paris of the late Middle Ages, Fridericus Gualdus,
the mysterious German in Venice whose portrait Titian had painted and
who was still living there in full vigor a century and a half later, and
finally the heir to his legend, the Count of St. Germain who reached into
Goethe's own time. The images of reclining beauty that Titian and his
short-lived friend Giorgione created return to Faust's vision within the
magic mirror, even as the violently contrasting images of the Flemish
grotesque painters and engravers do elsewhere in the "Witch's Kitchen."
From the next scene onward the story about Raphael's transformation of
a lovely young girl of the people into an immortal Madonna finds its
poetic parallel in Margarete.

For Part Two the dominant symbolic extension of the Faust figure is
to be found in the Plutarchian Timoleon, with important supplements

from his Roman parallel, Aemilius Paulus, and from Julius Caesar. The Timoleon extension, already suggested in the very first scene, becomes most obvious in Act Four and rises to highest significance in Act Five. But before we examine this symbolic complex more closely, let us look at the other figures who provided more limited or specific extensions at various points of the action. There are, first of all, the mythological and legendary figures from early Greek times. As I have shown elsewhere, the typical epic hero validates himself as a hero when he embarks upon a perilous voyage beyond normal space or time for the achievement of some important end. In the Greco-Roman epic the two chief exemplars are Odysseus and Aeneas; outside the great epic there are Jason and the other Argonauts, with two of them, Hercules and Orpheus, reaching beyond the Argonautic complex in their ventures into the realm of Persephone. For Faust the perilous voyage was the one to the realm of the Mothers; after it his venture into the realm of Persephone to attain Helen had to be relegated behind the scenes, with Manto openly drawing the parallel to Orpheus. Once he has attained Helen and is wedded to her, the symbolic extensions come from Menelaos, from Paris, but especially from Achilles, within the legend of his union to Helen in a new life on the island of Leuce; this is also analogous in the dreamlike reality-unreality outside normal place and time.

The poetic tradition of the perilous voyage is continued in the Renaissance epic, and here there are even closer analogies to the realm of the Mothers in the epics of Ariosto, Camoëns, Tasso, and Marino. Among the historical characters there is Agrippa again who magically won a battle for his sovereign analogous to that which Faust won for the Emperor. The poetic analogues are from Shakespeare: from Henry the Fifth who instructed his betrothed in his language even as Faust did Helen in his, and Prospero who also abjures magic in the end.

Mephistopheles brings Faust's action over against Philemon and Baucis into analogy to King Ahab's over against Naboth (1 Kings 21). Whether this is a true analogy or just another Mephistophelean twister to confuse the issue, as so often before, can readily be determined by examining the larger contexts of both events. On both sides the analogy breaks down, and it should have been noticed long ago that Mephisto here again is diverting attention from the true analogues. A closer, though far from complete analogue can be found in the history of colonial expansion, as in the removal of indigenous peoples to make room for new settlers or for the policies of a new regime. More truly in analogy to historic precedents is Faust's consequent vision of a free people on a free soil, kept unified by its struggle against hostile, destructive forces from without. Here the Dutch Republic offers the closest analogue in its struggle against natural forces, whereas the victorious struggle of a small people against overwhelming human forces has its analogue not only here but also in ancient Greece, medieval Switzerland, the young United States, and elsewhere. The blindness that leads to clearer creative vision has its precedents in a long tradition from Homer to Milton, even as does the tradition of the creative act of separating the land from the waters, not only in the divine act of Genesis, but also in the act of Apollo after the flood; other varied analogies come from Julius Caesar, the doges of Venice, Leonardo da Vinci, on to the Dutch and Frederick the Great. The "Prologue in Heaven" establishes an always recognized symbolic extension to Job. Dubious again, by contrast, is the analogue to Solomon and the "Song of Songs" suggested by Mephisto in "Forest and Cavern," though in other ways the historical and legendary Solomon offers analogies: in his colloquy with spirits, his constructive projects with spirit help, his wise rule, expansive trade, and sad fall in old age. The Moses analogue would be less dubious if it had not been overstated.

All of these, however, from the minutely specific to the more general, are relatively minor symbolic extensions when compared to the one great one from Plutarch and the two others that supplement it. At least four or five times in the course of a long life Goethe read the biography of a man that, with the omission of local and specific details and several episodes, can be generalized in the following outline:

A man highly esteemed for character and personal endowments became deeply involved in guilt. The blame for his act brought him to melancholy and dejection and drove him into solitude, remote from the company of man. Years later he was suddenly recalled to active life and at once demonstrated by effective action that time had cured him of his desperate soul crisis. Indeed, he became Fortune's favorite. His high efforts and brilliant actions had added to them a portion of good luck that at times rose to sheer magic. Thus at his most critical battle, against overwhelming odds, not only was there a dramatic omen in the skies (eagles and serpent), but, when the battle was joined, the very elements conspired to throw the enemy into confusion and panic, the whole culminating in a suddenly rising flood that brought about the final rout. The enemy camp was filled with vast treasure from which some soldiers enriched themselves personally, though he devoted the choicest of the treasure to the honor and adornment of his fatherland.

However, he himself did not return to the capital and to glory, but instead, after final victory, threw in his lot with the desolated people and country he had saved. He devoted all his energies to reconstructing and recolonizing the land long wasted and depopulated by chaos and tyranny. He ruled supreme until he succeeded in establishing a strong, free, self-governing state, then he turned over the government to the people themselves. Advanced in years, he lived in dignified, moderate prosperity, esteemed by all for his continuing good counsel, a citizen among free citizens. No good fortune ever being unalloyed, blindness overtook him in old age. He died mourned by all, and a decree was made to honor his memory for all time in an annual festival.

Thus, in excerpt and in outline, runs the life of Timoleon of Corinth and Syracuse, as Goethe read it in Plutarch's *Parallel Lives*, certainly in 1811, 1820, 1821, 1831, perhaps in 1826, probably also in 1798 or 1799, possibly once or twice previously. It stands in remarkable analogy to the life of the Goethean Faust at the beginning of Part Two and in the last two acts up to his great vision of the future of his realm.

So much is clear and simple, but the conclusions we can draw from this correspondence are perhaps not as obvious and clear-cut as they may appear at first sight. Let us, therefore, proceed step by cautious step, taking care to distinguish between the certain and the probable, the probable and the possible.

First of all, we must try to answer the question: Is this a genuine parallel or is it merely a remarkable but accidental resemblance? If we decide it is a real parallel, then the next step offers graver complications and uncertainties. We shall have to try to decide, Did the Timoleon analogue carry over (1) unconsciously from Goethe's reading into his poetic work? (2) consciously but covertly, with the poet merely borrowing a sequence instead of inventing his own? (3) consciously and with the more or less clear intent that the reader should become aware of the parallel and see it as a symbolic extension and implicit comment?

If we come this far, a host of further problems arises to be examined in the new light and from the new perspectives now opened up. There is, for instance, the technical matter of the genesis of the last two acts, but there is also the all-important matter of the poet's ultimate intention in these culminating scenes of Faust's life on earth.

At the very first question we have every reason to begin by being reserved and skeptical, in view of the numerous doubtful analogies dredged up in the past. For the fourth and fifth acts, as well as for earlier parts, specific "sources" have been found for all kinds of single motifs that were actually so commonplace in Goethe's day and earlier that it is clearly impossible to name any one source; in the case of somewhat rarer motifs it is, often as not, possible to find them equally well (or better) in several other works that Goethe is known to have read. And yet the traditional references are carried uncritically from one commentary to the next right down to our day. The danger of dubious analogy is especially great in the case of occult phenomena of the kind the poet used in the imperial battle of Act Four. Anyone who has looked about in the literature knows that such motifs occur over and over again through the centuries; anyone who has examined Goethe's reading in the matter knows that he did not have to rely on the Erasmus Francisci and Johann Praetorius usually cited, and also recognizes that he could not have received any new stimulus from his reading of Sir Walter Scott's *Letters on Demonology and Witchcraft* at the turn of the year 1830–31.

And yet, we must acknowledge that there is, after all, a vast difference between such dubious "sources" for single motifs or episodes and the Timoleon parallel extending through the better part of two acts. If anything comparable in scope and continuity has previously been adduced, it apparently remains unknown to modern *Faust* scholarship.

Graver doubts, however, may well arise when we read the life of Timoleon in full and set Plutarch's text over against the full text of Acts Four and Five of *Faust* (to line 11586). There is so much in the former that has nothing to do with the latter, and conversely. Hardly more than general is the analogy drawn between the soul crisis of Timoleon and that of Faust at the transition between the two parts of the drama. The origin is quite different (in Timoleon's case his consent to the murder of his brother who had made himself tyrant of Corinth, and his mother's bitter reproaches after the deed), as is the motivation for the return to the world of active life. Only the slow healing process of time and nature (in the one case presented realistically, in the other symbolically) and the strong positive turn to action in the great world are comparable. But then Faust goes through the varied episodes of Acts One to Three, which have only slight and single analogies to motifs in the Timoleon biography—though there are some striking analogies from other parts of Plutarch, well beyond the well known matter of the Mothers and the subsidiary one of the Pharsalian Fields.

In sum, the analogue of the soul crises of the two heroes and their return to active life would be weak if these stood in isolation instead of in a larger context. In the nature of things Goethe had to lead Faust through some such transition and would certainly not need any one literary model to show him how to do what human experience has demonstrated over and over again. However, this much at least may have happened: after the writing of the opening scene of the second part he may have observed this analogy between Timoleon and his Faust, and this observation in turn may have been the inciting incident that caused him to model the Faust of the last two acts so largely on the figure of Timoleon.

This mere possibility, at this point, tends only to reinforce the just doubts so far raised, and we need to adduce far more evidence for our case before we can have any assurance that it belongs in the realm of the probable rather than of the merely possible. Fortunately, there is more evidence, and of a fairly convincing kind.

Let us look first at the battle of Act Four. Many (not all) of the strange phenomena occurring in it and determining its outcome were also present, in part in a more naturalistic form, and equally decisive, in the great battle of Timoleon against the Carthaginians (XXVI–XXIX)

—right down to the final demoralization of the enemy by the suddenly rising (real) flood waters. The battle array and strategy, however, are quite different from anything in the Timoleon; all the more surprising, therefore, is the fact that they find their close correspondence in the immediately following "parallel" biography, that of Aemilius Paulus (XIII–XVI). There at the battle of Pydna King Perseus of Macedon disposed his troops on the slope of Mount Olympus in virtually the same unassailable position though with the same vulnerable spot: the inadequately guarded mountain defile through which the opposing troops pour and, in the historic case, overwhelm the defenders, in the imaginative case, come close to doing so until repulsed by the water magic. The occurrence of the decisive flood waters could perhaps be considered merely coincidental, if it were not reinforced in the Aemilius Paulus battle by a digression of Plutarch (XIV) on the bursting forth of the ground waters. These two together may well have confirmed Goethe in his decision to bring the imperial battle to such a whimsical and fantastic end. As I have shown previously, added specific features came from an episode in the *Danish History* of Saxo Grammaticus. And it is noteworthy that the motif in the fourth act deriving from his Cellini studies ("The necromant from Norcia, the Sabine," 10439) coincides in time with his Saxo reading and with his first intensive continued study of Plutarch at the turn of the century. Thus the poet, thirty or more years before the actual writing of the battle scene, apparently had all the elements for it in his hands. Significant also for Goethe's association of the Plutarch parallels to the *Faust* is the specific mention in Act Two of the Aemilius Paulus battle at Pydna as Chiron is carrying Faust alongside Mount Olympus (7465–68). If any commentator had looked up this specific reference in Plutarch's text itself, instead of in a handbook, he would have had before him the battle terrain and strategy of the fourth act.

For Faust the ruler in Act Five we find a vital strengthening of the main parallels of the Timoleon biography in another biography of Plutarch. The Timoleon contains the essential line of development from rescuer and realm builder, through autocratic ruler, to citizen among free citizens. But it has virtually nothing that parallels the details of actual constructive efforts in the rescue of his lands. These engineering achievements: dikes, harbor installations, canal, marsh drainage, colonization on new land, can be found together in one brief section of the biography of Julius Caesar (LVIII)—all this combined with a remarkable characterization of the "Faustian" impulse that did after all exist in classical antiquity despite what certain philosophers of history have tried to make us believe:

> Caesar's many successes, however, did not divert his natural spirit
> of enterprise and ambition to the enjoyment of what he had laboriously

achieved, but served as fuel for future achievements, and begat in him plans for greater deeds and a passion for fresh glory, as though he had used up what he already had. What he felt was therefore nothing else than emulation of himself, as if he had been another man, and a sort of rivalry between what he had done and what he proposed to do. . . . [There follows an outline of his military plans.] During this expedition, moreover, he intended to dig through the isthmus of Corinth, and had already put Anienus in charge of this work; he intended also to divert the Tiber just below the city into a deep channel, give it a bend toward Circeium, and make it empty into the sea at Terracina, thus contriving for merchantmen a safe as well as easy passage to Rome; and besides this, to convert the marshes about Pomentinum and Setia into a plain which many thousands of men could cultivate; and further, to build moles which should barricade the sea where it was nearest to Rome, to clear away the hidden dangers on the shore of Ostia, and then construct harbours and roadsteads sufficient for the great fleets that would visit them.

We at once recall that young Goethe projected a Julius Caesar drama about the time of the inception of *Faust*; we also remember his positive attitude toward this historical personage, then and later, despite the grave blemishes in his character. There is some not quite conclusive evidence that he had read the biography by 1772; if he had not, then almost certainly he was familiar, from one modern biography or another, with these engineering projects that Caesar had planned shortly before his assassination. Whether Goethe dropped his plans for writing a Caesar drama when he decided to use him as a symbolic extension in *Faust* or whether this decision came long after the abandonment of those plans, we do not know.

With all this corroborative evidence of major importance (I have omitted the wealth of smaller confirmative detail to be found in Plutarch) added to the unusually sequential intrinsic parallel, the possibility that the resemblance between the Timoleon and the Faust of the last two acts is a fortuitous one can hardly be entertained. We turn then to the more difficult second question with its three possible outcomes.

The question as to how consciously or unconsciously a poet proceeds in his creative activity can never be given a generally satisfactory answer. Not only do individual poets differ from one another in the degree of the deliberate and the involuntary that enters into their work, but any one poet will exhibit varying admixtures from time to time. In the case of Goethe we have the full range from almost completely submerged and subconscious creative effort, as the poet himself described it for certain dithyrambic poems of his youth such as "Wanderers Sturmlied," all the way over to the clear and obvious case of the first "Wanderers Nachtlied" ("Der du von dem Himmel bist") where he expected every reader to see the beginning in analogy to the Lord's Prayer and to interpret the poem in that spirit and against that background.

Rarely, of course, is the case that clear unless the poet himself has chanced to make a statement on the subject. In the Timoleon instance, as usually with the particulars of his *Faust*, Goethe maintained a guarded silence. Personally, therefore, I do not see how we can ever definitely know whether these processes were conscious or unconscious that, in the construction of the imperial battle, combined the phenomena in the Timoleon with the disposition of the forces in the Aemilius Paulus, adding certain single motifs from Camillus' battle against the Gauls in Plutarch, that of the early Greeks against the Gauls in Pausanias, as well from Cellini, Saxo, and assorted folklore. The same would be true in the delineation of Faust's last earthly activity that combined the general course of Timoleon's concluding career with the specific projects of Julius Caesar just before his death and with single motifs from elsewhere. The varying convictions of critics as to the nature of the creative process would, very likely, produce quite different conclusions, defended with equal warmth and eloquence. Perhaps the judicious conclusion would be that in the case of the Cellini and Saxo analogues, lying some thirty years back, and the folklore analogues, so general and widespread, the process of creative assimilation may well have been largely subconscious, whereas the repeated reading of Plutarch throughout life could hardly have left the Timoleon, Aemilius, and Caesar analogues in the realm of the subconscious, especially considering his conscious and specific reference to the battle of Pydna in Act Two. Likewise supporting such a conclusion would be Goethe's own observation expressed in his letter to Wilhelm von Humboldt of December 1, 1831, that the creative processes were on a highly conscious level during the final stages of his work on *Faust*:

> And through a mysterious psychological turn, which perhaps deserves to be more closely studied, I believe I have risen to a kind of production that in full consciousness brought forth that which still meets with my approval.

This much conceded, that he probably used the Plutarchian motifs consciously, the second part of the question—namely, whether he was merely borrowing a sequence here instead of inventing his own, or whether he had proceeded purposefully in the establishment of this parallel—can be decided with a greater degree of likelihood. Certainly he had no need to lean on Plutarch and was decidedly not lacking in personal inventiveness for the continuation of his *Faust*, as he clearly showed in the quite different synopsis of Part Two that he dictated late in 1816 for his autobiography (thus, clearly, as a reconstruction of his early plan of about 1775) but did not publish.

Even if we rested the case here, that would seem to leave us with the likely though not certain result that the poet developed the culmination of Faust's earthly activity in deliberate and conscious parallel to the Timoleon biography (with echoes from the Aemilius Paulus and the Caesar). Thus, to make the *Faust* another "parallel life" may have been a *jocus serius*, one of "diese sehr ernsten Scherze," as he described his work in his last letter, the one to Wilhelm von Humboldt of March 17, 1832—and not only here. That still would leave the question as to the poet's intent and purpose in developing the parallel to such impressive dimensions, this quite in contrast to the other, more limited symbolic extensions. The beginning of an answer can perhaps best be found in the text of Plutarch itself, in the introductory section to this pair of biographies:

> . . . I always cherish in my soul the records of the noblest and most estimable characters. . . . Among [the fairest of my examples] were Timoleon the Corinthian and Aemilius Paulus, whose Lives I have now undertaken to lay before my readers; the men were alike not only in the good principles which they adopted, but also in the good fortune which they enjoyed in their conduct of affairs, and they will make it hard for my readers to decide whether the greatest of their successful achievements were due to their good fortune or their wisdom.

Here the theme of virtue plus good fortune is set. It is continued in the remarkable Persephone-Ceres episode (VIII, so strangely related to another part of *Faust*) and more obviously in Plutarch's remarks (XXXVI) that Timoleon ascribed his success to Fortune (Τύχη), built a shrine in his house for sacrifice to Chance (Αὐτοματία), and consecrated the house itself to man's sacred genius (ἱερός δαίμων). The negative side of fortune comes not only in this hero's blindness, but more particularly in the sad fate of Aemilius Paulus when at the height of his fortune he lost one son five days before his triumph, the other three days after, and made the point himself in his moving funeral oration (XXXVI). Plutarch comments just previously (XXXIV):

> But after all there is, as it seems, a divinity whose province it is to diminish whatever prosperity is inordinately great, and to mingle the affairs of human life, that no one may be without a taste of evil and wholly free from it, but that, as Homer says, those may be thought to fare best whose fortunes incline now one way and now another.

The ironic parallel occurs in the paralipomenon where the Emperor bestows knighthood and fief on Faust, the chancellor intoning:

F a u s t u s, mit Recht der G l ü c k l i c h e genannt.

Faustus, *with justice called the* Fortunate.

With respect to virtue, this pair is probably preeminent among the all-too-human, all-too-imperfect Plutarchian heroes. Possibly a main point that Goethe wished to convey to us is that the hero of real life is, at best, a very human and fallible creature, and at less than best is still an authentic hero and offers yet another instance of some excellence of which mankind must continue to be mindful. At any rate, the poet indicates on another occasion, in the fourth book of his verse aphorisms (the "Zahme Xenien") that what separates him from his contemporaries and gives him a different concept of the nature of man is his continued reading of Plutarch:

"Was hat dich nur von uns entfernt?"
Hab immer den Plutarch gelesen.
"Was hast du denn dabei gelernt?"
Sind eben alles Menschen gewesen.

*"Tell us, what made you so remote?"*
*My reading in Plutarch and agreeing.*
*"What's in him that's so worth your note?"*
*Each one of them was a human being.*

After one has followed Goethe's example and continued to read one after the other of the lives of the noble Greeks and Romans, observing their changeful fortune, their lapses and rises in virtue, their good intent crossed by evil accident or impulse, one cannot help but dismiss the fashionable (though fading) invidious criticisms of Faust and the negative interpretations of his character and destiny. They are anachronistic and beside the point; they reflect the sickness of the post-Goethean era rather than the poet's intent. Even aside from his devotion to Plutarch, Goethe, from the nature of his character and art, cannot possibly be conceived as having anything to do either with the ideal hero or with his negative after-image. The Plutarch parallels simply add further confirmation to the fact that in his *Faust* he wanted to portray an authentic, and therefore imperfect, hero and wanted us to judge him by the standards of real life and accomplishment in an imperfect and changeful world.

It is clear, therefore, that Goethe's deliberate choice of the Timoleon analogue as an extension of the meaning and implications of his Faust was for him a matter of primary importance and consequence. He needed such prototypes since neither the historical nor the legendary Faust had the full dimensions requisite for his mighty purpose and intent. Here in Plutarch we have a true "Faustus Fortunatus" who at the height of fame and influence is not seduced into a life of self-indulgence in either luxury or power. He has and uses wealth and power, but uses them for his great creative, constructive efforts, in the service of the common weal that arose out of them. Caesar and Faust, equally unseducible, had, albeit less purely than Timoleon, even greater creative, constructive impulses toward turning yet one more area of chaos into cosmos, Faust being superior to Caesar in his Timoleonic vision of a free people on a free soil (and generally in character and standards), but like him in his impetuous, impatient nature, his intense, irrepressible drive onward when some great purpose was to be realized.

The rich context of symbolic extensions of the Faust figure that we touched on briefly before examining the more spacious Timoleon parallel does not, of course, exhaust the full range of allusiveness that the poet employs for the purpose of raising him to the full stature of a representative man. But it will suffice for our present purposes and we can turn to another character in the drama who experiences a varied amplification by means of successive symbolic extensions: Mephistopheles. However, this happens in a way notably different from the development accompanying the Faust figure. For one, whereas the symbolic extensions of the latter are only rarely accompanied by a change of costume or mask (as Plutus, as Delphic priest, as chivalric lord, as armored knight), the former goes on from black poodle and hippopotamus to wandering scholar, to cavalier on tour, to university professor (twice), to court jester, Zoilo-Thersites, Avaritia-Geiz, Phorkyas, Peter Schlemihl, warrior, pirate captain, and denizen of Hell. In the "Witch's Kitchen" especially, but also later, there are jesting remarks about the way he put aside his medieval costume, with horns, horse's hoof, etc., and accommodated himself to the new era. In the Martha episode he did manage to escape the sad fate of his Renaissance colleague in Machiavelli's *Belfagor*. Where he has greatest trouble in accommodating himself is in the ancient world; there he meets with one rebuff and humiliation after the other until he finally, as a last resort, makes contact with classical antiquity at the edge of chaos in joining the daughters of Phorkyas and adjusting his appearance to theirs. In the third act, where he continues in the Phorkyas role nearly to the end, he exemplifies with especial clarity an old observation about the mask, namely, that the assumption of a role can have an effect that goes well below the surface down to basic traits of character. His (her) role of housekeeper and nurse attendant comes to show striking parallels to the figure of Demeter in the Homeric hymn (as I indicated on an earlier occasion), to the extent that in the Arcadian scene he speaks in tones that are alien to Mephisto in his other masks. Of course, at this point he is quite cut off, by time and place, from his source of evil.

Even as symbolic extensions can be used to enhance and enrich major (and minor) characters, they can also be used to enrich and deepen the connotation of whole scenes. Let us see, by way of example, what happens when we follow up the poet's quite obvious indications of the relations of the "Classical Walpurgis Night" to Lucan's *Pharsalia*. Here only a few summary observations, because we shall have to examine the whole matter in detail in the next chapter. When we reach the sixth book of this epic, we learn in the description of the Thessalian plain (333–412) that it was originally flooded and uninhabitable. When it was drained, it became the place of origin of the Greek arts of civilization. A parallel with increment comes in Faust's subsequent vision of a land newly won from the flood tide and his final vision of this as the proper place for a new beginning of a society of free people on a free soil. The life-giving waters and the life-giving land can now exist productively side by side instead of chaotically intermingled. Indeed, there may be some intimation of a mythic symbolic continuity from Thales, Homunculus, Nereus, Proteus, Galatea, and the rest on to Faust's creative ordering of the seashore. Certainly the "Classical Walpurgis Night" moves from chaos to cosmos, from Erichtho to Galatea, from Faust's vision of the primordially monstrous to his attainment of the ultimate beauty that arose out of it.

# 10

# The Structure of Time

Wer nicht von dreitausend Jahren
Sich weiß Rechenschaft zu geben,
Bleib im Dunkeln unerfahren,
Mag von Tag zu Tage leben.

*Let him who does not make the treasure*
*Of three thousand years his own,*
*Stay in darkness, lacking measure,*
*Live from day to day alone.*

HE ROUND NUMBER of three thousand years for the heritage of European civilization came to have symbolic meaning for Goethe, also, and especially, in connection with his *Faust*. The implication is that one is not a full member of this civilization unless one has the commanding perspective over this range of time, can perceive and understand the sequence of its development. Without this vital extension one would have too little beyond the experience of one's own short span and narrow environment and so would fail to grasp the meaning of even this little segment. One would remain in the dark, inexperienced, be condemned to live from day to day, to repeat the mistakes of the past, instead of living in the larger time, greater spaciousness, and accumulated wisdom of one's cultural heritage.

To be sure, this heritage can be an oppressive burden also, a stifling prison, cutting one off from living in the present, which is, after all, the only time in which one can really live. This is in part Faust's dilemma when we first meet him and that is why he repeatedly and at length speaks of the heritage from the past, from his father's time and earlier, the ancestral stuff (408) with which he is oppressively surrounded, with which he can do nothing, which has become meaningless to him, as has the traditional learning. Faust himself, however, states in positive terms what is necessary if a heritage is to become meaningful (682–83):

Was du ererbt von deinen Vätern hast,
Erwirb es, um es zu besitzen.

*That which your fathers have bequeathed to you,*
*Go earn it if you would possess it.*

A heritage must be acquired, must be assimilated, must become a part of one's self if it is to be an enrichment instead of a burden.

Now Goethe consciously and deliberately took these words over from Ulrich von Hutten. We know this because in his autobiography he tells us that he read Hutten at the time of the writing of *Götz von Berlichingen* (and thus of the *Urfaust*) and he quotes *in extenso* the letter from Hutten to the Nürnberg humanist Wilibald Pirckheimer (October 25, 1518) that contained the stimulus for these *Faust* verses, not just at one point but at several, of which the following statement on ancestors and heritage is the closest:

> . . . but whatever their worth may be, this worth is not our own, unless through attainment we make it our own.

It is structurally as well as psychologically important that this positive note on heritage is introduced in the monodrama at the conclusion of a lengthy condemnation of the useless, burdensome baggage of the past. In shorter perspective it marks a turning toward an insight into the more positive values of his heritage. Somewhat later, and still within a generally negative setting, comes a stronger, personal confirmation when the crystal goblet recalls memories of a happy youth and his father's festive board. Almost immediately thereafter comes the final larger confirmation (with only one negative note) when the Easter Choruses bring back to mind the long tradition of his Christian heritage, the life wisdom that went with it, the sanctity of immanence, and the insight into the impious folly of his will to transcendence.

In longer perspective this first reevaluation, reassimilation of a heritage prefigures the far broader and more comprehensive assimilation of the full three-thousand-year-old heritage that occupies, in symbolic form, two whole acts of Part Two and sections of the other three. That it was the author's intent to make Act Three a symbolic synthesis of the three-thousand-year heritage we know from Goethe's own statements in letters to friends after he had finished writing it. A careful reading of the drama text will readily indicate that this intent of the poet extends also to Act Two and that this symbolic process includes Faust's attainment of personal mastery of the European heritage. One of Goethe's statements on his "three-thousand-year Helena" we have already quoted at length in Chapter Four. Let just one of the several others suffice at this point. On October 22, 1826, he wrote to Wilhelm von Humboldt:

From time to time I have worked away at it, but the piece could only be completed in the fullness of time, for it now plays on through a full three thousand years, from the fall of Troy to the capture of Missolonghi. This too can be considered a unity of time; the unity of place and of action, however, are, even in the usual sense, observed most exactly.

Let us then examine the time structure of the drama, as soberly, exactly, and factually as possible. To be sure, it is of the essence of the time structure that it is not clearly differentiated, but that there is an intentional blending of times, a montage, a superimposing of two or more times in an iridescent shimmer of phantasmagoric effect. This, however, gives us all the more reason for determining the individual images out of which this montage is composed. Only thus will we come to an insight into the framework of time and into Goethe's careful design for bringing together the three thousand years of Western heritage into one grandiose panoramic sweep.

The historic time of Part One is left indefinite. Externally in his autobiography Goethe tells us (especially in the paragraphs just before the Hutten letter) how deeply he was preoccupied with the Renaissance-Reformation period of the decades around 1500. Internally also there is evidence in abundance that specific traits of Faust, Wagner, Mephistopheles, also action sequences, unusual expressions and formulations have their closest precedence in that period and are intended to convey its spirit and flavor.

And yet, the young author was fascinated by this period just because it had such remarkable analogies to his own:

At this time the way to the epoch between the fifteenth and the sixteenth century was generally opened up and brought to life. The works of Ulrich von Hutten fell into my hands, and it seemed strange enough to see something so similar to what had taken place in his time again manifesting itself in our later days.

Thus it should not surprise us if the poet blends eighteenth century features into the work. Such anachronisms are inevitable even when an author tries to keep a work historically pure and authentic. But we have internal evidence that Goethe went beyond this, intentionally introducing anachronisms, designedly obvious at those points where they are introduced for humorous effect and conveyed by such appropriate characters as Wagner and Martha. Wagner, in his set piece of a humanist lament, complains of being so tied down to his studies that he barely gets to see the world on a holiday, "barely through a spy glass" (532). And Martha, when Mephistopheles brings her the news of her roving husband's death in Padua, pleasantly leaps in her thoughts to reading his obituary in the weekly newspaper (3012).

The intentional great anachronism in the "Prelude in the Theater," where the audience is assembled before the drama is even as much as written, prepares us for this jocoserious play with time (greatly intensified in Part Two), even as the serious announcement of the theme of the mystery of time in the preceding "Dedication" indicates that this is to become one of the major themes of the *Faust*.

In Part Two the several indications of time become individually clearer and more exact, though without ever escaping the ambiguities of blending and superimposition. Thus the Emperor, in the first and in the fourth act, is endowed with traits of character, certain acts and conditions, that remind us most strongly of Maximilian the First, whose time, just before and after 1500, also fits into the general scheme of things. We know that Goethe, at one stage of his planning, intended to introduce Maximilian and his court specifically into the drama, and the drama, as we have it, does in Act Four contain a variant of the three sinister allegorical characters from Maximilian's autobiographical verse romance, the *Teuerdank*, even as young Goethe's early Weimar poem, "Ilmenau," contains them in closer analogy. The mention at the beginning of the carnival scene that the Emperor had brought the new Renaissance pageantry with him from his Roman journeys (5068) is still essentially appropriate, considering Maximilian's Italian expeditions and sojourns and the Renaissance pageantry that came from Italy with his second wife. Even the episode of the Necromancer of Norcia at his coronation in Rome has in part the Renaissance background of Cellini; and, more strangely, the episode of the ghostly armies in empty armor added to the battle array has in part a Renaissance analogue from the legends that gathered around Agrippa von Nettesheim. However, the precedents for a battle between Emperor and Anti-Emperor are more generally medieval, from earlier centuries.

For the period around 1500, deeply involved as it was with the recovery of antiquity, saturated with its lore, speech, mood, and thought, the prominence of motifs from antiquity in Part Two is only a matter of course, even when it reaches the degree of dominance it does in Acts Two and Three. Appropriately here, even as the Renaissance reopened the way to pagan antiquity for modern man, so the realization of a Renaissance dream in the creation of Homunculus provided the specific guide to convey Faust to classical soil where alone he could safely reawaken from his dead faint to a new life. This is a task that Mephistopheles is unable to perform on his own, and Homunculus goes to great lengths in his first scene to emphasize the vast difference between his understanding and ability in this dilemma and Mephisto's helplessness and stupidity. After our close scrutiny of the latter's mendacities in Chapter One, we can hardly be so naive as to believe his concluding words in this scene that the Homunculus was his creature; indeed, the whole context, with his repeated humiliations, assures us that this remark was mere bravado to cover up his embarrassment. He also had to "cover up" in the last study scene of Part One when the aerial spirits exhorted Faust to a new life of creativity, something that no minions of Mephisto would ever do. Just as a normal everyday knowledge of folklore helped us to realize who and what these spirits really were, so a bit more of the same folklore will tell us who and what the Homunculus was and where he came from.

The lore of the folk tells us that the spirits of nature, though they lived on through the centuries, did finally die, and their death was complete because their souls were not immortal. Thus there are the many tales of such spirits who yearned for and sought human embodiment, since by becoming mortal human beings, they would also gain immortality of soul. In the tales themselves, typically in "Undine," the outcome is usually tragic, yet in tradition many a great old family claimed descent from such an embodied spirit of nature. Since such elemental spirits are also present in Paracelsian lore, even as is the alchemical creation of a homunculus, Goethe with whim and good humor as well as with the larger purpose he had in mind, endowed his Homunculus with the superiority over time and place of such spirits, as well as with their yearning for organic embodiment. The first, still artificial environment is provided by the alchemical mixtures and processes of Wagner, and indeed Homunculus addresses him as "Väterchen," "daddy." Mephisto he addresses as "cousin" and also as "rascal," and it is possible that the old rascal, in his dilemma, could have facilitated the entrance of Homunculus into the vial on this first preliminary stage toward real embodiment. Similarly for the aerial spirits of Part One there was a good-natured reciprocity with Mephisto as long as he was only being rascally, although they mourned every kind of destruction and nihilism, in which he reveled. Whenever he claims or suggests that he is being creative, let the reader beware. The realms of creativity are closed to him; he has the key and can show the way, but only in Faust's hand does the key glow and grow; only Faust can enter into the realm of the Mothers, can become the poet, the creative maker, can relive again the variegated course of the three thousand years. Mephisto is a mere facility and magic potency in this enterprise, an able stagehand who has to carry out his master's creative constructs. Goethe quite obviously wanted to make Mephisto's inferior position abundantly clear to us by the continuing series of humiliations to which he is subjected in this second act, first by the transcendent Bachelor of Arts, as we have seen, then by Homunculus, then by the whole series of creatures of antiquity. He of course must enter the realm of antiquity that Faust is entering, but he can do so only in the last possible and most ignominious form of a Phorkyad at the edge of chaos, the one place where this son of chaos can make contact.

In sharp contrast to Mephisto's limitations is Homunculus' range and penetration. After he describes Faust's dream of Leda and the swan (indicating the conception of Helen), Mephisto tries to be scornfully superior in his negation but is promptly put down and reminded of his inferior dark-age obtruseness. Homunculus at once sees that Faust must be translated out of his Gothic into a classical environment or he will certainly perish, and he declares (6940–43):

> Jetzt eben, wie ich schnell bedacht,
> Ist klassische Walpurgisnacht;
> Das Beste, was begegnen könnte.
> Bringt ihn zu seinem Elemente!

> *Just now, as I recall aright,*
> *'Tis Classical Walpurgis Night;*
> *This happens as the best event.*
> *Go bring him to his element.*

And a few speeches later, amid continuing ridicule of nordic Mephistopheles, he describes the place of the "Classical Walpurgis Night" (6951–55):

> Südöstlich diesmal aber segeln wir—
> An großer Fläche fließt Peneios frei,
> Umbuscht, umbaumt, in still- und feuchten Buchten;
> Die Ebne dehnt sich zu der Berge Schluchten,
> Und oben liegt Pharsalus, alt und neu.

> *This time southeastwardly our course is bound—*
> *An ample vale Peneios wanders through,*
> *Mid bush and tree, in moist and gentle bends;*
> *Up to the mountain glens the plain extends,*
> *Above it lies Pharsalus old and new.*

Now how was Homunculus able to recall swiftly that this was the anniversary of the battle of Pharsalus and the defeat of Pompeius by Caesar? How was he able to locate the place so accurately and know that on every anniversary the ghosts of the dead Greco-Roman past assembled here, out of all time? The answer can only be that this lay in his nature, that it was one of his attributes to be a repository of time, a kind of living historical chronology—in brief, the perfect initiator of Faust's ensuing voyage through time. He also knew of Faust's preceding perilous voyage beyond time and place to the realm of the Mothers and comments significantly in the next scene (7060–61):

> Wer zu den Müttern sich gewagt,
> Hat weiter nichts zu überstehen.

> *Whoe'er to Mother realm dared go,*
> *Has nothing more to overcome,*

indicating that no further venture could surpass this, thus also implying that a Persephone scene, if realized in the drama instead of being merely suggested, would be anticlimactic.

Let us chart this voyage through time, setting down the dates of the major stations as accurately as ancient history and legend have transmitted them to us. Such accuracy will not only be amusing to us, we shall see in the end that it had likewise been amusing to the poet and, what is more, symbolically significant. Here again, as elsewhere, the principle of multiple points of view prevails. When Faust reckoned that Helen was only ten years old when she was kidnapped by robbers and rescued by her brothers and Chiron, Chiron ridiculed Faust for such pedantry and added in summary (7433):

Gnug, den Poeten bindet keine Zeit.

*In sum, the poet is not bound by time.*

If we at once agree and note that this is certainly a true statement for this work of this poet, we will be not slightly taken aback when we find Helen in the next act (8850) confirming that she was ten years old when she was kidnapped by Theseus. Faust's very next words to Chiron draw the conclusion he desires (7434):

So sei auch sie durch keine Zeit gebunden!

*Then may she also by no time be bound.*

The first landing, at Pharsalus, is observed by the Erichtho that Lucan had associated with the place, and she introduces the scene with a reflective monologue. The question may possibly have been asked, though certainly it has never been adequately answered, as to why Goethe placed his own invention of a "Classical Walpurgis Night" in just that definite geographical region of the Thessalian plain through which the Peneios with its tributaries wanders, and why he timed its calendar date to August 8, on the spectral annual return of the eve before the battle of Pharsalus, which took place on August 9, 48 B.C. Would it not have been more appropriate to place it at one of the archaic locations of the Peloponnesus, closer to where Helen had her origins? And what bearing do Caesar and Pompey and the decisive battle between them have on Faust's quest for Helen or on Homunculus' quest for embodiment? On the whole, would not the Trojan plain have been a more appropriate place for the reassembling of the Homeric heroes and their successors through antiquity? After all, such a nocturnal Hellenic assembly was a product of Goethe's imagination, he was not bound by tradition and could have placed it where he wished. Clearly, the problem of time, our main concern here, turns out to be inseparable from the problem of place.

The poet's reasons for the time and place he chose are there, in the text of the *Faust* itself, but no one seems to have taken the trouble to follow up the obvious clue that he provides at the very beginning when he has Erichtho open the scene with her monologue. It must be added that in order to have her serve this purpose the poet had to tone down her character and attitude considerably, so that she is no longer the creature of unspeakable horror that the ancient poets depicted. Everyone knows, of course, and takes it for granted that everyone knows, that the Erichtho (though mentioned also by Ovid) derives from the frightening Thessalian witch who appears in one of the most sensational and memorable scenes of Lucan's *Pharsalia*. This should long since, to be sure, have caused the critics to read or reread the epic with the Faustian text in mind, in order to learn just why the poet modified her character so radically in order to have her speak the reflective prologue and just why Faust's voyage through time requires this particular beginning in place and time. What they seem to have done is merely consult the handbooks and their memories, and what the commentaries offer is no more than the surface facts of history and myth and then some symbolic reflections and interpretations in which specifically Pharsalian and Thessalian relations and allusions play no intrinsic part. They explain Erichtho (and the ghostly recurrence as a whole) as indicative of the eternal return, the union of myth to history, the coming of ever new life out of ancient origins. That is all well and good, but why then Erichtho, whose ancient lineaments unmodified would be most inappropriate for this role, whereas any number of other ancient figures (a Cassandra, a priestess of Delphi, a sibyl) would certainly be more appropriate?

What Goethe was doing here was making use of one of his favorite poetic devices, symbolic extension, a device that we examined in detail in the previous chapter. Thus the answer lies in the text of Lucan's epic, not indeed in what he said about Erichtho (who in *Faust* serves primarily to call attention to the intended symbolic extension) but in what he said about Thessaly and its relationship to the whole development of Greek culture and civilization. The "Classical Walpurgis Night" is centrally concerned with orgins, with the origins of Hellenic cult and culture from its monstrous primordial forms onward and, in the closing Homunculus scenes, it is concerned with the biological origins of life itself in the littoral sea. Faust, on viewing the sphinxes, griffins, and other weird mythic creatures from the transitional age of the new heroes and old monsters, suggests their function and symbolism in words of approval (7182 and 90):

Im Widerwärtigen große, tüchtige Züge.

.   .   .   .   .   .   .   .   .   .   .   .   .   .   .   .

Gestalten groß, groß die Erinnerungen.

*In the repulsive great and sturdy features.*

. . . . . . . . . . . . . . . . .

*The forms are great, great are the memories.*

This is a going back to origins. Out of such monstrous archaic origins there developed, in direct succession, the beauty that was Helen and the glory that was Greece.

Lucan and his predecessors tell us that these origins are to be found in Thessaly. This was the cradle of the Hellenic peoples, and when they were forced south out of this fertile plain by invaders from the north and west, they took with them an already highly developed mythic and heroic lore. Some of it continued to be located in Thessaly, some of it was, together with associated place names (Olympia, Eurotas, Peneios, etc.), transferred to once alien geographic features. However, not only the positive aspects of civilization originated in Thessaly but also the negative ones that became the bane of mankind and removed it from its primordial innocence. The two violations against nature most frequently mentioned by ancient writers, when they reflect on man's fall from golden-age simplicity and virtue, were plowing through the sea in ships and digging the metals out of the bowels of mother earth. The crucial passage in Lucan comes in Book VI (395–412) shortly before the episode of Erichtho, at the close of the long passage on Thessaly (English translation by J. D. Duff):

> In this land the seeds of cruel war first sprang to life. From her rocks, smitten by the trident of the sea, leaped forth first the Thessalian charger, to portend dreadful warfare; here he first champed the steel bit, and the bridle of his Lapith tamer, unfelt before, brought the foam to his mouth. The shore of Pagasae launched the ship [the *Argo*] that first cleft the sea and flung forth man, a creature of the land, upon the untried waves. Ionos, a king of Thessaly, was the first to hammer into shape ingots of molten metal; he melted silver in the fire, and broke up gold and stamped it, and smelted copper in vast furnaces; there it became possible to count wealth, and this drove mankind into the wickedness of war. From Thessaly the Python, hugest of serpents, came down and glided on to the land of Cirrha; for which reason also the laurels for the Pythian games are brought from Thessaly. From here the rebel Aloeus launched his sons against Heaven [the Gigantomachia], when Pelion raised its head almost to the height of the stars, and Ossa, encroaching upon the planets, stopped their courses.

Somewhat earlier, near the beginning of his description of Thessaly, Lucan tells how its erstwhile swamps became the later fertile plains, when Hercules here, in a different way, performed the creative act of separating the land from the waters that Faust was to perform in the final stages of his life (VI, 343–351):

The land which lies low in the depression between these mountains was once covered over with continuous swamps; for the plains detained the rivers, nor did the outlet of Tempe suffer them to reach the sea; they filled a single basin, and their only way of running was to rise. But when the weight of Ossa was severed from Olympus by the hand of Hercules, and the sea first felt a sudden avalanche of waters, then Thessalian Pharsalos, the realm of sea-born Achilles, rose above the surface— better had it remained drowned for ever!

It is to be remembered that when Chiron transports Faust from the upper to the lower Peneios and the vale of Tempe at the foot of Mount Olympus, he makes allusion (7465–68) to another decisive Thessalian battle fought there between the Roman republican Aemilius Paulus and King Perseus, with whom the great Macedonian empire of Alexander came to an end. Chiron himself, like the other centaurs, was Thessalian, but, unlike the others, he was credited with profound learning in medicine, music, and astronomy and became tutor of the older generation of heroes, Aesculapius, Hercules, Jason, members of the Argonautic expedition and their contemporaries, and also of Achilles who fought with the next generation of heroes before Troy. As we learn from Lucan, Pharsalus was the home of Achilles, and, as Faust reminds Chiron, Achilles' life-after-life on Pherae with Helen was a valid precedent for his own highest desire. It has always puzzled scholars why Goethe departed from tradition in making not Leuce but Pherae the magic place of this marriage. Since Pherae was a place in southern Thessaly, not far from the home of Achilles, the poet's "auf Pherä" (7435) clearly means on the heights (in a castle) above Pherae. In other words, the poet deliberately changed Helen's and Achilles' dwelling place from an island to a high place and thus brought them into even closer parallel to the Helen and Faust in the castle of Act Three.

Just as the first designation of scene, "Pharsalian Fields," and the monologue of Erichtho enabled the poet to indicate the symbolic extension to Lucan, just so the second (genuinely Goethean) designation of scene, "Peneios Surrounded by Waters and Nymphs," indicates another symbolic extension. The pictorial significance of the title has long been recognized and reference made to the related engraving attributed to Giulio Romano and its background in Philostratus' *Eikones*. Apart from *Faust*, Goethe's concern with Philostratus has been the subject of repeated studies, but in connection with *Faust* it would seem that no one has gone back directly to the text itself to see whether it may be of pertinence to the Thessalian origins and backgrounds of these scenes. Actually, there is much in Philostratus' work that bears upon the strange creatures and the strange events of the "Classical Walpurgis Night" and, beyond the details, upon the whole vividly pictorial nature of this succession of scenes. However, for present purposes, let us limit ourselves to several sentences from the description of the picture of Thessaly where Poseidon, in his role as Seismos, creates the passage for Peneios through the vale of Tempe to the sea (Book II, Eikon 14, translation by Arthur Fairbanks):

> . . . the Thessalians in early times were not permitted by the Peneius to have any land at all, since mountains encompassed the level spaces, which the stream continually flooded because it had as yet no outlet. Therefore Poseidon will break through the mountains with his trident and open a gateway for the river. . . . Accordingly he greets the plains as he sees that they are both broad and level like stretches of the sea. The river also rejoices as one exulting; and, keeping the usual posture of resting on his elbow (since it is not customary for a river to stand erect), he takes up the river Titaresius as being light water and better to drink and promises Poseidon that he will flow out in the course he has made. Thessaly emerges, the waters already subsiding.

Chiron, Achilles, Hercules, Jason and the Argonauts, Aesculapius, Aemilius Paulus—all go over by meaningful symbolic extension from Thessalian localities and Thessalian events into this one scene of the "Classical Walpurgis Night," Erichtho and Caesar entering earlier, Seismos and Nereus later. With such a close and intricate web of inter-relationships it becomes quite plain why Thessaly was chosen as the place for these scenes. Furthermore, time as well as place finds its best fulfillment here. The three decisive battles represent three crucial dates: the mythical Gigantomachia represents the decline of the primitively monstrous and the triumph of the Olympian pantheon, first in Hellenic religion, ultimately in classical art; Pydna and the defeat of King Perseus signify the eclipse of Hellenic glory by the rising splendor of the Roman Republic; Pharsalus and the defeat of Pompey signify the eclipse of that same Roman Republic 120 years later. Thus Thessaly is both the cradle and the grave of classical civilization. From the two destructive endings we are led back to the origins of it all in these same regions, not only to Achilles and the heroes before Troy, the fall of which, tradition says, occurred at a date equivalent to 1184 b.c., not only to the time of the building of the *Argo* in Thessaly and the launching of the Argonautic expedition during the previous generation, let us say about 1215 or 1220 b.c., but also, through the link of wise centaur Chiron, back to the preceding age of fabled monsters into the remotest past imagined by Hellenic man. In sum, it would be difficult, probably impossible to find a better time and place for Faust's entrance into antiquity at this initial point of his voyage through time.

This going back to remotest origins, however, is carried to the ulti-mate, to the origins of organic life in the littoral sea, by the singular adventures of Homunculus who attaches himself to the two disputing philosophers, Thales and Anaxagoras, whom time, the gap of over a century, did not allow to dispute in their earthly lives. Now in a strange

"Dialogue of the Dead" Thales (ca. 640–546 B.C.) disputes with Anaxagoras (ca. 500–428 B.C.) about the best way a Paracelsian Homunculus of about A.D. 1530 can come into authentic existence. Circumstances conspire against the vindication of Anaxagoras' basic assumptions, but Thales finds for Homunculus the way and means for entering into real life at the beginning stage of organic evolution. Here is another dying and becoming that can stand symbolically for the return of Helen from the spirit world to a new life on earth.

The beginning of the third act is the purely classical one of Helen's return to Sparta (1184), in the nearest possible equivalent of the language of the great Attic dramatists of seven centuries later. But the Phorkyas, despite all the connotations coming over from the Homeric "Hymn to Demeter," tears the delicate fabric of classical antiquity and brings Helen herself to a despairful incertitude about her time in past and present. Then after the ghostly transition takes place under the guidance of Hermes, the conductor of souls (this time in reverse), Helen is transported to another era. Already carried over into the new era is the Argonaut Lynceus, who indeed remains with Faust up to his last day on earth. The time of this scene is a blend of the two invasions from the North, the Gothic invasions around A.D. 400, represented especially by Lynceus and his gathered treasure, and then the establishment of Crusader strongholds and principalities in Greece around 1150, represented especially by the fedual lord, Faust, and by his knightly retainers. If we want an exact date, we may fondly remember that high point of chivalric pageantry realized at Mainz, Whitsuntide, A.D. 1184, a neat transfer of Helen from 1184 B.C.

With the death of Euphorion a further time transition is made to the Greek war of independence when there was another, supporting and idealistic, invasion from the North. The threnody to Euphorion becomes the threnody to Byron who died on Greek soil in 1824, and if we add this to the 1184 of the fall of Troy, we have only a few more than the 3000 years of which Goethe spoke.

On the voyage into antiquity the Middle Ages are quite rightly passed over, in the spirit of the Renaissance for which this was the dark age beyond which shone the light of antiquity. On the return, however, the main stages of the coming together of North and South are commemorated, in the spirit of the romanticism for which the Middle Ages again attained positive value and were to be included with antiquity in the new "progressive universal poetry." After the death of his son, Euphorion the Romantic, Faust returns to his emperor's times for a new start into a future era of a free people on a free soil. This new beginning, like the old beginning in Thessaly three thousand years earlier, comes after the creative act of separating the land from the waters.

Some years ago, on an impulse, I opened an atlas and traced Faust's aerial voyage on Helen's cloak back from Sparta-Arcadia to the Tyrolean Alps where the imperial battle of Act Four was about to take place. Faust tells Mephistopheles that on the way back he had observed a vast stretch of tidal flats with the sea surging fruitlessly over them and back again, purposelessly, leaving a chaos of what was neither land nor water. This sight offended his feelings of order and cosmos and challenged him to the creative act of separating the land from the waters. It would be interesting to see whether Faust could have encountered any such shore-line on his voyage north in the distant past; the commentators apparently have not done so and simply take it for granted that Goethe had in mind similar land gaining operations in North Germany and the Nether-lands, possibly together with a symbolic vision of the new United States of America. As a matter of ancient fact, the northern Adriatic that Faust flew over did have such shore lines, and if we think of them in connec-tion with the desolate swamps, islands, and lagoons that from the early Middle Ages onward were gradually transformed into the city of Venice and its environs, we have a visionary poetic prototype of the harbor, canal, and palace where Faust's last hours on earth transpire. On further investigation I found that I was not the first to have had this *aperçu*; Goethe's own Friedrich Wilhelm Riemer had it and briefly made note of it, and thus it is likely that others have also had it during the intervening years. What one must guard against is to take this observation as a new or revived dogma intended to displace all previous dogmas; that would be missing the point, as one always does when one tries to approach a work of the dimensions of *Faust* in a reductionist manner. The intention of the observation is exactly the opposite: to loosen up one's thinking and free it from any rigidly dogmatic commitment to any standard interpretation, whether on a small matter such as this or on a more important one. For example if one seeks for a remarkably close visual parallel to Faust's palace, canal, and harbor at eventide, one can find it readily in one of the beautiful harbor sunsets of Claude Lorrain. Every symbolic imaginative approach to a Faustian scene or sequence must remain an approximation so long as there is the possibility of a better one turning up that is closer to the poet's spirit and intent.

It is with such an attitude of open-mindedness that I hope the reader will also approach the next chapter, a chapter that for me too turned out to be a voyage of discovery into regions of which I had never dreamed, which I did not realize existed. Many a reader will find the implications disturbing, and more than disturbing, as I would also if I were unaware of the wonderful spirit of fun in which Goethe must have perpetrated this *jocus serius*.

# 11

# Proportions and Perspectives

E HAVE REVIEWED a large array of formative principles in the complex structure of *Faust*: the pervasive symbols, the primary themes and attitudes, the recurrent patterns, the contextual and configurative networks, the symbolic extensions in person, time, and place, the principle of the interlude both in symmetrical and progressive sequences, the coordinating structure of monodrama and polydrama. In surveying this wealth of formal components we are left with the total impression of a highly complex symphony, a polysymphony, if we can imaginatively project such a form. From our repeated observations of the way in which form fits function, we are assured that the poet remains throughout in masterful command of the whole and all its coordinated parts. And yet, the parts remain so bewilderingly complex in their interrelations and successions, in their mutual illumination and contextual signification, in their backgrounds and perspectives, in their sheer multiplicity, that we may have difficulty in following the author in his comprehension of the whole.

Can it possibly be that the poet, in his intentness on controlled and controlling form, developed yet another formal compositional device that would contain the whole in an all-encompassing framework? Possibly on the analogy of a carefully measured and balanced musical composition, even one in which mathematical calculation plays a part? Some of the greatest poets of past and present have done so without losing the respect of the critics, witness Vergil and Dante, not to mention the medieval poets in whose works the problem of the mathematical or architectonic structure is still under investigation. As for certain modern or recent authors of rank, a closer scrutiny may well reveal structures of which no one yet has an intimation, except in the few instances where they have been exposed. In the English novel of mid-eighteenth century such hidden structural features have recently also been discerned.

There is such an allover compositional network or framework in *Faust*, a fairly clear and obvious one at that, which anyone could have found during the past century and a half by simply making a table of the scenes. I anticipate in order to devaluate. This allover pattern is not on the same level of importance as the primary formative structures that we have examined in the previous chapters. It is instead subordinate to them, supplemental, a framework used with conscious intent for the more complete formal mastery of this exceedingly complex drama.

1

Nevertheless, it is a most remarkable device, in its total unexpectedness bordering on the sensational. Once it is pointed out, its obviousness will only add to this effect. We can be thankful that it was not discovered separately from and ahead of the principal forms. Its disclosure would have been so dramatic, it would have appeared to explain so much so easily and comprehensively that the more important aspects of the formal study of Goethe's masterpiece might have been seriously impeded. In my preliminary article on the form of the drama, "Patterns and Structures in *Faust*" (1968), I refused to give any details about this framework because even a brief summary description of it would give it a specious prominence over the more important structural principles and throw a short article such as that quite out of balance. I did live in fear lest someone make this discovery out of context and out of perspective, fear not of the mature and responsible *Faust* scholar, for he would certainly see it in its perspective and give it its due subordinate value, fear rather of the less responsible, who could find it because it is actually so easy to find, who would want to build a whole reputation on it, who would see and expose only the obvious and striking features of it, who would overlook the refined subtleties of it, the delicate and meaningful ambiguities, the final incertitude, and most of all the marvelous puckish humor of Goethe, who in a heaven not devoid of laughter may still be chuckling about this *jocus serius* at the expense of the all-too-serious, this strict form that mocks all the contemporary and later clichés about Goethe as the "Naturgenie des Hingeworfenen," the uncalculating genius of spontaneous and disordered utterance. Fortunately, there has been no isolated discovery of this framework; the friends and students to whom I have disclosed it have not made it public; and I can now, in the larger compass of a book venture to speak about it more openly, well knowing that some readers will disregard my words of caution and reservation, no matter how urgent they are, and yet hoping that in the larger setting and fuller perspectives most readers will give the device the subordinate place proper to it.

I came upon the encompassing framework years ago while working on an earlier draft of the present study and noticing the many and intricate interrelations that existed between scenes and groups of scenes of Part One and Part Two and also of scenes within each part. For further clarity and visibility of such relations I made a table of the scenes of both parts, numbering them for convenience. I found that Part One has 27 scenes and that Part Two has 27 scenes, and could not believe my eyes, for I had expected quite discrepant numbers in the two parts. To be sure, this much is actually very little: 27 scenes in each part could merely be one of those surprising coincidences that do happen and mean nothing. Furthermore, the actual count of scenes is subject to grave incertitude, not so much in Part One (where one detail of the count stands in doubt) as in Part Two where, first of all, Goethe's own (intentional) ambiguities in scenic division create difficulties enough, and where, secondly, the various editors' arbitrary changes in division (quite contrary to original manuscript and print) reduce the whole matter to chaos. Only the 1832 edition is free from the latter and generally reliable, the Weimar edition and a very few others largely so, the rest are more or less misleading. Not until a closer examination reveals that the coordination of the two parts is more likely to be design than accident, would it be profitable to examine the ambiguities and their significance. Then, and only then, will it become possible to proceed to the third, crucial stage that will reveal overall proportional relations between the two parts.

The possibility of chance diminishes the moment we look at the articulation of scenes within each part and compare them. If we divide approximately into thirds, the first nine scenes of the drama end with the "Witch's Kitchen" and include all the preliminary scenes before the Margarete drama. The first nine scenes of Part Two end with the "Laboratory after the fashion of the Middle Ages, extensive, cumbrous apparatus, for fantastic purposes," a striking grotesque parallel to the witch's kitchen with its "strangest kind of witch's furnishings." Then in Part Two come the scenes in classical lands, revolving about the quest for Helen, eight of them, nine if we include the "High Mountains," with its last cloudlike presence of Helen. In the last nine scenes Faust gains his new land, develops it, has the vision of a free people on a free soil, dies, is buried, and has his immortal parts carried to higher spheres. The middle scene of Part Two, significantly, is the one that follows "Rocky Coves of the Aegean Sea," and is entitled "Telchines of Rhodes," with its genetic pageant of life, the "stirb und werde," dying and becoming of Homunculus entering into organic life and its evolution, with the final chorus of praise to the four elements and life-giving Eros. This fourteenth scene completes the second act and therewith the preliminary parts before the concluding thirteen of Faust's earthly achievements in the winning of Helen and of a new realm, and then of his assumption after death into higher realms.

For the moment we have passed over the last eighteen scenes of Part One. Let us return to them. The middle scene of the entire 27, the second "Street," where Faust yields to bearing false witness, and the conclusion of the second nine, the second "Martha's Garden," where he is less than candid in answering Gretchen's questions and where her desires are also stronger than her scruples, certainly belong together, but they do so in another order, that of the thirteen scenes of the Gretchen tragedy, which we examined in an earlier chapter. To be sure, it is between the eighteenth and the nineteenth scene that the events occur that make the tragedy inevitable, and one could argue that here also Goethe observed the tripartite division, thus observing it throughout ($9 \times 3 + 9 \times 3$). However, the more natural divisons of Part One are: 9, 13, 5, or more exactly: 3, 4, 2; 6, 1, 6; 2, 3. Thus there is nothing mechanical about the poet's use of this device and it remains subservient to his larger intents. It is well to observe this from the beginning since his use of this framework is a far more subtle and complicated one than our observations thus far would indicate. This is already borne out by our observations in earlier chapters of the axial structure of the Gretchen tragedy and the unidirectional (not symmetrical) relation of the first three to the last three scenes of the drama, now viewed from the larger perspective of the present chapter.

Let us look at some of these closer relationships, both those previously suggested and the new ones brought to light when we behold the scenes grouped in order before us. The first three and the last three scenes of the whole drama can equally well be given the titles: (1) man as creator, (2) the comic *theatrum mundi*, (3) divine creativity—in the same order, not in reversed symmetrical order, for the reasons indicated near the end of Chapter Eight. In the ninth scene of each part, witch's kitchen and alchemical laboratory, where the stage directions already indicate the analogy, we see the paradox of cosmos arising out of chaos, sense out of nonsense. In the one Helen's name is mentioned for the first time, in the other Homunculus describes Faust's dream of the conception of Helen. In the eighteenth scene of Part One Gretchen's doom is sealed. In the eighteenth scene of Part Two Faust has his last vision of Helen as the cloud of her garment disperses, but he also has his first vision again of Gretchen in that small wisp of vapor that on rising does not disperse but assumes form. And it is she who appears again in the final scene of each part.

Several minor relationships may also be worth pointing out. There is an amusing analogy between the eighth scene of each part. On the surface, to be sure, the young freshman first appears in the seventh scene of Part One and reappears in full baccalaureate glory in the eighth scene of Part Two. In the eighth of One, "Auerbach's Cellar," however, we witness microcosmic self-stultification through alcohol, in the eighth of Two we behold a case of microcosmic self-stultification through a subtler, even more inebriating kind of spirit, that of the subjective idealistic philosophy. The analogue may be accidental, but on a more serious level and clearly intended, scenes eight and nine of both parts are scenes of chaos and interludes between major parts of the action. Since the interplay between chaos and cosmos is one of the chief symbolic movements that goes through the whole drama, it might be worthwhile to examine the succession of scenes further for such patterns.

In a sense we can do that in the scenes surrounding the Helena action proper. It should first be noted that scene sixteen of Part One, "Forest and Cavern," is the central scene of the Gretchen action, and that scene sixteen of Part Two, "Inner Court of a Castle," is the central scene of the Helena action. Thus the three scenes of the Helena action occupy the same position in Part Two as do the central scenes of the Margarete action of Part One and they turn out to have a similar though not the same axial arrangement. After all, there are only three of these scenes, with the medieval "Inner Court" flanked on the one side by the ancient palace of Menelaos in Sparta and on the other side by the ancient (and perennial) landscape of Arcadia. And yet, even as the imperiled cosmos of the Gretchen scenes is preceded by the chaos of "Auerbach's Cellar" and the "Witch's Kitchen" and is followed by the chaos of "Walpurgis Night" and "Walpurgis Night's Dream," just so the imperiled cosmos of the Helena action is preceded by the chaotic whirl of the "Classical Walpurgis Night" and followed by the chaotic whirl of the imperial battle in the mountains. It is to be noted that the one Walpurgis Night comes after the Gretchen action, the other Walpurgis Night comes before the Helena action; thus there is a symmetrical arrangement between the two actions as well as within each of them.

If we look more closely at each of these two chaotic whirls, an interesting articulation emerges. From another point of view this already came to our attention in the last part of Chapter Five. The first scene of the "Classical Walpurgis Night," the "Pharsalian Fields," site of the ancient battle and site of Mephistopheles' grotesque discomforts among the ancient monsters, at first seems to be under the sign of chaos; this is counterbalanced, however, not so much by the slight intimation of the new imperial order of the Caesars, but more importantly by the brief appearance of Faust with his discerning remarks on the beginnings of a great emergent order. The next scene, "Peneios Surrounded by Waters and Nymphs," is dominated by Faust and his view of the emergent order of the age of heroes, first in the vision of Leda and the swan, then in the conversation with Chiron, the tutor of the heroes. The next scene, "On the Upper Peneios," is a fivefold chaos: through the grotesque fantastic events on and around the new mountain heaved up by Seismos, the short-lived activity of its inhabitants, Mephisto's frustrating encounter with the Lamias, the dispute of Anaxagoras with Thales, and Mephisto's personally more satisfying meeting with the Phorkyads at the very edge of chaos. Finally, in the "Rocky Coves of the Aegean Sea" and the "Telchines of Rhodes" we see cosmos triumphant on the life-generating littoral sea, an ever emergent life order.

After the Helena act the succession, at first sight, appears to be parallel, with a central scene of chaos flanked by scenes of order. Actually though, what we have is something quite different: a surface order lightly concealing an intrinsic chaos. In the "High Mountains" Faust has his first vision of a new order, turning one portion of chaos, the tidal flats, into a new land, under the most ancient symbol of creativity, the separation of the land from the waters. The second half of the scene, however, continues with a view of the chaos into which the empire has been plunged by civil war, and, as Faust and Mephistopheles descend, they come upon the scene of battle, with the Three Mighty Ones already in tow. In the second scene, "On the Headland," comes the chaos of the imperial battle, at first view seemingly controlled by the well-chosen field and order of battle, but then with chaos compounded by the intervention of Mephistopheles and his sinister, grotesque auxiliaries, and finally the panic and flight of the enemy forces. In the last scene, "The Rival Emperor's Tent," there is a most ironic play between surface order and covert chaos after the male and the female plunderer are driven off by the imperial guard. Here the Emperor, now secure and at the height of his power, proceeds to establish the new order in the course of a kind of dramatic parody of the Golden Bull, actually establishing the new "order" by creating the conditions that will inevitably lead to a new collapse into chaos. His vexed words at the end, after the Archbishop has exacted such heavy ecclesiastical toll from him for the sinful use of magic in battle, are (11042):

So könnt' ich wohl zunächst das ganze Reich verschreiben.

*If I went on this way, I'd forfeit the whole empire.*

This is the culminating irony, for he has already done so.

The only brighter prospect here is that the Emperor resisted the Archbishop's final attempt at encroachment, on Faust's new land, and so this, unencumbered, can emerge into a new order—that proves, nevertheless, like everything human, to be encumbered. Here too Faust lapses into the chaos of guilt but emerges from it to the clarity of his final creative vision. In the beginning scenes of Part Two we also have this pendular motion between order and chaos. And so we see that this pair of polarities, already announced in the preliminary scenes of Part One, comes to be a dominant symbolic configuration of Part Two.

Of the other symmetrical balances in the drama, that of the two monodramas, discussed in Chapter Eight, is the most important. The initial monodrama comes as the fourth scene of Part One, the concluding one comes as the fourth and third from last of Part Two. Within these Faust's affirmation of life on earth as the proper sphere of man as well as his abjuration of a false transcendence comes in the fourth and fourth from last.

Minor and not necessarily significant instances of symmetry are as varied as the three following. In the tenth scene Faust first sees Gretchen, in the tenth from last, "High Mountains," comes his first new vision of Gretchen. In Part One the first study scene begins with Faust's survey of the faculties and their futile knowledge, the last study scene has, near its end, Mephistopheles' parodistic survey of the faculties for the "benefit" of the new student. Faust's second monologue in the first scene ends biblically with the Easter Choruses; after the Easter Walk his return to his study begins with his translation of the first words of the Gospel according to Saint John. Thus "Christ is arisen" is set over against "In the beginning was the Word."

## 2

If we stopped here, we should have the view of a neatly composed order enframing and disciplining this extremely complex work. If we did so, we should do less than justice to Goethe's deep skepticism about all such neat order without fractional residue, to the ironic manner in which he plays with such an order in at least one other work of his, to the whimsical humor with which he introduces ambiguities into such a neat order.

We have already seen that our symmetries and correspondences and successions do here and there fall short of perfection, and indeed were never intended to be mechanically perfect or to be seen as such, though on the other hand they are so close and carried through in such detail that the possibility of a chance or accidental sequence that could include all of these correlations is quite out of the question. Thus, we are probably facing aspects of that serious jest ("Spaß . . . an diesen ernst gemeinten Scherzen," "diese sehr ernsten Scherze"), that "open secret" ("offenes Geheimnis," "ein offenbares Rätsel"), at which Goethe several times hinted with an inward smile.

But the dubiety of the whole goes well beyond this intended imperfection. Let us first take a closer count of the scenes. If we are going to

be pedantically precise, we shall have to divide scene fifteen, "Garden,"
into two scenes, for the brief last part of it has a clear scene indication,
and thus "Garden Arbor" has every right to be counted as a separate
scene. The evidence of the first edition on this is clear and indubitable.
This would result in seven instead of six Gretchen scenes before "Forest
and Cavern" (thus fourteen in all) and would bring the count for Part
One up to twenty eight. But we must not only add, we must also sub-
tract: from the first edition onward the first three scenes are considered
preludial, and only after the third, the "Prologue in Heaven," comes the
half-title, "First Part of the Tragedy." True, Goethe brought the three
back into the drama proper through the corresponding last three scenes
of the drama, as we have observed. Nevertheless, strictly speaking, we
now have 3 preludial scenes plus the 25 of Part One.

In Part Two we have further ambiguities. In Act Three the first
scene is designated in the usual way: "Before the Palace of Menelaos in
Sparta," as is the second scene, "Inner Court of a Castle"—but only in
the modern editions. In the original editions there is no typographical
demarcation for either the second or the third scene. There are only
directions in parentheses, just like the stage directions in this act or
elsewhere in the drama. Thus again the ideological bias of the modern
editors, disregarding the importance of the poet's pictorial imaginative
intent, has falsified the text by supplying misleadingly clear and definite
scene divisions that are not present in Goethe's original text. The poet,
for special artistic purposes, wanted no sharp divisions in this act but
rather a dreamlike almost imperceptible blending over, as the nature of
the transition through the mist between the palace of Menelaos and the
inner courtyard of Faust's castle plainly shows. For the transition from
the castle to the Arcadian landscape Faust's immediately preceding lines
speak of "Arcadia in Sparta's neighborhood," and the stage directions tell
us: "The scene is entirely changed. Closed arbors recline against a series
of rocky caverns. A shady grove extends to the base of the encircling
rocks." This act had already appeared separately in 1827 in volume four
of the collected works, and the disposition was no different from that in
the first complete edition of 1832.

That would then leave us, at the moment, with 25 instead of 27
scenes for Part Two—just as we now have 25 instead of 27 or 28 for Part
One. Coincidence? Is Goethe smiling? All that the numerologist needs
now for the complete series is the 26 (24, 25, 26, 27, 28) and he does
have that, even though only by halves. However, rising above pedantic
precisionism as well as numerological occultism, common sense tells us,
on the one hand, that for the "Garden Arbor" there was no change of
stage scenery; this little bower was simply off to one side of the stage in
this scene "Garden." On the other hand, common sense is just as clear
in telling us that there is a second and a third scene in Act Three, in a

castle courtyard and in a sylvan landscape, each quite different from the archaic palace of Menelaos.

Another kind of ambiguity in scene shift occurs variously, for one in the first scene of Act Four, "High Mountains": when we reach the last sixth of it, not so much a change as a shift of scene to the middle range is suggested when the stage directions tell us about Faust and Mephistopheles (after line 10296): "They cross over the middle range of mountains and view the disposition of the troops in the valley."

The modern editions have not tampered with this shifting scene and have not changed stage directions into scene divisions, thus creating an unauthorized and unintended new scene. But in the case of another shifting or wandering scene they have intervened in a way that has impaired the understanding of the poet's intent. This hapless editorial intervention occurs in Act Two, in the "Classical Walpurgis Night." In the first place, there is no authority for inserting a scene division, "On the Upper Peneios," between lines 7079 and 7080. There is also no need for it. If the modern editors had merely consulted an atlas of antiquity, they would have realized that the initial scenic indication, "Pharsalian Fields" (before 7005), places the whole scene at the headwaters of the Peneios with its fanlike spread of tributaries. Furthermore, Homunculus' earlier words, quoted in the previous chapter (6952–55), about Pharsalus on the heights above the Peneios valley, make the poet's intent abundantly clear.

The second unwarranted insertion, "On the Lower Peneios" (between 7248 and 7249), relegating the real title, "Peneios Surrounded by Waters and Nymphs," to a stage direction, is an actual falsification of intent and saddles the poet with a painful blunder that he himself would not have committed. Quite obviously he would know that a river god in ancient art and imagination is traditionally represented as being at the source or at the confluence, not near the mouth. Here the god is even surrounded by the tributary "Waters." Thus the scene, in its beginning, is certainly upstream, at the confluence of the tributaries, at the Upper and not the Lower Peneios. And it is with appropriate symbolism that Faust here at the source has his vision of Leda and the swan. Soon thereafter, however, when he has mounted Chiron, he is borne swiftly through the night to the lower reaches of the Peneios, to the foot of Mount Olympus, where, at the battlefield of Pydna, as Chiron explains allusively, King Perseus of Macedon was defeated by Aemilius Paulus. Only when one understands this whole continuity will one be saved from drawing false inferences from the next, genuine designation of scene (between 7494 and 7495), "On the Upper Peneios" originally in the manuscript, then changed to "On the Upper Peneios as Previously" and so first printed. The action in the one scene has simply wandered downstream and in the next scene is back again at the headwaters where the seismic events take place and Mephisto at last finds kindred spirits at the edge of chaos.

Even here arbitrary editorial intervention does not stop: most modern editions have only one further scenic division, "Rocky Coves of the Aegean Sea," and willfully change the second, "Telchines of Rhodes," into a mere stage direction, to the impairment of the intended scenic balance and harmony as well as of the meaningful articulation. It will be clear, therefore, that any count of scenes or any picture of Goethe's intended divisions cannot be undertaken on the basis of the usual modern edition.

With such ill-starred intrusions removed, the real problem, the real question can be more clearly put. If Goethe consciously introduced the ambiguities actually present, or if he intentionally let them stand, could he have had any further motive beyond that of a salutary skepticism and irony over against any such numerical scheme? Quite possibly yes, a motive that becomes visible as soon as we take a second look at the new results. In Part One we have a new count of 14 scenes in the Gretchen action, just half of the new total of 28 (or 25 plus 3). In Part Two (if we apply the strict count also to "Burial," which in the original edition appears as a stage direction, just as does the later "Glory from above") the new count would apparently be 24 rather than 25, with the second half opening on the pageantry of the Aegean festival. For the aesthetic reasons indicated earlier, this symbolic event, celebrating the genesis to a new life, was developed here by the poet in the place of a more direct, literal Persephone scene in which Faust wins back Helen to life and light on earth. In both parts the sevenfold and the thirteenfold division play a role. By the old count there are 13 scenes in the Gretchen action and 13 scenes in Part Two to reach the new beginnings. By the normal count there are seven initial scenes in Part One before the double interlude and seven initial scenes comprising Act One of Part Two before the double interlude that begins Act Two. Altogether the ambiguity of the 24, 25, 27, or 28 scenes calls attention to the intricate interweaving of the frequent triadic groupings and the repeated use of sequences of seven, of nine, and (less conspicuously) of five and of thirteen scenes. In Part Two it is especially apparent how the seven sequence and the nine sequence overlap. The longest single scene of the drama, the third of Act One, the great carnival scene, illustrates the ambiguity of fluctuation between seven and nine in the groups or tableaus with which it begins. In the initial, premythological part there are nine such groups, but of these only seven are poetically realized, the other two are merely sketched. The mythological part begins with the three-times-three of the Graces, Fates, and Furies. After these comes the uncanny Zoilo-Thersites, then the unprogrammed group of Plutus, the god of wealth, and finally the culminating group around the great god Pan.

And so we could go on, proving nothing, simply revealing interrelations. In sum, here is an intricate complex of facts and phenomena, far too systematic and coordinated to be mere happenstance, revealing a side of Goethe for which we are not prepared, which from our accepted views about him we can hardly believe actually exists. If we feel, with the idealists, that a fact cannot exist if it conflicts with our ideas, then we will close our minds, reject these phenomena, and bury them in deepest silence—or, like Nicolai-Proktophantasmist in the "Walpurgis Night," request the phenomena to disappear after applying medicinal leeches as a cure against phenomena. If we have the more modern type of mind that gladly discards the most fondly cherished theory or hypothesis if it comes into conflict with facts and phenomena (which simply are there and will not disappear when we tell them to), then we may have to do some rethinking and refashioning of our image of Goethe the creative artist.

3

The whole matter becomes even more disturbing when we use simple line count instead of scenic division. The now generally accepted line count of *Faust* comes to 12,111. Let us divide this first into fourths and then into thirds. One quarter of the way through brings us to the scene where Faust learns of the arrangements for his meeting with Gretchen. Actually in lines 3027–28 Mephistopheles says:

> In kurzer Zeit ist Gretchen Euer.
> Heut' abend sollt Ihr sie bei Nachbar' Marthen sehn.
>
> *Quite soon now Gretchen will be yours.*
> *This evening you shall see her at her neighbor Martha's.*

One half of the way through comes the scene of the Emperor's delight with Faust's and Mephisto's magic conclusion of the carnival masque and the latter's "solution" of the financial crisis. Precisely at lines 6055–56 the Chancellor declares:

> So hört und schaut das schicksalschwere Blatt,
> Das alles Weh in Wohl verwandelt hat.
>
> *Hear then and see this most momentous leaf*
> *That has from all our woe brought us relief.*

Naturally, this is only the prelude to a further request from the Emperor: to bring Helen and Paris to view before him, as we learn in the next scene where Faust for this purpose ventures on his perilous voyage to the realm of the Mothers. Three quarters of the way through comes Helen's decision to go to Faust's castle and her command to Phorkyas to lead the way, with the chorus voicing its approval precisely in the ten lines around 9083. In the next scene comes her meeting with Faust. At each of the three quarters then comes the prelude to Faust's meeting with the chief feminine presences in the drama: Gretchen, the Mothers, and Helen, and at the close of the fourth quarter comes the culmination of all this with the Mater Gloriosa and the Eternal Womanly.

The division into thirds turns out also to be significant. One third of the way through brings us to the "Walpurgis Night" precisely (line 4037) where Faust expresses his desire to procede onward and probe the mystery of iniquity. Two thirds of the way through brings us to the "Classical Walpurgis Night," precisely at the point of first mention of "the realm of the lofty Cabiri" (8074), these "strangely unique," self-generating gods of no self-awareness (8075–77) who make their triumphal entrance less than one hundred lines later.

Now this is a symmetry of structure so perfect, so unambiguous as to make it appear to be in a different class from the scenic harmonies and symmetries previously observed. And yet, typically for Goethe, there is an ambiguity here too, as we shall see.

The question naturally arises as to how far all this goes. Is this play with mathematical-musical symmetries and repeat patterns unique for *Faust* or does it also extend to other works of Goethe? I could not answer this question because I had never looked for anything of the kind in his works. I had previously had no interest in doing so and no notion that there could be anything of the kind in them. These phenomena in *Faust* forced themselves on my attention, unexpectedly. To be sure, in one other work of his I had noticed analogous phenomena, so obvious and at the same time so playful, that I at first did not even think of making any connection. On second thought, the playfulness may be an associative rather than a dissociative factor.

It is a brief and minor work, "Weissagungen des Bakis," which I examined more closely and in fuller context some years ago in *The Soothsayings of Bakis: Goethe's Tragi-Comic Observations on Life, Time, and History.* It may be of some significance that they date from 1798, around the time that Goethe resumed his concentrated systematic work on *Faust* after a long interval. Here, as in the *Faust*, the numerological interrelations are not essential, not even high in importance. In the "Bakis" they simply add a few grace notes and echoes of confirmation to the themes and meanings that emerge from the poetic text, and I therefore paid only slight attention to them at the time and pointed out only a few of them. I here add further details. The 32 quatrains indicate that 31 days of the month plus the last one that, in content also, leads into a new cycle, here beyond the reaches of time. The factor of time is intrinsic to the whole group, and indeed images of time dominate the initial quatrains, as they do many a later one. The calendar of the month rules the numerical system, though far from exclusively. At the end of the first "week," at 7, we have the seven open and concealed faces that signify a completed cycle in the continuous revolving that leads to the end of all. In the "Sundays" of the month (1, 8, 15, 22, 29) we may observe more or less obvious beginnings of smaller cycles. The content of number 2 is appropriate for the first "Monday." Then there are the ominous "eleventh" hour and the triumphant high noon of the "Twelfth." At unlucky "Friday the thirteenth" the poet does reach the darkest point of his historical pessimism. Number 16 is at mid-point and appropriately dwells on the three faces of time, the mysterious equivalence of past and future flanking the present. Numbers 10, 20, and 30 may be related by the motifs of attraction and enjoyment, even as there may be a relation of 12 and 24 in the man of power. Of course, first and last, 1 and 32, are related in their dwelling upon the endless variety yet constancy of historic processes. The seven is naturally dominant, but, predictably, there seems to be no trace of any system of nine. There are also close connections in theme and content among quatrains for which no numerological interrelations can be established.

It is clear then that Goethe did use number relations as compositional factors to help hold together, also outwardly, a seemingly heterogeneous group of parts, but also to give an outward sign of certain inward relevancies and interrelations necessary for the understanding of the whole. These number coordinates never established such relationships, they simply underscored them, called attention to them. In the "Bakis" as in the *Faust* they are therefore useful though strictly subordinate; the intrinsic formal relationships of the work would exist without them but they would not be so clearly discernible without them.

Goethe presumably realized that they were useful but apparently he could not take them very seriously. We know from his own writings that he had an aversion to all mystical numerology, and from the *Faust* itself we know into whose mouth he put (2540 ff):

> Du mußt verstehn!
> Aus Eins mach Zehn.
>
> *This you must ken.*
> *From one make ten.*

and the rest of the "Witch's one-times-one." Goethe several times waxed sarcastic at the solemnity and seriousness with which his younger contemporaries attempted to extract profound metaphysical meanings out of this and similar texts of his. Actually, the whole is a calculated joke at the expense of the all-too-serious, a joke with an ironic satiric twist: that which seemed to challenge the most exalted speculative contemplation is actually subject to the simplest kind of arithmetic solution. All that we need to do is first add together the numbers 1 to 10 as they exist in the normal rational world, giving us 55, and then add together the set of numbers the witch derives from them: 10, 0, 0, 0, 7, 8, 1, 0, giving us 26. The witch's arithmetic, a kind of anamorphosis, tells us that Faust was fifty-five before the event and twenty-six after drinking the potion, thus by a second irony losing twenty-nine instead of the thirty years he had expected. Surprising only that he was "shortchanged" so little considering the company he kept. Then there is also the Cabiri numerology (8186 ff.) with the mock-serious playfulness of its 3, 4, 7, 8 increment. There is a deeper intent, of course, in this passage, but it has to be sought contextually, not numerologically, above all not too solemnly. Such instances should warn us that any interpretation of our findings in terms of weighty profundities is likely to miss the point and to be un-Goethean.

On the other hand, we do know from long-time observation that various persons and societies have tendencies and habits toward groupings in threes, and fours, and sevens, in triple triads, etc. We also know from aesthetic studies that natural harmonies and symmetries often group themselves effortlessly into such and similar configurations. If Goethe was aware or became aware of such tendencies in himself or such results in his literary works, he may have taken advantage of these natural tendencies and results to construct a convenient framework within which to arrange the "Fülle der Gesichte," the plenitude of visions, of his great masterpiece. That he did not give any emphasis to this system or force the work or any part into it, can be readily observed from the closing scenes of Part One. After the 3 + 4 + 2 + 13 (or 14) scenes, there are five left over, the double interlude of "Walpurgis Night" and "Walpurgis Night's Dream" and the three closing scenes of the fateful end, the futile attempt to rescue Gretchen from prison. The three concluding scenes, to be sure, harmonize fairly well with comparable parts of the work, all the more since the brief middle one is the appropriate grotesque interlude. But the Walpurgis Night scenes of Part One are not in a position comparable to that of any other double interlude, nor do they have any relation by position to any other comparable pair of scenes, except through the motif of chaos. They are there simply because that is where they functionally belong; nothing parallel to them is functionally required in any other comparable place in the drama. Goethe used the larger framework of numerical relations simply because he found it handy, but he changed no particular in the course of the drama simply for the sake of making it fit better into the framework, not even the position of the Valentin scene.

It was to be assumed that in the wake of these findings other investigators might be interested in making counts in other major and minor works of Goethe. Out of curiosity as to what they might find I did, when I reached this point, quickly look into a few of his works, and I must admit that the sevens, nines, and thirteens turn up with remarkable frequency. After the *Hermann and Dorothea* with its nine cantos, the *Elective Affinities* is the most obviously symmetrical, with its two books of eighteen chapters each and with neat divisions at the nine. The companion piece to the "Bakis," the "Four Seasons," is made up of 99 elegiac distichs, a fact worth mentioning at this point only because *Wilhelm Meister's Apprenticeship* consists of 99 chapters (counting the undivided sixth book, the "Confessions of a Beautiful Soul," as one unit). Here likewise, if we look at the half and the thirds, we come upon crucial thematic chapters. *Wilhelm Meister's Travels* at first view seems less amenable with its 41 chapters (plus the double section of aphorisms), and our faith in the casual and accidental is restored until we find that the sum total of *Meister* chapters is 140, and therewith the seven comes into the picture (as it does also, with typical Goethean ambiguity, for each part separately, with part one consisting of 98 chapters and one book, and part two of 41 chapters plus the apended aphorisms). By contrast, the earlier version of the *Travels* stayed with the nines in having 18 chapters. The *Werther* is resistant to a clear count, but if we omit the editorial intrusions and count only Werther's own dated entries, we have 39 such in Book One and 45 (+ 3 + 1) in Book Two, so that once again 3, 9, and 13 are prominent and 7 intrudes. Furthermore the middle entry is the critical one. The paradox remains that, first, Goethe made use of these number frameworks to good purpose and, second, they serve no vital purpose and he clearly did not take them seriously.

And yet, if he used them, even playfully, what kind of meaning did they have for him and from where on earth or in the heavens did he derive them? One thinks first of the Pythagoreans and their number speculations and at once looks to see what Goethe thought of them. As frequently, his attitude here also seems paradoxical. In his letter to Carl Friedrich Zelter (December 12, 1812), on a new system of notation by numbers, to which he reacted negatively, he calls himself "zahlenscheu," wary about numbers, and goes on to remark: "I have always avoided and fled number symbolism, from the Pythagoreans down to the latest mathematico-mystics, as something formless and cheerless." True, this is something of a modification of the attitude he expressed to Georg Sartorius on July 19, 1810, but if this were all, we could rest content with our general conclusions. Unfortunately, however, there is equally positive evidence that Goethe thought otherwise, at least during one period. That period comprises the years from 1796 to 1800 as a minimum, precisely the time during which he completed *Wilhelm Meister's Apprenticeship*, wrote the *Hermann and Dorothea*, the "Soothsayings of Bakis," the "Four Seasons," and other works here pertinent, as well as establishing the new numbered plan for *Faust*, writing the "Dedication" and other parts of it. Generally overlooked is the fact that in 1797 he wrote an essay in which numerology plays a prominent part, the "Israel in the Desert," this not published till much later in the notes and treatises added to the *West-Eastern Divan*. Near the end of the essay he makes his summary observations on "several numbers that can be called round, holy, symbolic, poetic," prominent among them the 7, the 40, and the 49. Then there is the letter to Schiller of August 1, 1800, in which he speaks of reading Franz von Baader's treatise on the Pythagorean tetractys of nature or the four regions of the world, 1798, and goes on to say: "Whether it be that I have in recent years become more friendly toward these modes of thought, or that he knows how to familiarize us with his intentions, the little work pleases me well."

We know that his interest was aroused, for some six weeks later, on September 13, 1800, he borrowed from the Weimar library Pierre Sylvain Maréchal's anonymously published *Voyages de Pythagore en Égypte, dans la Chaldée, dans l'Inde, en Crète, a Sparte, en Sicile*, a fictional, historical, topographical, biographical, philosophical work in five (plus one) volumes (Paris, 1799–1800). In chapter 52 in the first volume, on the Egyptian calendar, Penophius, the guide of young Pythagoras, explains to him the origins first of the lunar and then of the solar calendar. For Penophius the numbers 3, 4, 7, 9, 13, 27, 28 (that is, just the numbers we found prominent in *Faust*) are the basic ones. Here is a translation of the pertinent second paragraph:

> It is probable that the sun was not the first object of a contemplative worship of the peoples. The brightness of its light at first forced even the boldest of its early observers to lower their eyes, The gentle light of the nocturnal luminary was more accessible to our investigations. The ancient astronomers among the Brahmans of India divided the zodiac into twenty-seven constellations or moon stations before they divided it into twelve signs or houses of the sun. The moon, which traverses the circle of the stars thirteen times during one single tour of the sun, offers greater ease for the exploration of the celestial movements. The regularity of the phases of the moon, each seven days long, induced our ancestors to divide time into lunar years, and each lunation into four equal parts of seven days. They thereby found another advantage, I mean the accord of the seven days of the week, each bearing the name of a planet, with that harmonious concert which the heavenly bodies produce among themselves through the divine mingling of their diurnal movements; for the source and the principle of all true harmony, the noblest of all consonances is the diatessaron (the interval of a fourth).

This will do for present purposes, though there is more in Maréchal's account, notably in chapter 60, on the science of numbers, with details on ancient number symbolism.

4

The present chapter originally ended several pages earlier, but then after calling to mind the "Bakis" analogy, I took a swift glance at other major and minor works of Goethe and came to observations that were more than a little disconcerting and called for modifications of my earlier assumptions as to the scope and significance of the number patterns. However, there was still another surprise in store for me. Finding Goethe so fascinated by Pythagorean speculation just during the crucial period of new comprehensive *Faust* plans around 1798, I could not help but wonder whether the golden section, the golden proportion, held any interest for him. It seemed likely enough; his periodical, the *Propyläen*, 1798–1800, bears witness to his intensive concern at the time with problems of art and aesthetics, and this would naturally bring with it some concern with the problem of proportions, a problem long since familiar to him, of course, from his architectural readings, in Vitruvius, Palladio, and others. But did this general interest lead to any specific interest in the golden section? And if it did, were there any practical results issuing forth from it, in his *Faust* or elsewhere?

It would be easy enough to find out. In recent years a number of classical scholars, particularly George E. Duckworth, have made extensive studies of Vergil's varied use of the golden section or ratio as a compositional element in his works, and these investigations have been extended to other poets. Thus one has easily available what is essential both about the theory and the practical application of this principle of proportion. It is a matter of ancient and continuing observation that certain proportional relations in a work of art elicit the highest degree of positive response in the beholder and that these relations can be expressed in mathematical terms. Best known (though far from unique) among the pleasing proportional relationships is that of the golden section, and long since experimental tests have demonstrated that quite abstract figures (empty picture frames, for instance) were found to be the more pleasing to the beholder the nearer they came to corresponding to the golden section. Various investigators have found these proportions in nature in the whole range from plant life to man, most regularly and accurately perhaps in various conch shells and notably the chambered nautilus—a seashell that has inspired a famous ode. In works of art or in poetry there is naturally no rigorous mechanical conforming to these mathematical relationships; the artist proceeds by feeling rather than by calculation, though calculation seems likely in some instances, even as early as the Parthenon, and Vergil's employment of these proportional relations was in a number of instances remarkably exact.

In the proportions of a golden section the lesser member is to the greater member as the greater member is to the whole. This comes out as an irrational number, but approximately the lesser number stands to the greater as 1 does to 1.618; the greater stands to the lesser as 1 does to .618. With application to *Faust* there are here, as always in Goethe, amusing ambiguities. The line count of Part Two has long since been established at 7499; a few critics have discovered minor inconsistencies in the manner of that count though without much effect on the final result. The line count of Part One comes to 4612, including the six lines of the next to last scene, "Night, Open Field," but not the prose of the third from last, "Dreary Day. Field," which in the first edition comes to 60 printed lines. The total verse count for the drama is 12111. If we use the established figure for Part Two, then the ideal line count for Part One would be slightly under 4635. This would be 23 lines longer than the actual verse count or 37 lines shorter if the prose lines were to be counted as verse. This is a remarkably close approximation to the golden ratio, closer than most of those found in the Roman poets. Another approach to the matter produces equally striking results. It is a feature of the Fibonacci sequence (1, 1, 2, 3, 5, 8, 13, 21, etc.), in which each successive number is the sum of the two preceding numbers, that the further one progresses, the closer one comes to a golden ratio in any three successive numbers. Here the 24th, 25th, and 26th progression from one, if divided by ten, reads: 4636.8, 7502.5, 12139.3, surprisingly close to the Faustian line counts of 4612 (plus prose), 7499, and 12111 (plus prose).

We are at once reminded of a *Faust* paralipomenon (number 86) and induced to wonder whether we now understand why Goethe ever intended to include it in this drama:

> Und merk dir ein für allemal
> Den wichtigsten von allen Sprüchen:
> Es liegt dir kein Geheimnis in der Zahl,
> Allein ein großes in den Brüchen.

> *And mark this well: no useless lumber*
> *But maxim first in benefactions,*
> *There is no mystery in number,*
> *Yet there's a great one in the fractions.*

As supplement and extension we have Sulpiz Boisserée's report of a conversation with Goethe, August 11, 1815:

> It's just the way it is in music where one never gets a pure octave, instead in the second a new tone is always formed, a ninth part that one cannot accept as standing by itself alone and therefore distributes as a fraction into the whole. This fraction is what one encounters everywhere, in geology and in all nature. If one tries to resolve it totally, it can't be done, one will only confuse the whole; one must realize that there is something insoluble left and acknowledge that it is so, then one will get along.

Following this wisely modest precept, let us rest content. To carry the inquiry further forward from approximations to absolutes would only end in failure. Imperfection, unresolvable, is an intrinsic feature of natural relations, although the mind of man cannot resist forcing it toward unnatural absolute perfection even at the risk of destroying the very usefully and beautifully imperfect. If Goethe consciously and calculatedly introduced the mathematical-proportional features of composition that we have observed in his *Faust*, he would, for very good reasons of art and nature, also have introduced the ambiguities, uncertainties, and irresolvables that we have also observed. Indeed, he could not have avoided doing so. If, on the contrary, this whole framework of intricate compositional interrelationships was largely intuitive and spontaneous, arising out of an almost unprecedented inner sense of balance, proportion, and interrelationship, then these creative processes of his would have been, like any other work of nature, resolvable, explicable only to a certain (indeed quite generous) degree and for the rest go on, like the 3.14159. . . of pi or the 1.618. . . of phi, unresolved into infinity. This feature of the whole matter is highly symbolical, adding the further surreal dimension to the solidly real, and it would be a misunderstanding of Goethe's greater artistic intent to regret its presence in his masterpiece.

Whether Goethe's introduction of the golden ratio in *Faust* was conscious and calculated or was intuitive and spontaneous, at least one further question calls for an answer, however tentative and provisional the answer may be at this stage. The central question is: did this proportional division happen only once in a significant work? Or does it also occur elsewhere in Goethe in a clear and notable manner? Let us take at least a first brief glance, although at this stage, new to me as well as to the reader, it is merely a first glance.

If we turn to that other very different work of his that is always reckoned among his very greatest, the *Wilhelm Meister*, we can at once observe in the *Apprenticeship* that the middle chapter (Book IV, chapter 7), the fiftieth out of ninety-nine, comes much earlier than does the middle page of the novel—just as the middle scene of *Faust* comes much earlier than does the middle line. In the first edition some 587 printed pages of text are taken up by the middle of this fiftieth chapter (at volume II, page 235), leaving just over a thousand more (exactly 1005) to the conclusion of the novel. This is a somewhat less perfect though reasonably good golden ratio (better perhaps than the average Vergilian one): 587 : 1005 :: 1005 : 1592, whereas the nearly ideal golden ratio would be: 608 : 984 :: 984 : 1592. This would bring the page count to volume II, page 256, four pages along in chapter 10 of Book IV.

If we look at the content of these chapters, the results are even more impressive, for the novel here is at a real turning point. The forty-ninth, the last of the first half, brings to the gravely wounded Wilhelm the vision of "the beautiful Amazon," his guiding star thenceforward. Here too and with Wilhelm's ensuing slow recovery we have a symbolic death and resurrection. In the bisected middle chapter the vision of her and the tangible cloak from her hands dominate the first half and contrast sharply with the naked hostility and crass recriminations of the troupe in the second half. This in turn elicits Wilhelm's response in the next chapter (IV, 8), countering meanness with generosity. Then (IV, 9) comes his recovery under the loving, lighthearted care of Philine, and also her flippant paraphrase of Spinoza's ethical imperative ("And what if I do love you? it's none of your business"), to which Goethe himself called attention. Thereupon (IV, 10) she silently departs, leaving him along with Mignon and his memory of the lovely Amazon.

This place of division in the golden ratio is similar to the one in *Faust* in that the first part, relative to the second, is slightly too short, with the section actually coming early in the second part. For the *Travels* also the golden section comes just a page or two after the Pedagogical Province with its exposition of the "four reverences," "die vier Ehrfurcheten." For the two parts of the novel together the golden section comes just at the end of Book VI, the "Confessions of a Beautiful Soul." All this could still be considered a series of casual and coincidental approximations if it were not for the other, smaller work of his from 1797 (two years after the *Apprenticeship*, one year before his comprehensive new plan for *Faust*) that also has a 99-fold division, the "Four Seasons." Taken by itself and out of larger context, these "Vier Jahreszeiten" seem a strangely unsymmetrical production: with 18 and 19 distichs for spring and summer, then all of 46 for autumn, and only 16 for winter, a typically fragmentary product of Goethe's, developed with great spirit but then dropped before it was rounded out to proper balance—so the critics have inferred and concluded. But what happens if we do not jump to complacent conclusions but take the work just as Goethe left it? The first two parts of 37 distichs are related to the second two parts as a remarkably close golden ratio, with the section actually coming at 38, at the beginning of the third part. And again if one reads distichs 37 and 38, at the turning point, one cannot escape the conclusion that this was intended as a major division and central statement.

Out of the time of Goethe's special fascination with Pythagorean numerology and proportions came not only the complex or problematic works we have examined but also the most clear and seemingly unproblematic of his classical masterpieces, the *Hermann and Dorothea*, begun shortly after the completion of the *Apprenticeship* and finished within a remarkably brief time. Here the line count is clearly established as 2034 and, remarkably, the Pythagorean sectioning resolves almost without fractions as: 777: 1257 :: 1257 : 2034. Line 777 is Canto IV, line 181, and at this line, precisely, comes the statement on the turning point in the life of Hermann when he announces his declaration of independence to his mother and makes the transition from dependent child to responsible man.

To summarize: with *Faust, Wilhelm Meister,* and the "Four Seasons" the middle scene, chapter, seasonal division comes much earlier than does the middle unit in line, page, distich. It comes instead at, or rather just before, the place where the lesser of the two members of the golden ratio would ideally terminate. In *Hermann and Dorothea* the golden section and the turning point coincide with almost eerie precision. And I can add here, without further detail, that these are not the only works of his in which the position of the golden section comes at a division of major significance. Several other prose works of his show this phenomenon, even as do several long poems, especially of his earlier and middle periods. But it must at the same time be stated emphatically that other works of his, of real importance, show no indication of any such proportion, but instead reveal quite different formal relationships.

There may be a fairly simple and natural way to account for the number harmony and the Pythagorean proportions in *Faust,* or at least for the way in which they may have originated in Goethe's creative imagination. On May 5, 1798, he wrote to Schiller:

> I have carried my *Faust* a good piece further. Still at hand was the old, quite disordered manuscript; it has been copied and the parts placed in separate folders, one after the other, according to the numbers of a detailed outline.

This is not the time or place to examine the recent attempts (*Goethe Jahrbuch,* 1970 ff.) to reconstruct the whole of the numbered *Faust* outline of 1798 on the basis of the few numbered parts surviving in the drafts and paralipomena of this period. For us the important point is that this preliminary numerical outline of his for the whole drama may very well have called his attention to the potentially harmonious distribution of scenes for Part One, revealed what was still lacking for proper proportion and interrelation, and then, or more probably later, induced him to project a similar balanced, harmonious distribution (parallel with increment) for Part Two.

However it all came about, it is there, clearly discernible, an integral part of the work, and, as such, a feature to which we must pay careful attention, with at least half our care devoted to keeping it in its decently modest place among the formal, compositional features of the whole. Perhaps this factor was best put into perspective by Goethe's younger friend, Wilhelm von Humboldt, in a critical essay of 1806, "Latium and Hellas, or Reflections on Classical Antiquity." Reflecting on the creative powers of man: imagination, reason, and feeling, and the forms they employ: configuration, rhythm, and sentience, Humboldt continues (III, 140):

> To these, however, can probably be added a fourth, difficult to explain, hovering before true philosophizing the way metric pattern does before a not yet invented poem.

> This configuration stands under the eternal law of the mathematics of space, has all visible nature as its basis, and speaks to one's sensibilities in manfold ways.

> Rhythm originates out of the mysterious but indispensable relations of number, reigns over the whole of vibrant nature, and is the constant, invisible companion of feeling.

# Conclusion

# Form as Meaning

In looking back over the course we have traversed in our examination of the formal aspects of Goethe's Faust drama, we readily come to the conclusion that the means of articulation and construction used in the drama are of a variety and complexity well beyond the usual group of formal devices employed in a work of art. Such an unprecedented richness and subtlety in the interrelation of the formal elements, for which no one was prepared, has resulted in a critical confusion that was only redoubled when the conventional kinds of dramatic form were predicated for the drama and then not found. The end result was that the work was presumed by some to be formless and by others to be gravely flawed in form. In the several instances where genuine, intrinsic factors of form were found, they were seen in isolation, then necessarily thought to be of only limited relevance, with the result that even the true new insights could not prevent the work from being dismissed as fragmentary or discontinuous.

One further, relatively extensive series of steps was necessary. Only after all the main factors of form are seen, understood, and brought together: the four corner pillars of equivalence erected in splendid symmetry at the earthly beginning and end of each part; then the initial introduction of the primary themes and points of view, establishing precedents followed throughout the work; then the structural principle of the interlude; then the continuous fabric of theme, attitude, motif, symbol, with the patterns of repetition and variation; then the more encompassing phenomenon of echo structures; then the architectonic relationship of monodrama and polydrama; then the succession of symbolic extensions that give to the protagonist the world scope called for by a drama of these dimensions; then the equivalent time structure that symbolically gives the protagonist the world scope of a mastery over the three thousand years of our civilization; and finally the calculated harmonic mathematics that accompanies and makes manifest the equivalences, proportions, and perspectives of the whole, with the inevitable residuum of the ultimately unresolvable and indeterminable—only when all these come together, in total contextuality, do we attain to the necessary insight into the form of *Faust*.

If we were to designate the total form as polymorphous, we would have to take care not to think of this term as implying a mixture of forms but as designating a careful coordination of forms. In this connecion, in partial analogy, it may be possible to think of a great symphony with its very different movements, its very different themes and ways of thematic development and interrelation, with all of its complexity and diversity in the end still resulting in a unified work of art that may even (and probably does) have some of the aspects of a mathematical precision and distribution. This will be mathematical-artistic, to be sure, not mathematical-mechanical, as we have seen in several instances in the drama, notably that of the ending where the poet wisely refrained from adding a false symmetry that he had planned at an earlier stage, and achieved instead a unique and fitting artistic triumph in a recapitulation raised to a higher power and glory. The whole of this formal complex is perhaps too involved for immediate or even rapid assimilation by reader or listener. Such an assimilation may come only after a fresh reading of the whole drama with all these factors of form in mind; and further readings thereafter will probably bring further enriching of formal comprehension, possibly even new insights into intrinsic form. Such a pioneer study as this is bound to have its flaws and shortcomings, but after it the way is easy for others to do better. In the end the *Faust* will probably remain incommensurable enough, though, we may hope, no longer incomprehensible.

Another analogy that we could make would also be an imperfect one, but, with Goethe's principle of the elucidatory power of mutual reflection in mind, we may justly decide that by following the analogy through, we shall rather gain than lose. By looking to the field of architecture for our analogy, we have the double advantage that we can draw directly on Goethe and that the carrying out of an architectural plan, particularly one of large dimensions, can likewise go on through many years, be subject to many delays and changes of plan, and come to a final realization that both by omission and inclusion can surprise many a spectator who had from the beginning inferred quite a different continuance and completion. Such surprise may at first go over to disappointment and then to adverse criticism of the architect for not doing what he should have done. However, if the architect has truly remained in masterful (though flexible) control from beginning to end and if the critic is not opinionated, not dominated by abstract theory, but truly able to judge a work from its own point of view and function, he may come to the insight that the unexpected changes and surprising features of the final structure are truly in the service of the whole and, all things considered, represent better solutions than the ones previously planned or expected.

Yet we must be careful: with architecture as the analogue, there is the danger of lapsing into a prime fallacy. A favorite architectural analogy of the writers on *Faust* is that of a Gothic cathedral, centuries in the process of completion, with an end result quite different from the initial plan. This is a false analogy, if only for the reason that the continuance is out of the hands of the individual genius with the great architectural vision.

Far better, though also not in perfect analogy, is Goethe's own view of the creative processes of such an architectural genius facing a situation not ideally suited to the achievement of perfection and yet triumphing over the adverse situation and circumstances, even incorporating them masterfully into his final realization. That Goethe himself was a master in the creative use of the *objet trouvé*, I demonstrated long ago and now again in Chapter Nine. Goethe's use for purposes of symbolic extension, however, carries us beyond the scope of the present analogy.

The architectural genius whom Goethe most admired, Andrea Palladio, was also able to incorporate alien, seemingly even hostile extant elements into an inclusive plan and achieve a harmony of the whole. Just how he did so, the poet described during his Italian journey, in Venice, October 6, 1786, contrasting the perfect though uncompleted complex of the Carità with other completed though imperfect edifices. Although the analogy is a limited one, the critical attitude is an exemplary one, for us also:

> In those works of Palladio that are completed, especially in the churches, I have found much to blame, together with much that is most precious. While I was reflecting how far I was right or wrong over against such an extraordinary man, it was as though he were standing beside me and saying to me: "This and this I did against my will, but nevertheless I did it, because in this manner alone was it possible for me, under the given circumstances, to come closest to my highest concept."
>
> It seems to me, however much I think about it, that when he contemplated the height and width of an already existing church, an older building for which he had to construct façades, he simply deliberated: "How will you give the greatest form to these dimensions? Some parts of the detail you must, from the necessity of the case, put out of place or botch a bit, here or there an awkwardness will arise. Be that as it may, the whole will have a grand style and you will take joy in your work."
>
> And thus he carried out the great image that he had in his soul, even there where it was not quite suitable, where he was obliged, in the detail, to crowd or to mutilate it. . . .
>
> The way he thought, the way he worked becomes clearer and clearer to me, the more I read his works.

Even the very young Goethe already had this critical wisdom and modesty. He was not yet twenty-two when he went through the same critical process with Shakespeare that at thirty-seven he went through with Palladio. In his brief address for the Shakespeare day, 1771, he says of his revered master:

> Regarding Shakespeare I am often ashamed of myself, for it sometimes happens that on first glance I think, "I'd have done that differently." Afterwards I realize that I am a poor sinner.

Such an attitude can be exemplary also for the modern literary critic when he strives to attain to an understanding of Goethe and his masterpiece. Indeed it is the only one that can lead him to a true understanding of any great masterpiece of world literature. The critical method that Goethe, early and late, continued to use was what his older friend Johann Gottfried Herder had early designated as an openhearted adaptability and empathy, the intrinsic approach to the work of art, with due observance of its own inner laws and intentions:

> Every artistic creation carries within itself its specific standard of validity; this must be fulfilled intrinsically and can only be apprehended through an empathy that delights in adjusting to it.

This "anpassungsfreudige Einfühlung," this critical adaptability and empathy that gladly yields precedence to the work's intrinsic self, is the only fruitful one, the only one that will carry us beyond ourselves, beyond the limitations of our theories and perceptions. We no longer have to intellectualize that which is accessible only to the symbolic-pictorial imagination. We can simply relax, accept the work on its own terms, and enjoy it for what it is, since this is something far greater than we can make of it.

# Bibliographical Note

In the Preface I stated the reasons why I refrained from decorating this volume with the usual array of footnotes. I have no objection to footnotes as such; in the study that builds upon past scholarship and extends it in one direction or the other, footnotes may well be desirable, or even necessary, if the reader is to be able to differentiate between what is continuing tradition and what is being modified or added. However, in the study that takes a new start from the original literary text itself, finds that quite different basic premises are called for, and arrives at insights hardly (or not at all) suggested in previous studies, any normal learned apparatus would contain negative footnote after negative footnote pointing out how this or that particular scholar had missed this or that point or had taken his departure from this or that totally wrong premise. I do not see how there could possibly be joy in any such procedure. Such negativism would make it appear that there is nothing good about all such previous studies from different basic premises, whereas actually the different point of departure may lead to observations that are valuable from any point of view.

Even though for the present volume footnotes may be futile, some bibliographical information should be provided for the person who wants to see for himself whether my report on the previous consensus is reliable and fair and also whether I have conscientiously used the basic material on which my new exposition of the form and meaning of *Faust* are based.

Access to the previous scholarship is most easily and reliably attained through the excellent edition of Goethe's *Faust* by Erich Trunz (Hamburg, 1953), with its extensive commentary incorporating the results of *Faust* scholarship and with its select bibliography that provides an adequate first guide to the literature in the field. Fortunately, it continues to appear in ever new editions with revisions and additions. A few points have been scored against the volume, but these are more than compensated for by the treasure of new insights and interpretations coming from Trunz himself.

191

A reasonably complete bibliography of the *Faust* literature is a formidable affair and those who have examined the *Faust-Bibliographie*, edited by Hans Henning (Berlin and Weimar, beginning 1966, 5th volume by 1976) will see why an intelligently made small selection such as in Trunz is better for practical purposes, even though every other *Faust* scholar would want to do quite a bit of adding and subtracting. It does perhaps contain a number of "facade" works that add nothing to our knowledge or understanding and it omits some of the most original Austrian, English, and American contributions. An older edition unjustly neglected despite its rich commentary and occasional remarkable insights is the one by K. J. Schröer (two volumes, third edition, Leipzig, 1892–96, later editions till 1907 and 1903).

When Bayard Quincy Morgan was making his prose translation of *Faust*, he remarked to me with some indignation that the section in Trunz on "Goethe über seinen Faust" omitted vital Goethean material that was in contradiction to the editor's point of view and interpretation. True, every selection involves the danger of subjectivity, of bending the evidence to conform to preconceived notions. Therefore the *Faust* scholar will eventually want to turn to the complete bibliography and to the nearly exhaustive fourth volume (II, 2) of Hans Gerhard Gräf, *Goethe über seine Dichtungen* (Frankfurt, 1904), which contains on 608 pages the remarks and observations of Goethe and his contemporaries, together with valuable notes and commentaries upon them, altogether a work that is fortunately as intelligent as it is laborious. In progress is another work that will be of great value here when the *Faust* volume is reached: Momme Mommsen and Katharina Mommsen's *Die Entstehung von Goethes Werken in Dokumenten* (first two volumes, Berlin, 1958). Equally laborious, intelligent, and indispensable is the great collection of Goethe's conversations, Flodoard von Biedermann's *Goethes Gespräche* (five volumes, Leipzig, 1909–11). The great old Weimar edition of Goethe's works, letters, and diaries (*Großherzogin Sophie Ausgabe*, 113 volumes in 123, Weimar, 1887–1919) remains indispensable until one or the other among the more recent undertakings is carried through to completion.

Another edition of the works, letters, and diaries that offers decided advantages to the Goethe scholar is the *Propyläen-Ausgabe* (forty-five volumes and four supplementary volumes, Munich, 1909–14, 1920 to the mid '30s). It is arranged chronologically and thus offers the student many a new insight into what was going on in Goethe's mind at certain crucial stages of his development of *Faust*. It thereby affords an indispensable supplement to Gräf and does so equally perhaps through Heinz Amelung's three supplementary volumes, *Goethe als Persönlichkeit Berichte und Briefe von Zeitgenossen*. Hidden here, for instance, is part of the devastating evidence of how wrong Jacob Minor was in his pseudo-refutation of the report of Carl La Roche on Goethe's own concept of Mephistopheles (*Aus dem alten und neuen Burgtheater*, Zürich, Leipzig, Wien, 1920, 243–47), evidence that has been overlooked by all subsequent *Faust* scholars.

The *Goethe Jahrbuch* from 1880 to the present, in addition to its own contributions, has included reports on Goethe scholarship elsewhere in the world. Even better for keeping up to date on recent *Faust* criticism and scholarship is the annual *MLA International Bibliography* of the Modern Language Association of America. The seasoned Goethe scholar, of course, does not need most of the above information, and it is not intended for him. My aim has been to give the fewest possible number of titles of works that will most readily lead the student to all the rest that would be of use to him.

As for the translations of Goethe's *Faust* into English, I am in the unhappy position of not being able to recommend a single one wholeheartedly. The reasons for this I stated in the Preface as well as at several points in the text where it was crucial to have an exact English equivalent to the German wording and to the original language level. A recent translation for which I had high hopes because of the poetic talent and flair of the translator turned out in the end to be disappointing on both counts of faithfulness and language level, though I do hope that there may be a carefully revised new edition that will fulfill the great early promise. After each disappointment I find myself going back again to the translation of George Madison Priest that first appeared in New York in 1941. It was unfortunately allowed to run out of print a few years ago but decidedly deserves to be reprinted. If the reader will use it in conjunction with B. Q. Morgan's prose translation of both parts (Indianapolis, 1964), he will probably come to what is the nearest extant English equivalent to Goethe's own *Faust*. That still leaves sad mistranslations that can affect the meaning of the whole text, as for instance in the one line 11814 that we examined in Chapter One and in other passages of larger scope. However, Priest and Morgan remain the most reliable, and the Morgan as an added value includes a judicious selection of Goethe's own statements on *Faust*. As I indicated in the Preface and perhaps need to state more specifically here, all the translations from *Faust* and from the other works of Goethe in verse and prose that I have included in the text are my own. Wherever possible I compared them with previous translations, though several of the verse and prose passages have apparently never been translated before. The same was true of many of the other German and French texts here translated. With the Latin and Greek texts I was in a better position, for reliable English translations exist in the Loeb Classical Library and elsewhere. For the quotation from Plutarch I used the Bernadotte Perrin translation, here as elsewhere refraining from standardizing the spelling of proper names.

Of necessity I had to refer in the text to a number of earlier books and articles of mine that dealt with aspects of *Faust* and Goethe here pertinent. Indeed the present study is to some degree a synthesis of earlier insights and observations, and several sections of it are revised versions or paraphrases of earlier publications, or excerpts from them, though these passages are only a small portion of the whole. The earlier contributions through 1970 can be found listed in the bibliography by Morgan H. Pritchett included in the Festschrift, *Traditions and Transitions*, edited by Lieselotte E. Kurth, William H. McClain, and Holger Homann (Munich, 1972, 9–11). The years since then were largely devoted to publications in other fields, especially in Baroque and early American studies. Thus only two articles need to be added here: "Caveat for Faust Critics," *Studies in the German Drama: A Festschrift in Honor of Walter Silz*, edited by Donald H. Crosby and George C. Schoolfield (Chapel Hill, 1974, 89–101), and an earlier version of Chapter Ten of the present volume: "The Structure of Time in Faust," MLN 92 (April, 1977), 494–508. Possibly the first brief general outline of the present volume should also be mentioned separately: "Patterns and Structures in *Faust*: A Preliminary Inquiry," MLN 83 (April, 1968), 359–89.

Two further works not mentioned above that I found useful for this study were: Kurt May, *Faust II.Teil in der Sprachform gedeutet*, Berlin, 1936, and Monty Jacobs, *Deutsche Schauspielkunst*, in the new edition by Eva Stahl, Berlin, 1954.

# Index

**The Johns Hopkins University Press**

This book was composed in Palatino text with Fractur dropped initials and Palatino display type by Maryland Linotype Composition Company, Inc., from a design by Alan Carter. It was printed on 50-lb., Publishers Eggshell Wove, and bound in a natural finish cloth by The Maple Press Company.

Library of Congress Cataloging in Publication Data

Jantz, Harold Stein, 1907–
    The form of Faust.

    Bibliography: p.
    1. Goethe, Johann Wolfgang von, 1749–1832. Faust.
I. Title.
PT1923.J345      832'.6      78-1447
ISBN 0-8018-2080-4